DZOGCHEN FOREMOST INSTRUCTIONS: "A GARLAND OF VIEWS" BY PADMASAMBHAVA

WITH COMMENTARIES BY LONGCHEN RABJAM AND JU MIPHAM

BY TONY DUFF
PADMA KARPO TRANSLATION COMMITTEE

First edition, July 2015
ISBN paper book: 978-9937-572-84-2
ISBN e-book: 978-9937-572-81-1

Garamond typeface with diacritical marks and
Tibetan Classic typeface
Designed and created by Tony Duff

Produced, Printed, and Published by
Padma Karpo Translation Committee
P.O. Box 4957
Kathmandu
NEPAL

Committee members for this book: principal translator and book composition, Lama Tony Duff; assistant translator, Tamás Agócs; editorial, Jason Watkins of Purica; cover design, George Romvari of Purica.

Web-site and e-mail contact through:
http://www.pktc.org/pktc
or search Padma Karpo Translation Committee on the web.

CONTENTS

Introduction vii

1. The authors ix

2. The basis of Padmasambhava's teaching, the *Guhyagarbha Tantra* ix

   2.1. Explanation of the first part of the thirteenth chapter by Longchen Rabjam xii

   2.2. Explanation of the first part of the thirteenth chapter by the author of this book xii

3. About Padmasambhava's teaching xv

   3.1. The purpose of the teaching xv

   3.2. The title of the teaching xvi

      3.2.1. More about foremost instruction xvii

   3.3. Content of the teaching xviii

4. An explanation of the eight categories of view xix

   4.1. The worldly views xix

      4.1.1. Phyal ba or Vacancy xxii

      4.1.2. Charvaka or Sweet Talkers xxiii

      4.1.3. Paryantika or Bounded xxv

      4.1.4. Tīrthika or Those at the Brink xxvii

   4.2. Beyond-worldly views xxix

5. A short explanation of the nine vehicles and their views xxix

5.1. The conventional vehicles xxx
5.2. The unconventional vehicles xxxi
5.3. The unconventional vehicles more fully explained xxxii
5.3.1. The pinnacle teaching of Great Completion xxxv
5.3.2. The version of Great Completion taught here xxxvi
6. Great Completion xxxvi
6.1. Origin and meaning of the term great completion xxxvii
6.2. Mis-translations promoting misunderstanding xxxviii
6.3. Etymology of Great Completion xxxix
6.4. Levels of the Great Completion teaching xl
7. Terminology xl
7.1. Realization xlii
7.2. Superfact and fiction xliii
8. Other matters xlv
8.1. Sanskrit xlv
8.2. Further study xlvi

An extract from "Dispelling the Darkness of the Ten Directions" by Longchen Rabjam 1

Foremost Instruction "A Garland of Views" by Padmasambhava 19

An Annotational Commentary Called "A Warehouse of Gems" to the Great Master Padmasambhava's "Foremost Instruction 'A Garland of Views'" Compiled by Jamyang Lodro Gyatso 33

Glossary of Terms 89

Supports for Study 111

Tibetan Texts

A Garland of Views 115

A Warehouse of Gems 123

Index 157

INTRODUCTION

This book presents a teaching that Padmasambhava gave his disciples that was recorded in writing and given the title *Foremost Instruction "A Garland of Views"*.[1]

The teaching is an explanation of the thirteenth chapter of the root tantra of the Great Yoga or Mahāyoga vehicle, a chapter which sums up in one place the main views present in the samsaric worlds and the views leading to emancipation, the views of the nine vehicles. It then focusses on the meaning of the most profound of all those views—Great Completion[2]—in relation to deity practice taught in Mahāyoga.

Padmasambhava's teaching—and the thirteenth chapter too—covers a lot of material in a short space, so, unless the reader is well acquainted with the subject matter, there will be many places where the meaning will not be obvious. Further explanation of the teaching is usually obtained through oral instruction or written commentary. There are a number of written commentaries to Padmasambhava's

---

[1] Tib. man ngag lta ba'i phreng ba.

[2] The Tibetan term "dzogchen" means "great completion". It is the proper name of a system of dharma and also of a view, in which case it is capitalized. It is also the general name for the level of great completion that is the next level above completion, as will be explained in this book; in that case it is not capitalized.

teaching, for example there are two in Jamgon Kongtrul's compendium of texts called *Treasury of Oral Instructions*[3] and four in the massive compendium of important Nyingma texts called the *Extremely Vast Word of the Nyingma*[4].

The written commentary most commonly used these days to unravel Padmasambhava's *Garland of Views* text is called "Mipham's commentary". The great Nyingma scholar Ju Mipham Namgyal [1846–1912 C.E.] annotated a copy of Padmasambhava's text between formal sessions of meditation. Later, Jamyang Lodro Gyatso of Zhechen Monastery, a monastery with which Mipham was affiliated, edited the annotated text into the form of a commentary to Padmasambhava's text then published it under the title *An Annotational Commentary called "A Warehouse of Gems" to the Great Master Padmasambhava's "Foremost Instruction 'A Garland of Views'" Compiled by Jamyang Lodro Gyatso*. The commentary was a compilation of Padmasambhava's text in its entirety, Mipham's extensive personal notes edited into it to make a clear commentary to it, and subject headings for it that had been written by the first Jamgon Kongtrul. The entire commentary has been included in this book, where it provides the main explanation of Padmasambhava's teaching.

The basis for Padmasabhava's teaching is the thirteenth chapter of the *Guhyagarbha Tantra*, so that also has been included in this book. Moreover, the chapter of the tantra is very terse, so the relevant portion of the most famous commentary to the tantra called *Dispelling the Darkness of the Ten Directions*, written by Longchen Rabjam, has been included in order to provide even more clarification of Padmasambhava's teaching. Thus, although this book is centred around Padmasambhava's teaching and Mipham's commentary to it, the book has the grand feature of making much of the meaning of the all-important thirteenth chapter of the *Guhyagarbha Tantra* available

---

[3] Tib. gdam ngag mdzod.

[4] Tib. rnying ma'i bka' ma shin tu rgyas pa.

in English in a way that has not been done before. This is truly a cause for rejoicing!

Tantras and their commentaries are notoriously difficult to understand, so it generally accepted that complete explanations from a lineage holder are needed in order to translate them. Therefore, I need to say here that I received complete teachings on Padmasambhava's text, Mipham's commentary to it, and both the *Guhyagarbha Tantra* and Longchen Rabjam's commentary to it in the late 1990's at Zhechen Monastery in Nepal from the great scholar Khenpo Padma Tsering of Śhrī Singha College at Dzogchen Monastery, Tibet.

1. The Authors

In a book like this it is standard practice to write about the authors in order to rouse faith in the reader. However, much has been written in English about the authors Padmasaṃbhava, Mipham, and Longchen Rabjam whose works have been included in this book, so I will not say more about them here.

2. The Basis of Padmasambhava's Teaching, the Guhyagarbha Tantra

Padmasambhava's teaching is an explanation of the thirteenth chapter of the *Guhyagarbha Tantra*, the root tantra of all the Mahāyoga tantras of the Nyingma tradition. This tantra is held in the highest esteem by Nyingma practitioners. It not only contains in one place the meanings of all the many tantras of Mahāyoga, but is known for its extreme profundity and remarkable clarity. It is something that all Nyingma practitioners want to hear in order to have a complete basis for studying and practising the inner tantras of the nine vehicles.

The tantra begins with primordial space manifesting in the form of tathāgata Samantabhadra in union with his consort. The consort becomes the cause of the tathāgata manifesting in speech, which comes forth as the various profound topics of Mahāyoga. Each time she presses Samantabhadra, another chapter of the tantra appears. The first to twelfth chapters contain explanations of the creation stage or deity practice of Mahāyoga. The thirteenth chapter starts the explanations of completion stage meaning *the stage of completing the creation stage* by completing the necessary work of joining creation stage with superfactual truth[5]. The root tantra's remaining chapters through to the final chapter twenty-two deal with various related matters.

The thirteenth chapter is in two parts: a listing of views with Great Completion mentioned as the highest and an explanation of the view of Great Completion as it applies to the deity practice of Mahāyoga given in the form of foremost instructions to ensure that the meaning of the Great Completion view is correctly understood. As a matter of interest, the thirteenth chapter is only three folios long in Tibetan, with the first part being about one folio in length and the second about two folios in length.

In its own words, the chapter starts by introducing itself like this:

> The chapter which, of the just-as-it-isnesses of the *Guhyagarbha*, presents the extremely secret level, the foremost instruction of the essence.

"Essence" there means Great Completion which is the very essence of all teachings of the nine vehicles. Foremost instruction is clearly explained a little later in this chapter. Great Completion is described as the most secret level of all the teachings of the secret, meaning the teachings of the Vajra Vehicle.

This chapter is important to practitioners of the deities of the Mahāyoga because it very clearly shows how the view of great completion of the Atiyoga vehicle is to be joined with deity practice of the Mahāyoga vehicle. However, it is not important only to Mahāyoga

---

[5] For superfactual truth, see the glossary.

practitioners; because it expresses the view of great completion so clearly it is also important to anyone practising the inner tantras of Anuyoga and Atiyoga.

The chapter continues with the preamble needed to set the stage for the teaching of the chapter. It says:

> Then the tathāgata, who is all maṇḍalas of the vajras of enlightened body, speech, and mind in the ten directions and four times collected into one, with great joy entered equilibrium on the samādhi that displays clouds of the extremely secret essence, the samaya of all dharmas being primordially spontaneously-existing in great completion, and then for that purpose expressed the following.

The chapter continues with the actual teaching of the chapter. This is in two parts. The first part consists of two, four-line verses. The first verse presents a summation of all views, starting with worldly views and ending with beyond-worldly views. Note that the views are presented in order, from lowest to highest, with "nature secret" being the name for the pinnacle view of great completion. The second verse states where these views are to be found and then who knows their meanings and is thus a teacher of them:

> The meanings of the ones which do not understand,
> wrongly understand,
> Partially understand, and do not understand the authentic,
> And of taming, intent, secret,
> And nature secret,
> Are fully shown by letters assembled into designating
> terms, the grammatical names,
> And the grammatical phrases based on them;
> The hidden and concealed meanings brought forth from
> within their complex
> Are present in the vajra teacher's mind.

The chapter then moves on to its second main part. This part explains how the pinnacle view of great completion applies to the practice of the deities of Mahāyoga. The explanations are given in the form of foremost instructions both to fully convey the meaning of great completion and to ensure that that meaning does not become wrongly understood.

2.1. Explanation of the First Part of the Thirteenth Chapter by Longchen Rabjam

Longchen Rabjam's commentary to the *Guhyagarbha Tantra* called *Dispelling the Darkness of the Ten Directions* is a massive commentary that is is regarded as the gold standard amongst explanations of the tantra, so it is important to read. Longchen Rabjam's entire commentary to the thirteenth chapter was too long to present here, so the commentary to the first part has been included in the book. To put it here in the introduction would have cluttered the introduction, so it has been placed at the beginning of the body of the book, before Padmasambhava's teaching. It is strongly recommended that you read it now, before continuing with the introduction.

2.2. Explanation of the First Part of the Thirteenth Chapter by the Author of this Book

As you have understood from the foregoing, the purpose of the thirteenth chapter of the *Guyhagarbha Tantra* is to show the meaning of the highest view for transcending the world, Great Completion, as it applies to the practice of Mahāyoga. To do this, the teacher of the tantra, Samantabhadra, enters a concentration that will display the meaning of the samaya or commitment connected with this level of the view, the samaya of all dharmas primordially spontaneously-existing as great completion. He then expresses that meaning in speech, which was later recorded as the tantra.

He starts by listing the views from lowest to highest in this world, using eight categories.

The first two categories constitute views that do not lead to transcendence of the world. First is the category of not understanding the authentic[6] at all. According to Padmasambhava, this contains two separate views which come together under one heading because they are equal in simply not understanding the authentic—views called Phyal ba and Chārvāka. Second is the category of wrongly understanding the authentic; Padmasambhava explains that this also contains two separate views that come together under one heading—views called Paryantika and Tīrthika.

The remaining six categories contain the views of the nine vehicles, all of which are views that lead to transcendence of the world. Of them, first there is the category of partially understanding the authentic, which is the shared view of the Śhrāvaka and Pratyeka vehicles. Next is not fully understanding the authentic, which is the nature of the view of the Bodhisatva vehicle. Taming is the view of the Krīyatantra vehicle. Intent, meaning mind working in a certain direction, is the view of the Yogatantra vehicle. The view of Ubhayatantra, which sits between and is equal parts of the two views just mentioned, is not mentioned because it has already been included simply by the explanation of the preceding two. The secret is a level of view that includes the two different views of the inner tantras, Mahāyoga and Anuyoga. The eighth and final category of view is the pinnacle of all views in the human world. It is the "nature secret" view, meaning that it too is at the *secret* level of the inner tantras like the views in the immediately preceding category, but it is a step higher again, sitting at the very secret or extremely secret level; it is the view of the Atiyoga vehicle, in which "*nature* great completion"[7] is explained.

---

[6] "The authentic" is a phrase commonly used in this book. It means reality, what is truly or really or authentically the case.

[7] For nature great completion see the glossary.

How and where do the meanings of those eight categories of view become known in this world? The *Guhyagarbha Tantra* goes on to explain this point. The explanation is very elegant but is based in a Sanskrit way of thinking about speech and grammar that will be lost on most English readers, so the next paragraph re-states what the tantra says so as to make it accessible.

The meanings of those eight categories of view become known in this world through articulated speech which has been written down in the form of texts, treatises, tantras, and so on. In English, articulated speech is said to arise from letters which are put together to make words, which are put together to make meaningful expressions in the form of phrases, clauses, sentences, and so on. It is similar, though not exactly the same, in Sanskrit and Tibetan languages, where articulated speech is said to arise from letters, which are put together into terms designated to have a meaning and which are called "grammatical names". Those names are similar to but not the same as nouns of the English language; they are the most fundamental part of speech to provide meaning. Letters are also put together to produce what are called in those grammars "phrase linkers" and other related parts of speech which do not have meaning in themselves, but which, when joined to grammatical names—which do have meaning—become the conditions for further meaning to appear. According to those grammars, the combination of a grammatical name and phrase linker produces a "grammatical phrase". Those grammatical names and phrase linkers and grammatical phrases are then put together to make meaningful expressions.

The body of writing in texts, treatises, and so forth is a complex of such letters and the structures of speech built up from them. Texts and so forth containing this complex that concern profound matters, especially the "secret" and "nature secret" matters of the inner tantras, are so deep in meaning that the meaning often will be naturally hidden. And, on top of that, because these matters can be damaging to those who are not ready for them, it is regarded that they must be kept secret by deliberately concealing them.

Who knows all of the meanings—both those that are obvious and those that are hidden and concealed—of all the levels of view contained in such texts, treatises, tantras, and so on? And who, because of knowing them, can impart them to another, for example to ourselves as we seek what is meaningful? Those meanings are present in the mind of the vajra master or guru, who then imparts the meanings of all those views to others.

It is possible to look at the wording of this first part of the thirteenth chapter and think that it is talking about Samantabhadra's presentation of this chapter of the tantra. Because of that, some Tibetans in the past have explained that these two verses mean that the teacher of the tantra, Samantabhadra, who had the meanings of all the views present in his enlightened mind, was expressing those meanings in the pure field of Akaniṣhṭha using grammatically correct language. That would be at once an explanation of the process of the tantra coming into the world and a validation of the extremely profound meaning—of great completion—that will be expressed in the second part of the chapter. However, Longchenpa disagrees, saying that the meaning is the literal meaning of the words, which I have explained just above.

An important point that comes out of this first section is that, if you really want to know these meanings that have been written down in texts, you have to go to a vajra master who has the meanings fully in mind and can therefore correctly impart even the hidden and concealed meanings of the tantra to you, and you have to apprentice yourself to him.

3. About Padmasambhava's Teaching

3.1. the Purpose of the Teaching

Padmasambhava must have taught the *Guhyagarbha Tantra* to his disciples many times, given its importance. The tantra is not easy to read or understand and tradition says that the disciples had become afraid that they would forget its contents, especially the thirteenth chapter. Therefore, he composed a teaching on that chapter in the form of a short but clear reminder or memory aid, so that his disciples could remember the details of the views, vehicles, and so on presented in that chapter. That is why he starts the teaching by saying:

> This is a reminder that contains the particulars of the views, vehicles, and so on.

3.2. The Title of the Teaching

The text of the teaching has a title, as expected. However, Buddhist teachings given orally normally did not have a title, so how did the title that appears in the text of his teaching come about and what does it mean? You will see that, at the end of the teaching, Padmasambhava composed a one-verse prayer in which he mentioned that his teaching was a "secret garland of views".

His teaching was "a garland of views" because, following the thirteenth chapter of the *Guhyagarbha Tantra*, it consisted of a string of views taught one after another. It was "secret" because the bulk of the teaching was concerned with the views of secret mantra.

Secret mantra can be taught in several ways. The best type of instruction is called "foremost instruction". The thirteenth chapter of the *Guhyagarbha Tantra* says directly that it includes foremost instructions. Padmasambhava explained those in his teaching and added his own foremost instructions as well.

Mipham explains this point of foremost instruction in his own words when commenting on the verse of prayer at the end of the teaching. He points out that Padmasambhava gave his explanation using the authoritative statements in general of the Buddhist lineage, then embellished those basic instructions with the foremost instructions contained in the chapter as well as his own in order to ensure that the audience was locked onto the intended meaning of the basic instruction. Thus, the outstanding feature of the teaching aside from its being an explanation of a garland of views, was that it came with foremost instructions on those views in general and especially on the main subject of the chapter, Great Completion. That this is the case can be seen in Longchenpa's explanation of the opening section of the chapter:

> Then he expressed the following for the purpose of expressing superior foremost instructions.

Therefore, when the teaching was committed to writing it was given the formal title *Foremost Instruction "A Garland of Views"*.

3.2.1. More about foremost instruction

Foremost instruction is one of several types of oral instruction, the one which is foremost amongst all types of instruction. It most often comes as instruction given personally that carries the full weight of the teacher's experience or includes very private and potent instruction which the teacher has received from his teacher and which has possibly come down through many generations of the lineage.

The particular quality of foremost type of instruction is that it goes right to the heart of the person being instructed and connects the person very directly to the meaning being presented. It is not just a "pith" or "key" or "oral" instruction as is so often translated, but is the foremost of all types of oral instruction, the one that has the ability to get right into and move the mind of the person who is being instructed.

A second quality of foremost instruction is that it is usually kept private, simply because it has been given specially to the person receiving it. It is usually very specific to the person and the subject being taught. When the subject matter is very profound, as is the case with the great completion being taught in the thirteenth chapter of the tantra, foremost instruction is usually regarded as being very secret and is deliberately concealed. This is done as a matter of compassionate behaviour for two reasons. Firstly, if very secret topics are heard by those who are not ready for it—which is most people—they will not only not understand it, but it could be very dangerous for them. Secondly, foremost instruction quickly loses its potency when it is spread about, so it is kept secret in order to maintain the potency of the instruction for the sake of those who can benefit from it.

Mipham points out that the foremost instructions in this teaching are given as a form of special assistance. The audience gains a correct understanding of the subject matter through the general authoritative statements used in the teaching and then foremost instruction is used where needed to ensure that the audience is locked into that understanding and does not stray from it. This, which is another reason in general for using foremost instruction, is very much part of the thirteenth chapter and Padmasambhava's teachings on it.

The title given to the text of Padmasambhava's teaching reflects the fact that the teaching contains the most special type of instruction and should therefore be given an extra level of respect in general. Moreover, the foremost instruction in this case is on the most secret of all topics, Great Completion, so the teaching should be treated with the utmost reverence. And, given that this foremost instruction is on a topic that is most secret, it should be kept concealed.

3.3. Content of the Teaching

Padmasambhava starts with a single sentence that gives the purpose of the teaching that will follow.

He then gives the body of the teaching, simply following the content of the thirteenth chapter of the root tantra and explaining the main points as he goes. Thus, he first explains the eight categories of view that include all the views that do and do not lead to transcendence of the world. He then explains the highest of those views, Great Completion, as it applies to the deity practice of Mahāyoga. Finally, he explains the foremost instructions at the end of the thirteenth chapter and adds his own. In that way, he covers the two main parts of the thirteenth chapter.

Following that, he adds a brief presentation of the austerities and yogic conducts entailed by the eight categories of view. He then closes the teaching with a single verse of prayer which prays that the beings who have the capacity to use the teaching will come into contact with it. The written teaching was given a very short colophon simply to show the end of the text.

4. An Explanation of the Eight Categories of View

It should be obvious from the foregoing that the purpose of the thirteenth chapter of the tantra is to expose all of the views from lowest to highest present in the worlds of sentient beings and then to explain the highest one, Great Completion, in relation to the overall topic of the tantra, the deity practice of Mahāyoga.

To do that, the chapter mentions eight categories of view. These categories of view need to be identified first and then need sufficient explanation that Padmasambhava's teaching, Longchenpa's commentary, and Mipham's notes on them can be understood.

The eight categories of view begin with two categories of view that are worldly, that do not transcend the world. They end with six categories of view that contain the views of all of the nine vehicles, views that are beyond worldly, that do transcend the world.

4.1. The Worldly Views

The first category of worldly views is the category "not understanding" the authentic and the second is "wrongly understanding" it. It is important to understand the difference between the two. Although the first category is called a "view", it should not be thought of as the type of view that is deliberately taken up. For this category, view means the mind-set in general of beings who have no understanding of anything beyond what is in front of them. As Mipham points out, it is a very stupid mind-set, where stupid means "the stupidity that comes with not having gained any knowledge, for example, by learning".

The second category is a step further than that, representing views that have been deliberately taken up or developed in connection with religion, philosophy, and so on. And, of all such views that there could be—right and wrong—this category specifically refers to the views which are wrong or twisted versions of what is actually the case. In other words, this is not simply not understanding what is actually the case, but is the deliberate acceptance of a view which, although thought to be correct, is actually wrong. Even though it might be the view of a religion whose adherents believe it to be a view leading beyond the world, precisely because it is a twisted version of what is actually the case, it is still a worldly view.

The tantra mentions those two categories but does not give any information about the sort of views that would fall into those two categories. Padmasambhava, who lived in mainstream Indian culture for most of his life before going to Tibet, explains a total of four views known to the Indian culture of his time—Phyal ba, Chārvāka, Paryantika, and Tīrthika. Most readers of this book will have no sense at all of what these refer to and the explanations of them found in Padmasambhava's teaching and Longchenpa and Mipham's commentaries to it will probably be unclear to say the least. Therefore I have tried to explain them in a way that will allow the reader to connect with them.

The first thing to say about this is that the views of Indian philosophy and religion are complicated. It takes some study to sort out what is what and who is who in relation to them. You might find it worthwhile to look up the four names given above on the internet; you will quickly understand that there is no simple definition for most of them and you will see how some of them have changed meaning over the course of time.

Next, it is an important point that Padmasambhava does not use those four names as names of specific religious, philosophical, or whatever views, but uses them as names for *basic types of view* that function as collectors of all of the many specific worldly views. In fact, there is an enormous number of worldly views—we could even say there are as many as there are sentient beings in the entirety of samsara—but if you isolate a set of views that are the basis for all of those views and which therefore contain all of them, there are these four basic types.

For example, the term "Chārvāka" was originally brought into use when one Indian philosopher used it specifically to refer to a group of fellow materialists. It quickly spread and became a general term for all types of materialist and other non-religious approaches to life. Padmasambhava uses the term only in the latter sense, never in the former, and the same is true for the other three. Likewise Tīrthika, which Buddhists starting using in the Buddha's time, was originally intended to refer to those who had embraced orthodox Hindu religious practice but was also used at times to mean everyone who was not a Buddhist. Padmasambhava uses "Tīrthika" only to indicate the basic type of view of a religion or philosophy having a wrong view of eternalism.

In short, the four are not four worldly views but are four basic types of worldly views.

There is one last point that should be mentioned here. The tantra speaks of eight types of meaning. This is initially understood as the meaning of eight types of view that are contained in the writings that constitute texts, tantras, and other written works. However, the last six categories are also the nine vehicles of Buddhism. Therefore, these texts, tantras, and so on could also contain the meaning of vehicles. However, the first two categories we are discussing now, of worldly views, apparently do not fit into the nine vehicles and perhaps the first category does not fit into the category of being a vehicle at all. Padmasambhava does not address this in his teaching, but both Mipham and Longchenpa do.

Longchenpa says that the meaning contained in these texts, tantras, and so on is intended not only to include views but to include all of the vehicles that there possibly could be. Thus, the first category of view can be considered to be an aspect of a vehicle that the Buddha did teach, called "the vehicle of gods and men" and the second category could also be understood in the same way. This vehicle of gods and men can be taken in two ways: as a purely worldly vehicle used by gods and men to get themselves into the happy rebirths of humans and up but also as a precursor to the nine vehicles in which case it could be seen as a path leading indirectly to transcendence. When Longchenpa is discussing this, he uses the words "left as it is" to indicate that the vehicle of gods and men could apply to these first two categories if the definition of the vehicle is the first one just mentioned, in which the vehicle is understood to be just what it is—thoroughly worldly—and without any further attempt to make it out as an adjunct to the beyond-worldly vehicles.

Having covered all of those points, we now look at the four basic types of worldly view. Padmasambhava explains that there are two types of view for the first category of not understanding—Phyal ba and Chārvāka—and that there are two types of view for the second category of wrongly understanding—Paryantika and Tīrthika.

4.1.1. Phyal ba or Vacancy

The lowest of the four views is called "Phyal ba" in Tibetan—no-one is sure of the original Sanskrit. In Tibetan Buddhist literature, it is mostly used to refer to a kind of empty but dead experience; it is a wrong approach in which one mistakes emptiness for a kind of vacant spread of dead, flat sameness. The experience of it is like a vacant lot of land on which there is nothing sprouting up, nothing happening, just a kind of vacant, dead space.

It is easy to join that understanding to the mind of people who simply plod ahead with life, having no higher aims let alone religion or philosophy that they pursue in an attempt to live a more meaningful life. Especially, they have no understanding even of cause and effect, an important point because even a small understanding of how cause and effect works changes a being's outlook, providing the being with an approach to life that gives some chance for a better existence.

This is the mind-set of the most ordinary of ordinary of beings and also the most common type of being when all the abodes of samsara are considered, a mind-set with which the being just blindly goes through life without any understanding that his actions might have any effect at all. Moreover, this mind-set has no higher aim at all.

Mipham explains that this view of "phyal ba" meaning "vacancy" is the worst possible approach to life, and that it is the state in which most beings in the bad migrations—hell, preta, and animal—live. In relation to that, another sense of this view comes with the expression "had a vacant look". Mipham himself says that beings with this view are "stupid as cattle", which fits exactly with the common expression "seeing the vacant look in the eyes of cattle".

Yet another way to understand this term is "humdrum"; the humdrum life of the ordinary human who has no understanding of even the most basic aspect of cause and effect and who just lives from day to day with everything turning into a kind of monotonous grey landscape of life experiences. Sound depressing? In a certain sense, that is correct—from the very bright perspective of a practitioner who understands the realities of life and approaches life in a higher kind of way, this vacant view is a very dull one.

4.1.2. Charvaka or Sweet Talkers

The next view is called "Chārvāka". The word "Chārvāka" was first used in the 7th century C.E. by the Indian philosopher Purandara, who referred to his fellow materialists as "Chārvākas". By the 8th century, the terms Chārvāka, Lokyātika, and Bṛihaspatya were used interchangeably to signify materialism, even though each of those names originally referred to a specific school of view. In other words, the word has come to be used in many ways.

Padmasambhava uses it as the name of a basic type of view. As with Phyal ba, this is a view of stupidity, called not understanding in the tantra, and is not a deliberately taken up view. Where Phyal ba was used to convey the sense of a vacant, dull mind-set, Chārvāka is used to convey the sense of someone who has some understanding of cause and effect but rejects thoughts of past and future lives and all that they imply either because of not believing in that or because of not wanting to be concerned with all it entails.

"Chārvāka" as originally used means "sweet-talkers" in the sense that Purandara's fellow materialists could speak compellingly about their view. The Tibetans did not translate it literally but in a way that implies though does not directly say, "materialism". The official translation from Sanskrit into Tibetan is "rgyangs 'phen pa", meaning a mind-set in which a person *tosses* or throws *far* away all thoughts about past and future lives, concentrating solely on making himself comfortable in the present life, without any thoughts of higher aims. There is also a second translation into Tibetan, "rgyangs phan pa", meaning a mind-set of thinking that there is only this life and nothing else before or after, the approach of *benefiting* this life alone, throughout this life as *far* as it goes; this type of person is pre-occupied with this life and happiness in it and has no connection to higher aims of any kind.

In this view, there is some understanding of cause and effect and for that reason it is said to be a better view than the vacant view. Here, cause and effect can be on the simple level of knowing that if you plant a seed and provide the right conditions, a certain result will be obtained; it does not have to have the higher sense that it has in Buddhism where cause means a karma made in mind and effect is what follows, making the being, for the sake of future lives, very careful of how he lives life now. In this case it can simply be that, if you smile at your enemy and stab him in the back the right way, you can get the position of rulership of a president, dictator, etcetera. Or, it can be that you understand that you can use oracles, astrology, shamanism, or any of the many other worldly methods available to create conditions for your own success or at least absence of failure in this life.

The "Chārvāka" basic type of view includes all sorts of approaches to life that we are well aware of these days, for example most materialistic approaches to life fall into this category. Not thinking about past and future lives, most people these days focus on this life, yet have enough education to know cause and effect sufficiently to know that if they do things right, they will get success and avoid failure in this life. The very hedonistic lifestyles of many people on our planet are another version of this mind-set; they might even claim to have a religious view, but they essentially put that to the side and focus on using what they have learned to get the most enjoyable life possible.

4.1.3. Paryantika or Bounded

Paryantika and Tīrthika views fall into the second category of view mentioned in the root tantra. These are not views that entail basic stupidity in regard to what is real, but are views that beings have deliberately developed or accepted because of seeking meaning for life. Moreover, they are views which, from a Buddhist perspective, are wrong or twisted understandings of what is actually the case.

According to the explanations given in Buddhist texts, this second category of view is comprised of various types of Hindu view. The Hindus themselves assert five or six major Hindu schools whose views can be reduced to being views either of nihilism or eternalism. "Paryantika" here is used to indicate views of nihilism and Tīrthika is used to indicate views of eternalism, with each being typified by specific Hindu schools. However, the right way to understand these two categories of Paryantika and Tīrthika is that they collectively refer to all deliberately assumed views of nihilism and eternalism. For example, most followers of the Christian religion as it stands today fit exactly into the Tīrthika category. Many disaffected youth have a materialistic-nihilist mind-set which is actually a case of not understanding what is real; most of them in my own direct experience are representative of what Padmasambhava is calling "Chārvāka", but there are those who have developed very strong views or who have taken up nihilistic philosophies of life and they fall into the category here of "Paryantika".

The term Paryantika has many meanings, all connected with the idea of a boundary or being bounded. In this case, it has the specific meaning of a view of a "bounded" life. This is a nihilistic view in which life is believed to have a beginning and end, with absolutely nothing coming before or after. It is believed that the events of life arise without cause, that the being then simply dies and ends—is annihilated—and that, moreover, no effects whatsoever arise from living that life. With this view, mind also simply ceases, so the possibilities of emancipation, knowledge of a buddha, and so on also are denied. It is a very cut and dried view in which life happens and ends and that is all there is to it.

In India, the term "Chārvāka" was and still is used in the way just described to refer to people who had an atheistic or materialistic sort of nihilist approach but who just followed that out of ignorance rather than having a well-developed philosophy that they had taken up. For example, the term was used to refer to the views of followers of the tenets of a divine being named Bṛhaspati who had written a series of sutras called the Bṛihaspatya sutras. Again, Chārvāka in that case is a view of simply not understanding what is actually the case, whereas this Paryanta view refers to those who have developed an actual view of nihilism.

In the latter half of the 1900's it was considered amongst Westerners that there were very few examples in Western culture of people with truly nihilist views, though materialism and atheism were burgeoning and there were many examples of the Chārvāka type to be found. At this point, in the early 2000's, nihilism as defined in Paryantika is more widespread in the world as a whole. I have seen around the world that, with the extreme economic crashes that happened at the turn of the millennium and the difficulties of globalism, rising populations, and so on, the younger generation has developed more of the view signified by Paryantika approach: there's nothing before or after, life just happens, without karmic cause and effect—even if the simple fact of cause and effect has been accepted—and at the end you die and there is nothing more, like an oil lamp that has run out of oil.

4.1.4. Tirthika or Those at the Brink

The term "Tīrthika" was used by the Buddha and his followers to refer to those whose view was a deliberately taken up religious view which, although it had the good effect of getting them firmly positioned at a stepping-off point to enlightenment, was wrong. Used in that sense, Tīrthika includes followers of both nihilist and eternalist views, but the bulk of Hindu schools had an eternalist view so Tīrthika was usually used by Buddhist to refer specifically to them.

Hindus themselves say that they have five, sometimes six, main schools of thought of which all but one has a view of eternalism. Padmasambhava mentions three of them in his teaching and Longchenpa lists five. However, alternative lists with yet other schools included or removed could be made following what the Hindus themselves say about their schools.

Regardless of how the views for Tīrthika are enumerated in Padmasambhava's and the other commentaries here, the point is that this basic type of view called Tīrthika includes all views believing in a conceptually-projected eternal personal self. Most Hindu schools call it the "atman". Christians and others call it "the soul". There are so many religious-type views that have this idea and all of them belong to this basic type of view called Tīrthika. They have in common that what they believe to be ultimately true is actually nothing but a conception projected onto what is actually the case. Thus all of them belong to the second category of being wrong, distorted, or twisted—

all ways used to say the same thing—views. Note that these words "wrong" and so on are not being used pejoratively against the religions and so on holding this type of view, but are just a flat statement of the same.

Having explained that, we should turn to the very interesting etymological meaning of "Tīrthika". Unexpectedly, we find that it sheds some light on how Buddha related to the followers of these views which he proclaimed were wrong.

"Tīrthika" was used to mean someone who has not entered the authentic path to enlightenment spoken by the buddhas, but who has entered a spiritual path which gives them a firm footing, a stepping-off place, at the edge of the river leading to enlightenment. That is what the term actually means. Given all the other ways that the Buddha could have referred to the many Hindus of his time, this is a very kind way to speak of them. The Buddha could have used a term that set them as non-Buddhists—as with the term "outsider" which means they are not in the only real teachings, those of the Buddha. However, this term Tīrthika includes them as fellow travellers on the journey to true enlightenment, even if they have started out with a view which is incorrect. Jeffrey Hopkins has translated this as "forders", meaning those at the edge of a water crossing. It is more like "those at the brink", which has the positive sense of going forward that "Tīrthika" contains.

Following on from that, it should be noted that, although Tīrthika refers to those who are non-Buddhists, it does not mean "non-Buddhist". The term "non-Buddhist" includes all kinds of non-Buddhist, for example including all of those who have Phyal ba, Chārvāka, Paryantika, and Tīrthika views—the views that do not lead to transcendence of the world. The term "Tīrthika" on the other hand is much more restrictive, referring only to those who, though they are not Buddhist, have progressed to the point where they have taken up a view that sets them firmly in position to enter the true path to enlightenment.

4.2. Beyond-Worldly Views

The remaining six of the eight categories of meaning are views that lead to transcendence of the world. They are also, as explained earlier, vehicles to the same. These views and vehicles all are, of course, Buddhist views and vehicles. The Buddha taught many types of vehicle. For example, a single vehicle, three vehicles, four vehicles, nine vehicles, and others with even more vehicles. The remaining six categories of meaning are actually a presentation of the views and vehicles of a path to enlightenment comprised of nine vehicles. Padmasambhava's teaching and the commentaries included here all explain how the six remaining categories incorporate the nine vehicles and their views.

Padmasambhava and the commentaries teach the nine vehicles in their defined sequence going from lowest to highest. Moreover, the view is primarily taught, with the meditations and fruitions of the vehicles receiving less mention. Mipham's commentary gives some explanations of why Padmasambhava has taken that approach.

The view and vehicle at the pinnacle of the nine vehicles is the view of Great Completion taught in the vehicle called Atiyoga. That vehicle and its view is presented at the end of the presentations of the vehicles and views below it. Then, as is done in the root tantra, the view of Great Completion is explained extensively in relation to the deity practice of Mahāyoga and foremost instructions are provided to back that up.

5. A Short Explanation of the Nine Vehicles and Their Views

This section is designed to expose enough of the meaning contained in the vast terminology of the nine vehicles that the reader will be able to make some sense of the teachings on the nine vehicles in this book.

There were two main periods in which the Buddhist teaching came into Tibet, called the older and newer spreads. Padmasambhava's teaching of the nine vehicles was taught as part of the older spread of Buddhist teaching that happened in Tibet. It is maintained by the Nyingma or "Older" Tibetan tradition of Buddhist teaching. A newer way of presenting the Buddhist teaching came into Tibet about three hundred years later, at the time of the newer spread, one which is maintained by the newer Tibetan traditions of Buddhist teaching called the Kagyu, Sakya, and Gelug schools. The newer way of presenting the teaching uses a presentation of three vehicles, not nine.

The nine and three vehicle presentations are essentially the same, with the first two of the nine vehicles contained in the first of the three vehicles, the third of the nine being the second of the three, and the remaining six of the nine belonging to the third of the three. Both styles of presentation do present the views, meditations, and conducts of Buddhist teaching in their entirety. However, there are differences between the presentations of the two systems, and this is most obvious at the higher levels, the levels of the tantras.

Thus, another feature of this book is that it gives very clear presentations of the views of the nine vehicles on their own terms and using their own terminology. These presentations will help clarify the confusion regarding the nine vehicles and how they work that is prevalent amongst non-Tibetan practitioners at the time of writing. Especially, they will clarify why "Dzogchen" is actually "Great Completion" and not "Great Perfection" and many other details related to that.

5.1. The Conventional Vehicles

The first three of the nine vehicles are the śhrāvaka, pratyekabuddha, and bodhisatva vehicles. Mipham points out that they can be collectively called "vehicles of characteristics" because all of them pay attention to characteristics known through conceptual mind as part of the journey to enlightenment. In more friendly English, we could say that these are "conventional vehicles" because they approach their journeys through the use of conventions. Mipham's commentary gives some explanation of that.

The conventional vehicles are categorized in the root tantra as follows. The śhrāvaka and pratyekabuddha vehicles have views which are similar enough that they both belong to the third category, partial understanding. The bodhisatva vehicle has a view which belongs to the fourth category, not fully understanding the authentic. Why these three are categorized in those ways is clearly explained in the teaching and commentaries.

5.2. The Unconventional Vehicles

The remaining six of the nine vehicles constitute the unconventional vehicles of Buddhism, vehicles that do not follow the approach of the conventional vehicles just described. They are called "secret mantra vehicles" or "vajra vehicles". They are "secret" because they present spiritual truths which can be dangerous if misused or given to someone who is not ready for them and they are "mantra" because they *tra* protect the enlightened *man* mind, keeping it manifest for the practitioner. They are called "vajra vehicles" because they are "vehicles" that can take a practitioner to enlightenment specifically by relying on the innermost core of what ordinary people think of as mind, a core which is "vajra" or completely indestructible. There are many other names for the unconventional vehicles and all of them, including the ones very briefly explained just now, can be explained at great length in order to give a deeper understanding of the view, meditation, and conduct of these paths to enlightenment.

The unconventional vehicles are categorized in the tantra as: "taming, intent, secret, and nature secret". What these four categories refer to and how they represent the remaining six of the nine vehicles is clearly explained in the teaching and commentaries.

5.3. The Unconventional Vehicles More Fully Explained

It would be useful to give a presentation in plain English of the six "unconventional" or "secret mantra" or "vajra vehicles" of the nine vehicles.

First, there is yet another name for these vehicles, which is "tantras". That name comes for two reasons. Firstly, tantras are texts that appeared in the human world long ago containing the unconventional teachings leading to enlightenment. Scripturally speaking, the teachings of these vehicles come from tantras, therefore, they are tantric vehicles or just "tantras". Secondly, tantra means "continuity", so tantric teachings are a special and profound kind of teaching that show reality as a thread running through the practitioner's life. This explanation relates to the point that these are unconventional teachings that do not primarily focus on conceptual facts or conventions as the way to tread the spiritual journey, but focus on the practitioner's direct experience of his world. This latter meaning of tantra is very profound.

The six unconventional vehicles of the nine vehicles include all tantras. These tantras and hence the vehicles are divided into two sets of three.

The first set is comprised of Krīyatantra, Ubhayatantra also called Charyātantra, and Yogatantra. Krīyatantra means the *tantra* concerned primarily with physical *activities* as the means for attainment[8].

---

[8] Skt. siddhi. "Attainment" throughout this text means the siddhi or attainments gained by the successful use of a vehicle. Generally speaking, there are two attainments, worldly and supreme. The former are things like the ability to fly, and so on, which are powers that can be developed but which in themselves do not provide or are not signs of

(continued ...)

Yogatantra means the *tantra* primarily concerned with the practice of *yoga* as the means for attainment, where yoga specifically means the use of one-pointed meditation to join with reality. Ubhayatantra means the *tantra* which is *half one and half the other*[9]; it is named that way because it incorporates equally the approaches of Krīyatantra and Yogatantra. Its other name Charyātantra means the *tantra* of a certain *conduct*, referring to the fact that its conduct or approach is half one and half the other. In other words, the two names Ubhayatantra and Charyātantra are actually saying the same thing.

The second set is comprised of Mahāyogatantra, Anuyogatantra, and Atiyogatantra. As with Yogatantra, each one is a *tantra* primarily concerned with the practice of *yoga* as the means for attainment. Mahāyogatantra means "the great yoga tantra", setting it a step above outer Yogatantra. Anuyogatantra means "the yogatantra next in the sequence", setting it above Mahāyogatantra and below but approaching Atiyogatantra. Atiyogatantra means "the yogatantra farthest along" in the sequence, indicating its position at the pinnacle position, past all the other eight vehicles which sit below or come before it.

The usual explanation of these six tantras is that the first three of the tantra vehicles are "outer tantras" and the last three are "inner tantras". Padmasambhava gives a slightly different explanation of the six tantras. He says that Krīya and Charyā are outer tantras. Then he says that there are two types of Yogatantra: the first is outer Yogatantra and the second is inner Yogatantra, with inner Yogatantra consisting of Mahāyogatantra, Anuyogatantra, and Atiyogatantra.

---

[8] (... continued)
liberation. Supreme siddhi is realization of Mahāmudrā or Great Completion which does provide liberation.

[9] "Ubhaya" reflects the correct Sanskrit; it is almost universally corrupted in Tibetan texts where is it written "upaya" or "ubaya". The first mis-spelling has misled non-Tibetans to thinking that it must be "method tantra" and the second has everyone scratching their heads.

The two styles of explanation end up meaning the same but Padmasambhava's explanation gives a clearer indication of the meaning of "yogatantra".

Going further with that, outer yogatantra is then called "The Tantra of Capability". Capable here means "capable of withstanding opposing forces" for the various reasons explained in Mipham's commentary under the presentation of Yogatanta.

Then, the three inner tantras are collectively called "anuttaratantras" meaning "unsurpassed tantras" because they are the top level of tantra as a whole within the tantra teachings.

It is a feature of Unsurpassed Tantra that its whole teaching and practice is contained within what are called "the two stages", the stages or we could say phases of creation and completion. Very roughly speaking, creation stage is the phase in which you create yourself as a deity and completion stage is the phase in which you then complete that by thoroughly conjoining it to reality. Furthermore, all Buddhist practice has both method and prajñā aspects, with method corresponding to creation stage and prajñā corresponding to completion stage.

The lower of the three unsurpassed yogatantras, Mahāyogatantra, emphasizes creation stage which emphasizes method, therefore it is called "method" tantra. Mipham's commentary has a very nice explanation of this point. The middling one, Anuyogatantra, emphasizes the completion stage in which method and prajñā are being deliberately connected together, therefore it is called "completion" tantra. The highest one and the pinnacle of all vehicles, Atiyogatantra, emphasizes completion stage but does it at the highest possible level in which everything is not method and prajñā being deliberately connected together as with Anuyoga, but is already in its primordial or timeless state of unification, therefore it is called "great completion" tantra.

5.3.1. The pinnacle teaching of Great Completion

As the names "completion" and "great completion" suggest, from a certain perspective there is not much difference between the view of the completion and great completion tantras. It really comes down to unification: great completion is special because it takes the stance that everything is already the great unification, thus everything is already buddhahood and therefore nothing needs to be done—enlightenment is already spontaneously existing. This is borne out by what Padmasambhava teaches at the end of his explanation of the view of "completion", Anuyoga:

> If that could be done as existing without endeavour, spontaneously, and if it could be done equally at all times and places, then it would be no different from great completion. However, here in the mode of completion, application is laden with effort and rigpa is only partially joined. It is understood as a moment in time—as an instant in which everything is complete.

Atiyogatantra, which has the view of great completion, does go a step further. In its view, it is not a moment of rigpa that is aimed for, but an unending total experience of rigpa that is not pursued with the use of conceptual approaches but is known in direct perception to be the one sphere containing everything, the one sphere in which everything always has been, always is, and always will be utterly complete. That sums up the pinnacle view of great completion in just a few of my own words, though words that do not exceed the tradition of its explanation. Padmasambhava's teaching in *Garland of Views* gives a long explanation of the vehicle of great completion, the highest spiritual teaching available in the human world.

Padmasambhava was, of course, one of the most important people involved in bringing the Atiyoga teaching into Tibet. Longchenpa was the greatest exponent of that teaching, and Mipham was a central figure in the later transmission of it. Thus, this book not only includes an extensive teaching on the great completion of the pinnacle vehicle of Atiyoga, but includes teachings on that subject by some of the key figures in its transmission.

5.3.2. The version of Great Completion taught here

Some non-Tibetan readers might find that Padmasambhava's explanation here of great completion is different from what they have come to think of as great completion. That will be because they are used to hearing the innermost level of the great completion teaching of the purely Atiyoga vehicle.

Each of the three inner tantras can be presented according to the influence of one of the three inner tantras. For example, there is Mahāyoga of Mahāyoga, Anuyoga of Mahāyoga, and Atiyoga of Mahāyoga. These days what many non-Tibetans think of as great completion is actually the great completion of the Atiyoga of Atiyoga level. Padmasambhava's presentation here of great completion is the Atiyoga style of the presentation of Mahāyoga, that is, it is Mahā Ati of Mahāyoga.

I can imagine some people who I have met being disappointed to hear this or even denigratory of Padmasambhava's teaching because it does not come up to the expectations they have of hearing only the great completion of the innermost level of Atiyoga of Atiyoga teachings. That would be as much of a mistake as their obvious clinging to the teachings of great completion. A careful reading of the teaching will reveal many fine points about the great completion teaching that, when approached with a pure motivation, can only lead to a deeper understand of great completion.

6. Great Completion

There have been a number of misunderstandings in general amongst non-Tibetans of the view of Great Completion and its terminology. Even the name itself, not being well understood is often mistranslated as "great perfection" and the like, which has the singular effect of leading the students in the wrong direction and preventing them from being able to understand the many threads of meaning connected with the term.

Padmasambhava's instructions on the view together with Longchenpa and Mipham's clarifications make it easy to see how some of the specialized terms of the inner tantras are used and especially how terms like "completion" and "great completion" function within the overall presentation of the nine vehicles. To assist with that, I have included this short section on great completion.

6.1. Origin and Meaning of the Term Great Completion

"Great completion" is used in several ways in the teachings of the nine vehicles. The one that most people are familiar with is its use as the proper name of a system of dharma that came from a land called Uḍḍiyāṇa which is thought to have been in what is now the Swat region of Pakistan. The Tibetan translations of the tantras of the Great Completion system of teaching that were brought into Tibet say that the name of this system in the language of Uḍḍiyāṇa was "mahāsaṅdhi", a Sanskrit word meaning exactly "the great juncture". Some people have criticized this observation, saying that a Sanskrit word would not have been "the language of Uḍḍiyāṇa", but I am merely reporting what the tantras brought from Uḍḍiyāṇa and translated into Tibetan say. Either way, it is totally accepted amongst Tibetan masters of this system of teaching that the name for the system in Sanskrit at least is "mahāsaṅdhi".

The point here is that the name for the system, "mahāsaṅdhi", means "the great juncture" or "the great point at which things come together". Tibetans translated this name with "rdzogs pa chen po", which literally translated into English is "great completion", not "great juncture". However, the words "juncture" and "completion" have the same meaning in this case; they refer to that one all-encompassing space, that one great juncture, in which all that there could be—whether enlightened or unenlightened, whether belonging to nirvana or samsara—is complete. That is exactly what the Tibetan texts say and what my own Tibetan teachers have taught me in Tibetan, put into plain English.

The name "great completion" is not only the proper name of a system of teaching, but also refers to an all-inclusive space that beings including humans could realize[10] as a result of following the teachings of that system. When a being does realize it, there is nothing more to be realized or done because all is complete within that being's space of realization. In a Buddhist way of talking, the great completion is the final realization, a realization with which truly complete buddhahood has become manifest.

Furthermore, as is seen clearly in Padmasambhava's teaching, "great completion" is used to indicate the fact that, whereas Anuyogatantra presents "completion" in which male and female principles are deliberately connected together in an attempt to produce their unification, Atiyogatantra presents the greater level of that, in which their unification is an already accomplished fact. And continuing on from that, another term "greater completion" is also seen, with the meaning that the great completion teaching teaches a *greater* level of *completion* than any of the teachings in the vehicles below it.

Those are the meanings and usages of great completion.

6.2. Mis-translations Promoting Misunderstanding

The Great Completion system of teaching has its own, extensive vocabulary, with each item in that vocabulary signifying an important meaning. Small changes to the meaning of these words can cause a student of the system to go off in completely the wrong direction. For example, "great completion" is often called "great perfection" in English, but that is a mis-representation of the name that takes the audience in a wrong direction, away from what the actual wording

---

[10] For realization see the glossary.

"great completion" points toward. It points to a final space of realization that is not a state of perfection but one that contains both perfection and imperfection. The name is not intended to connect us with the idea of perfection but with the idea of the juncture of all things perfect and imperfect, a state of realization in which all things are complete.

Longchen Rabjam's definitive explanations in his revered text *The Dharmadhatu Treasury* make it clear beyond a doubt that the meaning of the name is "great completion", exactly. He mentions in several places that the point of the name is the "inclusion of all dharmas within a single unique sphere of wisdom"—which echoes exactly what the original name from Uḍḍiyāṇa says. Moreover, Padmasambhava's teaching here, because of the way it has been composed, makes this point clear without the slightest ambiguity.

6.3. Etymology of "great completion"

The standard explanation of the etymology of "great completion", for instance as found in Longchenpa's various works, is that *completion* means that all phenomena are included at once in a single unique sphere of self-arising wisdom. Padmasambhava mentions this explicitly in several places in this text, for example in the section on "single cause" and for example saying that "completion means the completion of all accumulations of merit and wisdom".

In the tantras in general, *great* is used to distinguish something known by wisdom in direct perception from the same thing known by dualistic mind as a concept. Thus, one explanation of *great* completion is that it is not the completion understood through the use of concept or through deliberate attempts to connect together method and prajñā and as explained in the "completion" section of Padmasambhava's teaching here, but the greater version of that, the actual state of completion known without the use of concept-based endeavour, in the sphere of spontaneously-existing self-arising wisdom.

6.4. Levels of the Great Completion Teaching

The Great Completion teaching as a whole is divided into three main sections, with each section being more profound than the previous one: Mind, Space, and Foremost Instruction sections. Of them, the Foremost Instruction section contains the most profound teaching of Great Completion. This section is sometimes further divided and sometimes not. When it is divided further, the most profound level of it has several names, the most common of which are "nyingthig" meaning "quintessential" and also "unsurpassed" and "extra-secret" Great Completion. The quintessence extra-secret unsurpassed level of teaching is the most essential teaching of reality that has appeared in our current era of human society. You will recall that, in the opening to the thirteenth chapter of the *Guhyagarbha Tantra*, it says that Samantabhadra will teach the "essence" teaching, which has exactly that meaning.

As explained earlier, the Atiyoga tantras, which are the scriptures that are the basis of the great completion system of teaching, can be presented from different standpoints. Atiyoga of Atiyoga will be pure Atiyoga teaching that will have the levels culminating in the quintessence extra-secret unsurpassed teaching described just above. There is also, as explained earlier, an Atiyoga approach to Mahāyoga, which is the approach used in Padmasambhava's teaching here. There is likewise Mahāyoga, Anuyoga, and Atiyoga of Mahāyoga and so on for Anuyoga and Atiyoga.

7. Terminology

There are many subtleties of meaning in the nine vehicles and there is an extensive technical vocabulary for conveying those meanings in Tibetan. The texts in this book present those profound meanings and do so with the heavy use of that technical vocabulary. Therefore, this book will not be an easy read.

Some people want a book like this about profound topics but complain when they find that it is not an easy read. This is unrealistic. The material in the original Tibetan texts in this book is not easy to read, even for Tibetan experts! In fact, without an explanation of the texts from someone who understands their meaning and, on top of that, years of personal training in the topics involved, it is simply not possible to gain an in-depth understanding of these texts.

When we hear that someone has rejected a book like this because it is too hard to read, we feel sad because that person has missed all of the jewels in the treasure mine of these texts because of not being willing to make the effort needed to understand the texts. Therefore, we encourage you to pick the book up and read it through several times. Each time you read it, you will find that new dimensions of meaning will open up. Even then, it has to be said that, in Tibet, you would not understand these texts by reading them yourself. The texts would be explained to you by someone who had received explanations of them from someone else knowledgeable of them, and so on and then you would read the texts over and again, and ask for clarification of points that you could not understand. Therefore, you might also consider reading this book and then taking it to a learned person of the Nyingma lineage who could explain it to you in depth.

Some other people complain that we use non-standard terminology in our books. They say that the terms involved have already been settled for English and that we are wrong for not using them. In fact, we tread the tightrope of using current translation equivalents as much as we can while continuing the work of improving the translation vocabulary. In truth, it is absurd to be saying that after forty years we have settled English translation terminology—the Tibetans took over four hundred years to do that to a point where the basic vocabulary was settled and even then there were translators for several more hundreds of years doing their work in Tibet. In short, we have a long way to go when it comes to translating the extensive technical vocabulary in use in these texts and, with that, we at Padma Karpo Translation Committee have committed ourselves not to being popular but to working at getting the meanings of the Tibetan texts into English as best as we can. Note that we provide footnotes and an extensive glossary containing explanations of all unusual or less-well-known terminology.

7.1. Realization

The most difficult term in the texts translated here was the Tibetan word "rtogs pa" which is used very heavily throughout the texts presented in this book. The difficulty is that the original term in Sanskrit "avagamana" and the Tibetan word too, has several connotations. Although it is nearly always translated into English as "realization" and "to realize", it actually has a much broader meaning. The base meaning of the Sanskrit term is "correct comprehension", "correct understanding" of something. One specific aspect of that base meaning is the sense of "realization" which is either a final comprehension or a high level direct understanding of some truth.

This term is not only used heavily in the texts in this book but is used with both meanings just mentioned freely interchanged. Reading the Tibetan, you can allow for this because of knowing the connotations packed into one word. However, you will see that Mipham has to clarify the meaning of this term in Tibetan, sometimes specifying it as "comprehending" or "understanding" and sometimes as "realization". In other words, even in the Tibetan it is sometimes a problem to know what connotation is actually in use. On the English side we do not have one word with these connotations, so a difficulty of correctly presenting and understanding the text in English easily arises.

For example, in the presentation of the view of great completion, you will come across what are called "the four realizations". You will see that some of the four realizations refer to simply understanding that something is so. For example, for the first realization "of a single cause" Mipham takes the trouble to gloss it as meaning first hearing about and then coming to know clearly, intellectually, that there is a single cause; in current English dharma language we would not call this realization. The fourth of the four realizations which is direct perception of rigpa is "realization" in the sense of direct realization of a higher truth; in current English dharma language we would call this realization. Therefore, we have four complete comprehensions, some of which are understanding and some of which are realization.

This same term appears in other places, too, and again with varying meanings. For example, in the section on the eight categories of view at the beginning of the thirteenth chapter of the tantra, it speaks of "not understanding, wrong understanding, partial understanding, and not understanding the authentic ..." In fact, the first two mean "understanding" and the second two are more like "realization".

7.2. Superfact and Fiction

There is a pair of especially important terms in the Buddhist vocabulary. They have to be mentioned because the original Sanskrit terms for them have very a specific meaning, a meaning which is crucial to being able to understand texts on views and vehicles. The original Sanskrit terms have long been translated into English as "absolute" and "relative", as for example in absolute truth and relative truth. However, these translations are so far from the meaning of the original terms that explanations using them cannot be properly understood or even understood at all. After years of research, I settled on "superfactual" and "fictional" for the two terms respectively. These two terms very accurately convey the meaning of the original Sanskrit terms. Moreover, they are etymologically correct, so they really do serve to translate any literature of Tibetan Buddhism that uses them. You will find a partial explanation of the why's and wherefores of these two terms in the glossary under "superfactual" and "fictional". You will find a much longer explanation in my *Illuminator Encyclopaedic Tibetan-English Dictionary*.

Despite the fact that the new terms superfactual and fictional are correct in every way, some people do not like them and even argue against them. I have seen that these people fall into two main groups. One group is so used to using absolute and relative that they cannot conceive of change. That is, of course, not a sound reason to reject the correct terminology, but it is amazing to see how difficult it is to change the mind of these people, even when it will result in their being able to properly understand—probably for the first time—the materials they have been reading for so long.

The other group has a mistaken understanding of the original terms because of the use of absolute and relative and wrong explanations they have been given of these two English terms in this context. The original Sanskrit does not talk about an "absolute" but speaks, literally, of a superior or higher type of thing known. The original Sanskrit likewise does not speak about relativity and most especially does not speak about the interdependent origination that is behind the so-called "relative truth". If you have heard "relative truth" explained in terms of interdependent origination, the person teaching you simply did not know what he was talking about. The original Sanskrit means "a fiction" and it is used in reference to what deluded sentient beings make up for themselves, something they believe to be true but which is just a fiction made up by their deluded minds.

Some people, not understanding the fullness of the Buddha's teaching on the two truths, say "How can there be fictional truth? If it is one, it cannot be the other!" However, they are mistaken. The Buddha explains very clearly that this is a fiction made up by sentient beings' delusion that those sentient beings believe to be true. In terms of what the Buddha said, it is exactly correct that fictional and truth are paired together to describe what is known by deluded beings.

Some people will probably still be thinking, "These terms cannot be right!" However, look at what Mipham, one of the greatest Tibetan Buddhist scholars of recent times says in his commentary in here to Padmasambhava's text:

> ... the wording "superfact" is used because of its etymology of *super*ior wisdom's *fact* or object and its more general meaning that it is the superior of all attainments possible.

And he goes on to say:

> The "fictional" is confused consciousness together with its appearances. "Fictional" is used because it is classed as something which obscures the fact of the authentic or which is a fiction, a concept, made up by the adventitious confusion of the rational mind.

Please note that these are literal translations of Mipham's words, not translations that have been worked around to make the terms "superfact" and "fiction" fit with what he says. His very words show that "superfact" and "fiction" are how the original terms have to be understood. Moreover, if you read these definitions of his carefully, you will find out some interesting things about superfact and fiction. Certainly you will find out that absolute and relative do not in any way convey the actual meaning intended.

There is still much work to be done in accurately translating Tibetan Buddhist terminology into English. This little exercise should show you that, even if you have been using certain English terms for a long time, they are not necessarily correct. We need you, the audience to have an open mind. If you are open, then we as translators can do the work of finding terminology that accurately translates Tibetan Buddhist terminology, then explain it to you, and you can help by having it accepted. That would be to everyone's benefit.

8. Other Matters

8.1. Sanskrit

Sanskrit terms are an important aspect of the technical explanations found in the commentary. They are properly rendered into English with diacritical marks, therefore, for the sake of precision, diacritical marks have been used with them throughout this book.

The IATS system of transliteration of Sanskrit, the one generally in use in academic circles, is hard for non-scholars to read. Therefore, we have modified that system slightly to make the transliterated Sanskrit more readable even when the meaning of the diacritical marks is not understood. This same approach seems to be commonplace amongst translators of Tibetan Buddhism. In it:

ca is written as cha ;
cha is written as chha ;
ṅ is written as ṅg ;
ṛ is written similarly as ṛi ;
ś is written the way it sounds, as śh ;
ṣ is written similarly as ṣh .

The other letters for transliteration are used in the same way as they are used in the IATS scheme. In general, if you do not understand the system, simply read the letters as though they did not have the diacritical marks and, with our modified system, you will have a good approximation to the actual pronunciation.

8.2. Further Study

Padma Karpo Translation Committee has amassed a range of materials that will assist the reader to understand the teachings in this text; see the chapter at the end of the book for the details.

Longchen Rabjam's massive three-part anthology of texts called *The Great Completion Resting Up Trilogy* contains very extensive explanations and definitions of the nine vehicles and how they work to convey a practitioner to enlightenment. In particular and as with this book, there is a special emphasis on the Great Completion teaching that comprises the ninth vehicle and how it fits with the other eight vehicles. Padma Karpo Translation Committee is working on a translation of the entire trilogy. It is a major work that will take some years to complete, so it is not noted in the chapter on further study at the end of the book, where only published works are listed. However, it will provide a complete resource for serious practitioners when it does become available.

Lama Tony Duff, director
Tamás,Agócs, translator
Padma Karpo Translation Committee
Swayambunath,
Nepal,
July 2015

Plate 1. Longchen Rabjam Drimey Ozer.
Mural on the wall of Dzogchen Monastery,
Tibet, 2007. Photograph by the author.

Commentary to Chapter Thirteen of the *Guhyagarbha Tantra* From Longchen Rabjam's *Dispelling the Darkness of the Ten Directions*

The Meaning of the Essence, Completion Stage

This has three parts: seeing the connection to the chapter's meaning, explaining the chapter's meaning, and summarizing the current section.

1. Seeing the Connection to the Meaning

So far, the tantra has shown the creation stage of the path. Now, in order to show the completion stage of the path, it says:

> Samantabhadra, the teacher who dwells as all the maṇḍalas of the vajras of enlightened body, speech, and mind of all the tathāgatas of the ten directions and four times collected into one, playing in the great joy of unsurpassed wisdom entered the equilibrium of the samādhi that displays to those having supreme good fortune clouds of the essence just-as-it-isness[11]. Those are the clouds of the samaya of all the dharmas of the

[11] "Just-as-it-isness" refers to what the *Guhyagarbha Tantra* ascertains in each of its chapters, so "essence just-as-it-isness" means the just-as-it-isness ascertained by this chapter called "essence", where "essence" specifically refers to the great completion, the most essential of all teachings.

appearances and rebirths of samsara and nirvana being primordially spontaneously-existent in the great completion, a samaya which has the nature of being extremely secret from those who are not suitable vessels. Then, in order to express superior foremost instructions[12], he spoke like this.

2. Explaining the Meaning

This has two parts: showing in general that the meaning of the secret is in the vajra master's mind and explaining the meaning of Nature Great Completion in detail.

2.1. Showing in General That the Meaning of the Secret is in the Vajra Master's Mind

This has three parts: identifying the meaning; where that meaning is; and who un-mistakenly teaches that meaning.

2.1.1. Identifying the meaning

Generally speaking, the ultimate meaning of each of the vehicles comes about in relation to the master who teaches each of them. In particular, the ultimate meaning of Nature Great Completion which is hidden and concealed in the words of the tantra and agama texts resides in the guru's mind, so if one wants the oral instructions, one has to get on with pleasing the guru.

Now in relation to that, there are inconceivable, inexpressible vehicles and countless fields of buddhas and levels of abodes of sentient

[12] "Superior foremost instructions" means ones connected with great completion. The instructions given in the tantra in prior chapters were foremost instructions on the creation stage level of the path. The instructions given in this chapter are the superior level of foremost instructions on the great completion stage or Ati yoga.

beings, so there is a distinct level of uncertainty involved with attempting to do so. Nevertheless, in this current age of the Good Aeon and this Endurance World, buddha lamps are on show and when each of the modes—inferior, superior, and twisted—of vehicles and their textual traditions are collected, there are eight altogether.

Of the eight, the first one is characterised as not understanding the meaning of the authentic. It corresponds to the majority of beings, those who have not taken up a defined system of tenets. For them, what is meaningful is to find a good situation and no more than that. Thus, this is the vehicle of gods and men left as it is, without further interpretation, a vehicle which simply accomplishes the good migrations. This vehicle has the meaning of propelling beings into the abodes of gods and men in the desire realm by way of the ten virtues and of producing for them the realms above that of the meditative absorption[13] and formless realms by way of their meditations. A Middle Way text says of this[14]:

> The worldly ones' right view ...

One person[15] has asserted that this first one encompasses both the Phyal ba and the Chārvāka views, due to which it ends up not relating to former and later lives and not being classified as a vehicle. Still, the meaning of the vehicle of gods and men mentioned earlier in the context of the five vehicles[16] and the meaning of all possible

---

[13] Skt. dhyāna. This is another name for the form realms.

[14] This is a quote from the *Precious Garland* by Nāgārjuna. The whole verse says, "Whoever comes to have the worldly ones' right view will not enter the bad migrations for at least one thousand aeons".

[15] ... Padmasambhava in his teaching ...

[16] The five vehicles, taught in an earlier chapter of the tantra, is a standard formulation which includes both vehicles that do and do not lead

(continued ...)

vehicles come together here, so this category is referred to as a vehicle left as it is, without further interpretation[17]. Note that the case of Phyal ba and Chārvāka being included within Tīrthika, which itself is wrong view, is not related to this.

Wrongly understanding the meaning of the authentic characterises the Tīrthika teachings. When the wrong views involved are enumerated, they are inconceivable in number, but they collect into four with a view of permanence and one with a view of nihilism which altogether are known as the five divisions of Tīrthika. The four with a view of permanence are: the followers of Nyāya who advocate Iśhvara as permanent; the followers of Viṣhṇu who advocate Viṣhṇu as permanent; the Saṃkhya who claim their prime principle to be permanent; and the Vaiśheṣhika who claim atoms to be permanent. They are the followers of Akṣhipāda, Ṛiṣhi Kapila, Kanāda, and

---

[16] (... continued)
to enlightenment. The first of the five, the vehicle of gods and men, is the one that does not lead to enlightenment. When that vehicle's meaning is taken literally, without further interpretation, it is the vehicle that beings follow in order to find a happier situation within samsara, which will either be a higher birth in the desire realm driven by merit or a birth in the form or formless realms driven by meditative absorption. However, when its meaning is interpreted, it can be a vehicle that leads to enlightenment, though only indirectly. The reasoning here is that the vehicle as it is literally expressed becomes a basis for births in the good migrations of humans, and so on. Thus it is not a basis for attaining enlightenment. However, when that is interpreted, because human and certain god realm births can be a basis for the attainment of enlightenment, the vehicle can be said to lead to enlightenment, though only indirectly.

[17] Mipham says that this can be a view without a vehicle and explains why. Longchenpa is even more clever, showing that this can be considered to be the "Vehicle of Gods and Men" but in a way that there is no deliberately taken view with it.

Ulūka[18]. There are various ways of referring to the one taking a view of nihilism: "Chārvāka" or "Sweet-talkers" or "Wearers of Space", all of which are understood to be the god Bṛihaspati[19].

All five advocate a self. The ones with a view of permanence assert a self or prime principle[20] that is permanent, singular, and independent[21] and assert it as a pervasive nature controlling the physical

---

[18] This is not correct, though that is not surprising given the complexity of the matter. Akṣhipāda was the founder of the Nyāya school, Ṛiṣhi Kapila of the Sāṃkhya, Kanāda of the Vaiśheṣhika, and although Tibetan philosophical texts generally give Ulūka as a founder or co-founder of the Vaiśheṣhika, Indian sources say that he was simply a very ancient figure whose views were similar to those of the Vaiśheṣhika. The followers of Viṣhṇu are followers of the Vedas.

[19] This too is muddled. Bṛihaspati is the name of an ancient Hindu god known from well before the Buddha. He is said to have written his views in what are called the Bṛihaspatiya sutras. People who follow those sutras are regarded as people who follow a sort of materialist view that has nihilist tendencies. Much later, in the 7th century C.E., an Indian philosopher coined the term "Chārvāka" in reference to his materialist associates, a term whose literal meaning is "Sweet-Talkers". However, "Chārvāka" soon came into wide use as a name for all sorts of schools of materialistic thought. The Jains, who are known for wearing no clothing and therefore are called "Wearers of Space" also have a materialist-nihilist type of view. Thus, to say that those three are names for followers of the writings of the god Bṛihaspati is simply incorrect. What is intended here for the one view of nihilism is in fact all the various Hindu schools that have a truly nihilist view. Padmasambhava in his commentary to this thirteenth chapter correctly names them with the term Paryantika, which has been explained in the introduction.

[20] Saṃkhya posits a prime principle which is permanent, the others all posit atman or self which is permanent.

[21] Buddha pointed out that seeing anything as permanent, singular, and

(continued ...)

elements[22] that resides in the heart of all sentient beings, and they assert that the eternal gods Iśhvara, Viṣhṇu, and so on are what propels a being into the higher levels and into the bad migrations. The nihilists say that a self suddenly happens in the mother's womb, stays during life, then is annihilated at the time of death. They are "the Paryanta of earlier and later bounds" who assert that life has a starting point with no lives prior to it and an ending point with no lives subsequent to it, and that there is no emancipation and no all-knowing[23]. Therefore they are called Paryanta or Chārvāka[24].

Thus, when the Tīrthika are summed up, they come down to having the two views of permanence and nihilism.

---

[21] (... continued)
independent fits with the way that sentient beings in general perceive the things of their world. He showed that the three are wrong views because an analysis of the things of the world shows that they actually are impermanent, manifold, and dependent.

[22] The elements here refers to what are called the great elements that comprise the physical world—earth, water, fire, air, and space.

[23] Paryanta is a commonly used term literally meaning "bounded all around" and Paryantika is a person who has that view. "Bounded all around" means that life just begins with nothing before it and ends with nothing after it. With that, it is also accepted that in between those bounds everything just happens, there being none of the karmic cause and effect that happens when there is a stream of lives. Therefore, people having this view also assert no emancipation from samsara and also no all-knowing wisdom of a buddha.

[24] This type of nihilist strictly speaking has the Paryanta or "no bounds" view. However, it has often been called Chārvāka by both Hindus and Buddhists because Chārvākas have that sort of nihilism implicit in their materialist view. Therefore Longchenpa says what he says but note that this usage of Chārvāka is not the same as in Padmasambhava's teaching.

Next, partially realizing the meaning of the authentic characterises both the śhrāvaka and pratyekabuddha vehicles. They have that character because they lead to liberation from samsara through the realization of a one-fold and one and a half fold absence of self respectively.

The śhrāvaka followers divided into four main groups that further divided into a total of eighteen sub-schools.

Seven schools divided off from the Sarvāstivāda school: the Kāśhyapīya, the Mahīśhāsaka, the Dharmaguptaka, the Bahuśhrūtiya, the Tāmrasatīya, the Vibhājyavādin, and the Mūla-Sarvāstivādin. Their lineage was from Rāhula-subhadra, the son of the Bhagavat, who came from the Kṣhatriya caste. They speak the "Well Constructed" or Sanskrit language. The cloth swatches of their outer robe are from nine to twenty-five in number. Their symbols are the utpala, lotus, jewel, and emerging tree-leaves.

Five schools divided off from the Mahāsaṃghika school: the Pūrvaśhailavarga "the group dwelling in the eastern mountains"; the Uttaraśhailavarga, "the group dwelling in the western mountains"; the Haimavatavarga, "the group dwelling in the Himalaya snow mountains"; the Prajñāptivādin "those advocating examination"; and the Lokottaravādin "those advocating transcendence of the world". Their lineage was from the Elder Mahākāśhyapa who came from the Brahmin caste. They speak the Prakrit language. The cloth swatches of their outer robe are from nine to twenty-three in number. Their symbols are the svastika coil and the endless knot.

Three schools divided off from the Sthavira school: the Jetavanīya, the Abhayagirivādin, and the Mahāvihāravasina. Their lineage was from the noble Mahākātyāyana who came from the literate caste. They speak the Apabhraṃśha language. The cloth swatches of their outer robe are from nine to twenty-one in number. Their symbol is the conch.

Three schools divided off from the Mahā-sammitīya school: the Kaurukullikavarga, the Āvantakavarga, and the Vātsiputrīyavarga. Their lineage was from noble Upālī who came from the caste who does this and that[25]. They speak the Piśhāchi language. Their cloth swatches are the same as that of the Sthaviras.

All of them realize the absence of self of persons and aggregates grasped as mine, and nothing more than that, through which they manifest the fruition.

The prayekabuddhas can be divided into three: those who mostly live communally, who partially live communally, and who living by themselves are rhinoceros-like. Their view is that they realize the absence of self of persons and realize that the grasped-at externals have no nature, so they realize a one and a half fold absence of self. And, their view is that at the time when they end rebirth, they accomplish a self-enlightenment that is realized without actually relating to a guru but through the dharmatā of interdependency shining forth of itself and are liberated by that realization. Having been liberated in that way, they do not speak out to show the dharma in words.

Not understanding the meaning of the authentic—of actuality—with nothing left out characterises the vehicle of characteristics. It asserts the cause of a sentient being accomplishing the two accumulations which carried out through many countless aeons produces a fruition of primal buddhahood being accomplished. The vehicle divides into two: Mind Only and Middle Way schools.

---

[25] ... meaning the śhūdra caste, which is the lowest of the four castes of Hindu culture, also known as the outcastes. The name given in the text comes from the fact that the other three castes all have specific tasks in life, whereas the outcastes do not ...

The former asserts that the appearances of the external environment are mind. Then it asserts that, at the level of superfact[26], that mind is self-knowing wisdom without the dualism of grasped-grasping[27]. One sub-school—called the True Aspectarians—claims that there are true superficies in the wisdom and a second—called the False Aspectarians—claims that there are false superficies in it. *Avalokiteśhvara's Yogic Disciplines* says:

> Those who claim that the things appearing in various ways are one's own mind and that that mind moreover in superfact is personal, self-knowing wisdom[28] without the dualism of grasped-at and grasper[29] should be known to have two factions that come from their advocating the nature of that wisdom to be either true or false.

The Middle Way also has two sub-schools. The Autonomy school asserts that these various appearances have the nature of being established in the fictional, where they are illusion-like, and of being without establishment in superfact, where they are like space. The Consequence school asserts that these various appearances are always without nature, thus appearing like the eight analogies of illusion, and that they are free of all elaborations' extremes, thus are without

---

[26] For superfact, see the glossary.

[27] For grasped-grasping, see the glossary.

[28] Tib. so so rang rig ye shes. The term translated here as "personal" is sometimes translated as "individual". The meaning is that each person has self-knowing wisdom and knows that directly for himself, not that the self-knowing knows each knowable individually. The term emphasizes that self-knowing wisdom is something that each person has and will know for themselves through practise of the path.

[29] The term "grasped-grasping" is an abbreviation of a phrase that shows the two sides of dualistic consciousness in a Mind Only style of presentation. In that system, duality comes in the form of mind being the grasper that knows objects and also being the object grasped-at by it.

establishment anywhere at all and are beyond the stains of the four extremes.

All of them claim that the view—the dharmatā[30] of the emptiness of two selves—is first resolved and then, by the path of putting aside non-virtue and practising virtue, the fruition is accomplished after that. When the view of this vehicle is assessed by the vehicles above it, those higher vehicles assert that all dharmas are realized as absence of self and presence of equality. However, compared to the higher ones, this vehicle with all of its subdivisions included: does not see the meaning they expose of all dharmas equally being primordially buddha; does not realize the nature of being without adoption and rejection because of karma and affliction itself shining forth as wisdom; and has fewer means and encounters more difficulties, so asserts an accomplishment of the fruition that takes a very long time. That is why it is referred to as "not understanding the authentic".

In regard to that, one person asserts, "There is no difference between the vehicle of characteristics and the vehicles of the tantras in terms of their prajñā, but the latter is superior in terms of its methods". However, that is mixed up. The latter is special and higher in terms of method, so the prajñā posited in relation to it must also be special, and on top of that, where in the Prajñāpāramitā vehicle does it assert the accomplishment of buddhahood with all dharmas being present in a maṇḍala and with this very mind right now not having been changed in the slightest? Thus both prajñā and method are higher. As the *Lamp of the Three Modes* says:

> Not stupid in regard to even one fact,
> Having many methods and without difficulties,
> And having a standpoint of being for those of sharp
> faculties—
> The secret mantra vehicle is special because of that.

---

[30] For dharmatā, see the glossary.

Therefore, what is being explained here is that there is a blind-spot, some stupidity, within the approach of Prajñāpāramitā.

In addition to that, *Presentation of the Three Vehicles* says:

> Because of referring to complete purity and
> Because of the forces of companions and conduct
> The vehicle of the intelligent ones
> Is known to all as the great of the great[31].

And the *Method Lasso* says:

> The exceptionally marvellous great mode of secret mantra
> Is among all paths, the great short path;
> Is among all methods, the non-mistaken superior one;
> Is among all prajñās, the special prajñā.

In relation to that, the tantra that tames the bad conduct of the three doors by making ritual cleanliness and austerities primary is Krīya-tantra. It can be divided into three: accomplishing the deity based simply on arousing enlightenment mind[32], accomplishing the deity based simply on austerities and fasting practice, and accomplishing the deity based simply on permission to turn the attention to the deity. In addition to that, astrology and calculations of the right time to start any activity are used for liberation.

The tantra of the use of mind is Yogatantra, where the Sanskrit term "apīpra" indicates the use of a mental approach in particular, which in turn means that the deity is accomplished primarily by means of

---

[31] Vajra Vehicle is the great version of the Great Vehicle. It pays great attention to the complete purity aspect of mind and uses the forces of samaya and yogic behaviour to achieve its goals.

[32] Skt. bodhichitta. The term "bodhichitta" has been translated in this book as enlightenment mind. See the glossary for more.

mind in one-pointed samādhi. In addition, in this case there is no accomplishing the deity without first obtaining the empowerment.

The tantra that clearly reveals the enlightened body, speech, and mind secrets[33] is Mahāyogatantra. It is not to be shown to those engaged with the vehicles beneath it who have rational minds strongly clinging to conceived things, so it is secret. When divided it consists of: father tantra which primarily shows creation stage; mother tantra which primarily shows completion stage; and non-dual tantra which primarily shows unification.

The marvellous meaning of the secret whose nature is primordial spontaneous-existence is the meaning of great completion that shows mind and wisdom to be self-appearing, the great gadgetry of illusion. This, which is not the domain of everyone, is especially secret due to its entity, nature, and methods. When divided it consists of: the great completion of unified creation and completion showing non-dual mind and wisdom; the great completion of primordially-liberated mind inspace primarily showing mind; and the great completion of luminosity-dharmatā primarily showing wisdom.[34]

---

[33] "Secrets" here specifically refers to the secrets of enlightened body, speech, and mind, meaning realities of enlightened body, speech, and mind which are hidden in an undeveloped sentient being and which, if brought out, become the indestructible, un-degrading vajras of enlightened body, speech, and mind of a complete buddha. See three secrets in the glossary.

[34] Tib. klong. "Inspace": there are several words in Buddhism used for meanings similar to space. This term has the specific meaning of the interior space that happens to a person of something known in direct, personal experience. It refers to the sense of being in a particular space. Here it is used to signify that realization has become a full-time, ongoing experience. You could also say "the great completion of total immersion in the space of primordially liberated mind".

The last three items mentioned are Great Completion or Ati yoga's

(continued ...)

The meaning[35] to be understood is all of the meanings of those individual modes of vehicle.

2.1.2. Where that meaning is

The meaning of all those vehicles is present in the texts that express them. In those texts, the meaning has been written starting with letters. Vowel and consonant letters have been assembled into terms designated as conventions, thus making grammatical names from the letters, like for example the letters "ma" and "ma" can be placed together to make the term "mama" which has been designated as a convention for "mother" and which is a grammatical name. Then many grammatical names have been assembled into grammatical phrases. Using them, verses then sections then whole treatises and then all the tantras in each class of tantras have been produced, with each having in it the meaning to be expressed by it and each fully revealing that meaning.[36]

2.1.3. Who un-mistakenly teaches that meaning

Those texts in general have present in them the meanings they are to express in words. In particular, the words concerning the nature secret essence contained in this *Guhyagarbha Tantra* have hidden in them the meanings of all dharmas being primordial buddhahood, and so on, which are by nature difficult to comprehend. And, those words, which it is not all right to broadcast in the realm of ordinary people, are kept concealed because their profound secrets would not

---

[34] (... continued)
internal divisions of mind, inspace, and foremost instruction sections.

[35] "Meaning" here refers to the meaning to be understood through this thirteenth chapter of the *Guhyagarbha Tantra*.

[36] Sanskrit and Tibetan grammars use a system for building meaningful expressions that is different from the English system. It is explained at length in a footnote to this part of the explanation of the tantra that can be found in Mipham's commentary later in this book.

be understood by ordinary people due to their absence of fortune. The meanings having that nature of being hidden and concealed that have been made visible with, as was said, "the A string and KA string symbols ...",[37] are present in the mind of the vajra master who teaches the meaning of the tantra without error, so they come from him and him alone.

One person says in reply to that, "The meanings are brought forth in Akaniṣhṭha by the teacher, Samantabhadra. Your saying that the meanings are brought forth by a vajra master for ordinary beings bears no relation to that. If it were true, then someone other than the teacher of the tantra would be bringing forth the meaning contained in this tantra, and then how could Samantabhadra himself be giving the explanation and bringing forth the meaning?![38] That makes no sense!" That is what he says, but it is nothing more than him not having understood the meaning.[39]

---

[37] "The A string and KA string symbols" is a quote from an earlier chapter in the *Guhyagarbha Tantra*. It is part of the explanation of how the vowel (A string) and consonant (KA string) symbols or letters are combined into written conventions that are used to making mentally-known meanings visible to another.

[38] In the tantra, Samantabhadra is responsible for teaching the tantra itself. The person saying this does not understand that the wording here in the tantra is not talking about the origin of the teaching of the tantra—Samantabhadra—but about the person who knows the meaning of the vehicles and teaches them to disciples.

[39] The section of commentary up to here explains the first part of the thirteenth chapter of the *Guhyagarbha Tantra*. It continues from here with the explanation of the second part of the chapter, which concerns the view of great completion applied to the creation of a deity in Mahāyoga and includes foremost instructions to ensure that that meaning of great completion is not misunderstood.

2.2. Explaining the Meaning of Nature Great Completion in Detail

This has three parts: the actual showing of the profound meaning of the essence, the way that it is superior to everything else, and the vessel who shall be instructed ...

Plate 2. Padmasaṃbhava and his manifestations.
Mural on the wall of Dzogchen Monastery,
Tibet, 2007. Photograph by the author.

Foremost Instruction, "A Garland of Views" by the Great Master Padmasambhava

This is a reminder that contains the particulars of the views, vehicles, and so on.

I prostrate to the bhagavat youthful Mañjuśhrī and the vajra dharma.

The mistaken, countless views of sentient beings in the worldly realm collect into four basic types: Phyal ba, Chārvāka, Paryanta, and Tīrthika.

Phyal ba is not understanding in relation to the existence and non-existence of the causes and effects of all dharmas, a total stupidity. Chārvāka is not understanding in relation to the existence or non-existence of past and future lives and is accomplishing rulership, wealth, and power for this life alone, done in reliance on the words privy to the world.

Paryanta takes the view that cause and effect for all dharmas does not exist and that all dharmas produced in one life are adventitiously-produced dharmas that are finally annihilated. Tīrthika takes the view that an eternal self which is conceived of in all dharmas exists and, as well as that, takes a view of the existence of effects without a cause, a wrong view of cause and effect, and a view of a cause existing without an effect.[40]

Those are views of ignorance.

There are two types of path that transcend the world: the vehicle of characteristics and the vehicle of the vajra.

The vehicle of characteristics is of three types: the śhrāvaka vehicle, the pratyekabuddha vehicle, and the bodhisatva vehicle.

The view of those who have entered the śhrāvaka vehicle is as follows. In their view, the view of non-existence from the outset—nihilism—and the view of existence of permanence, and so on, which the Tīrthikas and their like conceive of in all dharmas through over- and under-statement, are non-existent like a rope seen as a snake. For them, the atoms of the four great elements that make up the aggregates, dhātus, and āyatanas, and so on and consciousness are viewed as superfactually existent and the four types of fruition are gradually accomplished through meditative cultivation of the four truths of the noble ones.

The view of those who have entered the pratyekabuddha vehicle is as follows. They are in accord with the śhrāvakas in viewing that the eternal self that the Tīrthikas and their like conceive of through over- and under-statement for all dharmas is non-existent. However, they have the distinction of realizing absence of self in one part of dharmadhātu, the form aggregate, and, moreover, when they attain the fruition of a self-enlightenment it will not have been through relating to a spiritual friend as the śhrāvakas do but by the force of past

---

[40] Note the difference between the way of talking in the previous paragraph and in this one. The previous paragraph sets out two views which are cases of simply not understanding. This paragraph sets out two views that have been deliberately produced and are cases of taking a certain view or stance.

habituation with which they realize the profound meaning of the dharmatā by way of the twelve links of interdependent origination, then attain the fruition of a self-enlightenment.

❁ ❁ ❁

The view of those who have entered the bodhisatva vehicle is as follows. They assert that all of the dharmas of total affliction and complete purification in superfact are without nature and in the fictional are existent as mere illusions, their individual characteristics unmixed with that of the others. They assert that the fruition at the end of coursing in the ten pāramitās and gradually traversing the ten levels is the accomplishment of an unsurpassed enlightenment.

❁ ❁ ❁

The vehicle of the vajra has three types: the vehicle of Krīyatantra, the vehicle of Ubhayatantra, and the vehicle of Yogatantra.

The view of those who have entered the Krīyatantra vehicle is as follows. From superfact in which there is no birth and cessation, in the fictional one meditates on the body of the deity's form, and accomplishment happens primarily through bringing together the devices of body-images, mind-symbols, mantra-recitation, ritual cleanliness, set times, planets and stars of the zodiac, and so on, and through causes and conditions.

❁ ❁ ❁

The view of those who have entered the vehicle of Ubhayatantra is as follows. From superfact in which there is no birth and cessation, in the fictional one meditates on the body of the deity's form and accomplishment happens through reliance both on the samādhi of meditation possessing the four suchnesses and on devices and cause and conditions, and so on.

❁ ❁ ❁

The view of those who have entered the vehicle of Yogatantra is of two types, that of the outer yoga vehicle, the tantra of capability, and that of the inner yoga vehicle, the tantra of method.

The view of those who have entered the vehicle of outer yoga, the tantra of capability, is as follows. Accomplishment does not come through primarily holding to external devices but through primarily doing the yoga of meditation. The meditation is done using a samādhi on male and female deities without birth and cessation in superfact and on a totally pure mindstream having a similarity to that to meditate on a noble one's form body having the four seals.

The view of those who have entered the vehicle of inner yoga, the tantra of method, is of three types: the mode of creation, the mode of completion, and the mode of great completion.

The mode of creation is as follows. It asserts creation in steps by the three types of samādhi and accomplishment by displaying the maṇḍala in steps and meditating on it.

The mode of completion is as follows. While not wavering from the male and female deities without birth and cessation in superfact and not wavering from the dharmadhātu central channel the fact of not thinking discursively, in the fictional one meditates on the clearly evident bodily form of a noble one and on equality and on being unmixed, and by that meditation there is accomplishment

❁ ❁ ❁

The mode of great completion is as follows. All dharmas worldly and beyond worldly being inseparable, they are primordially the nature of the maṇḍala of enlightened body, speech, and mind. That is realized then meditated on.

Going further, tantra says:

> The limbs of the vajra aggregate are
> Known as the five complete buddhas.
> All of the many āyatanas and dhātus
> Are the maṇḍala itself of bodhisatvas.
> Earth and water are Locanā and Māmakī,
> Fire and wind are Pāṇḍurā and Tārā,
> And space is Dhātvīṣhvarī;
> The three rebirths are primordially the complete purity.

All of the dharmas of samsara and nirvana primordially unborn and illusions capable of performing functions are primordially the nature of the ten male and female sugatas, and so forth. Therefore, all dharmas are by nature nirvana: the five great ones are in nature the five females; the five aggregates are the buddhas of the five families; the four consciousnesses are in nature four bodhisatvas; the four objects are in nature the four goddesses of beauty; the four faculties are in nature four bodhisatvas; the four times are in nature the four offering goddesses; the body faculty, its consciousness, its object, and the enlightenment mind arisen from them are in nature the four wrathful ones; the four bounds of permanence and nihilism are in nature the four female wrathful ones; the mental consciousness is in nature the enlightenment mind vajra, Samantabhadra; and its objects, compounded and uncompounded dharmas, are in nature the female maker of dharmas, Samantabhadri. Moreover, their nature is primordially manifest complete buddhahood, it is not that they are made by the path.

Like that, all compounded and uncompounded dharmas in the ten directions, three times, three realms, and so on are never split off from one's own mind, which has been said like this:

> One's own mind discriminated
> Is itself buddha, bodhisatva;
> Is itself the three worlds;
> Is itself the great elements.

It has been said like this:

> All dharmas reside in mind.
> Mind resides in space.
> Space does not reside anywhere.

And:

> All dharmas are empty of entitiness.
> All dharmas are primally complete purity.
> All dharmas are universal luminosity.
> All dharmas are by nature nirvana.
> All dharmas are manifest complete buddhahood.

This is the great completion. (Note in text: The mode of great completion is the accumulations of method and wisdom being complete in this mode of the fruition dharmas existing spontaneously, the factual situation entered.)

Conviction in that mode of great completion happens via the path of the four types of realization. The four types of realization are: realization of single cause, realization through the mode of syllables, realization through blessing, and realization in direct perception.

Realization of single cause is as follows. All dharmas in the superfactual are unborn so are not individualized, and in the fictional have the characteristic of illusion so are not individualized, and the unborn-ness appears as various illusions like moons in water, able to perform functions, and the illusoriness without entity is unborn so all these dharmas are inseparable fictional and superfactual and are thus realized to be of a single cause.

Realization through the mode of syllables is as follows. The unborn-ness of all dharmas is realized to be A, the nature of enlightened speech. Their unborn-ness appearing as illusions able to perform functions is realized to be O, the nature of enlightened body. The rigpa realizing such, the wisdom of illusion without edge and centre is realized to be OṂ, the nature of enlightened mind.

Realization through blessing is as follows. It is realizing that, as for example the power to bless white cotton cloth into red exists in the dye, so the power to bless all dharmas into buddhahood comes through being blessed by the power of the modes of single cause and syllables.

Realization in direct perception is as follows. Knowing that all dharmas primordially residing as buddhahood is not contradictory to authoritative statement and foremost instruction, rather than relying on the mere words of authoritative statement and foremost instruction, this is realization entailing a deep-seated conviction in rational mind, through one's own rigpa in direct perception.

Conviction by the path is as follows. The meaning of the four types of realization, rigpa itself, is a yogin's path. Moreover, it is not the kind that looks forward to the time of a fruition of a cause deliberately made, rather, it is one of realizing it by oneself in direct perception and gaining conviction in it.

For that, the three characteristics will finalize the meaning. The mode of the four realizations, rigpa, has the characteristic of knowing. Doing the habituation to it again and again has the characteristic of engaging. The power of habituation to it having made it manifest has the characteristic of fruition.

The three characteristics reveal the relationship, need, and core need. The relationship is as follows. Everything designated as the dharmas of total affliction and complete purification is primordially the personage of enlightened body, speech, and mind and by nature the realm of buddhahood, and the meaning of being blessed is realized, which has the characteristic of knowing the cause, so they are related in meaning because of being the cause of accomplishing unsurpassed buddhahood.

The need is as follows. Everything designated as the dharmas of total affliction and complete purification, and the five medicines, five nectars, and so on is taken without the use of adoption and rejection into the great equality of primordial buddhahood, which has the characteristic of engaging. That is a need because of being the cause of accomplishing unsurpassed buddhahood.

The core need is as follows. Because everything designated as the dharmas of total affliction and complete purification, and in particular the five medicines, five nectars, and so on is spontaneously existing without adoption or rejection in the state of the great equality of primordial buddhahood, the samsara of rebirths itself the nature of unsurpassed buddhahood spontaneously exists in the characteristic of nirvana, so it has the characteristic of fruition. It is the wheel of ornamentation of unending enlightened body, speech, and mind now seen in direct perception, which is the core need.

For that, one has to be diligent at a yoga in which the meanings of approach, close approach, accomplishment, and great accomplishment become spontaneously existing.

Approach is knowing enlightenment mind; it is the realization of all dharmas being their nature of primordial buddhahood without accomplishing it by a path or contriving it by the use of antidotes.

Close approach is knowing oneself as the deity; it is the realization that all dharmas being the nature of primordial buddhahood I also am the nature of the primordial deity, not that the deity is something now to be accomplished.

Accomplishment is the creation of the female consort, it is the realization of a primordial female consort that comes from the great female consort, the realm of space, with that space itself appearing as and performing the functions of the four great female consorts—earth, water, fire, and air.

Great accomplishment is the connection of method and prajñā. From the prajñā of the five great female consorts and their emptiness space come the male consorts, the buddhas of the five aggregrates, in wishlessness connected together by way of being primordially already unified. From them come the enlightenment mind brother and sister manifestations whose nature is the fact of primordial buddhahood. Within that fact, illusion plays in illusion and there is a stream of great bliss illusion which just as it happens is kept in equilibrium with the fact of signlessness, not-referencing, space. Thus having turned into inspace, without endeavours for its production, it is spontaneously existing; the four types of māra also are tamed then the fact of finalization is accomplished.

Entering the primordial unsurpassed maṇḍala whose sphere is the totally undelimited immeasurable palace of the wish-fulfilling jewel of the primal complete purity of all dharmas moreover is to hear the texts of the vehicle of method which opens the eyes. Understanding their meaning is to see the maṇḍala. Having understood it, doing the habituation is to have entered it. Having entered it, its having become manifest is to have gained great attainment.

❁ ❁ ❁

That mode is great completion's final meaning. One spontaneously enters the level of the Great Assembly of Letter Wheels; beings of the very best mental ability will get the meaning of primordial buddhahood in direct knowledge of primordial buddhahood then will go on to have habituation to it in a flash, but that is not the usual way. Most beings who hear this will, no matter how they contemplate it, not develop the conviction of its truth and profundity. Due to the difficulty the minds of average people have developing conviction in it and understanding it and due to that person's not understanding its truth and profundity, when they try to experience it, it comes out the same as everyone else's usual experience. Saying, "They are false", they will denigrate the best type of beings and develop an attitude of rejection. Because of that it has to be utterly secret, which is why the instruction was given that "it is the secret vehicle".

That being so, until the mind that realizes the meaning of all dharmas being primordial buddhahood has been produced, if the vehicles below this one are to be used to work for the sake of migrators, so that those to be tamed are not damaged, the master must be expert in the faults of samsara, the good qualities of nirvana, and the entirety of all the vehicles. Otherwise, if there are some areas he does not know, it is widely stated that he should not hold the position of master.

❁ ❁ ❁

The particulars of view will also entail specific austerities and yogic conducts. The ones that do not have austerities are the worldly Phyal ba and Paryanta. There are four types in relation to those who do have them: the worldly austerities of the Chārvāka and Tīrthika; the austerities of śhrāvakas, the austerities of bodhisatvas, and the austerities of the unsurpassed ones.

Phyal ba have no austerities because of their stupidity regarding cause and effect. Paryantikas have no austerities because of their view of nihilism. Chārvākas have the austerities of ritual purity, and so on in order to make this life better. Tīrthikas perform the austerities of rejecting the body, relying on the five fires, and so on, and have wrong yogic conduct in order to purify the eternal self they believe to exist.

The śhrāvaka austerities are, as it says in the *Vinaya*:

> Do not do the slightest evil deed and
> Carry out a perfection of virtue,
> And tame one's own mind entirely—
> This is the teaching of the Buddha.

With the view that all the dharmas of virtue and non-virtue are individually existing both in fiction and superfact, they carry out the austerities and yogic conducts of living in virtue and abandoning non-virtue.

The bodhisatva austerities are, as it says in the *Bodhisatva Vows*:

> Not acting for their sakes when it would create a suitable
> condition,
> Not engaging in menacing and so on by magic.
> Because of having compassion and loving kindness
> And mind not going wrong in regard to virtue ...

If you are held by great compassion, any dharma whether virtuous or non-virtuous that you do will not corrupt the vows; the bodhisatva vow in brief is to set great compassion as the basis then act.

The unsurpassed ones' austerities are, as it says in the *Sutra of Great Samaya*:

> If he is utterly certain of the buddha vehicle, then
> He might act in the five afflictions and desirables,
> But like mud to a lotus,
> For him, the disciplines will be perfect.

Because of the primordial equality of all dharmas, there is no attending to compassion and no abandoning of anger. For those who do not understand such it is not that compassionate activity does not arise. As primordial complete purity has been known through the view, so austerities and yogic conduct will be carried out as complete purity.

Like a blind man who naturally opens and regains his eyes,
If there is a supreme being who
Has the capabilities of prajñā and method shine forth,
May he come into contact with this secret garland of views!

Foremost Instruction "A Garland of Views" is complete. Virtue!

Plate 3. Ju Mipham Namgyal
Mural on the wall of Dzogchen Monastery, Tibet.
Photograph by the author, 2007

An Annotational Commentary called "A Warehouse of Gems" to the Great Master Padmasambhava's Foremost Instruction "A Garland of Views" Compiled by Jamyang Lodro Gyatso

Namo Guru Padma Mañjuśhrī

Glorious buddha born of a lotus,
Holder of the store of all-knowing wisdom,
Teacher of the various vehicles,
Orgyan knowing the three times, protect me!

Here, *Foremost Instruction "A Garland of Views"*, a treatise that cannot be disputed, given as verbal instruction by the great master Padmasambhava, is explained in three parts: preface, main part, and conclusion.

1. Preface

This has two parts: the title and the expression of worship.

1.A. The Title

The *Guhyagarbha*, which contains the glory in general of all the tantras and authoritative statements that show the way that all dharmas are spontaneously existing in primordial great completion, says:

> The meanings of the ones which do not understand,
> wrongly understand,
> Partially understand, and do not understand the authentic,
> And of taming, intent, secret,

And nature secret,
Are fully shown by letters assembled into designating
terms, the grammatical names,
And the grammatical phrases based on them;
The hidden and concealed meanings brought forth from
within their complex
Are present in the vajra teacher's mind.

Those verses list the views transcending and not transcending the world that correspond to the different levels of mental capacity of beings. There are the views that do not understand, the two worldly ones Phyal ba and Chārvāka; that wrongly understand, the two outsiders, Paryanta and Tīrthika; that only partially understand, the two of śhrāvaka and pratyeka; that do not understand the authentic, the bodhisatvas who dwell in the pāramitā approach; of taming, Krīyatantra; of mind, Yogatantra; of the secret, meaning inner mantra with both creation and completion stages, starting with Mahāyoga; and of the nature secret, which has the mode of great completion.

Especially, those verses outline the path of complete liberation comprised of nine vehicles—śhrāvaka, pratyekabuddha, and bodhisatva; Krīya, Charyā, and Yoga; and creation, completion, and great completion—and their fruitions.

The guru himself made ***a reminder that contains***[41] in a short text all of ***the*** different ***particulars*** that reveal ***the views, vehicles, and so on*** mentioned in those verses, which he made in order to alleviate the fears of the king and subjects, twenty-five in all, and others who were worried that they would forget them. A title was then given in accordance with its meaning.

[41] The words of Padmasambhava's text in its entirety are woven into the explanations given by Mipham. In the translation here, they are marked off like this using bold and italic and, in publications where colour is supported, are additionally marked off in colour.

I.B. The Expression of Worship

In conformance with the Vehicle of Characteristics, ***I*** first ***prostrate to the*** deity of prajñā, the ***bhagavat youthful Mañjuśhrī***. A bhagavat is someone who has *defeated* the two obscurations together with their latencies and *possesses* the six good qualities of the goodness of cause and effect pāramitā, so has *transcended* the two extremes of rebirths and peace[42]. This bhagavat has the *youthful* style of a conqueror's son, is *mañju* or *gentle* because the dharmatā is divorced from the painful pricks of elaborations, and has the *śhrī* or *glory* of being endowed with the two aims. ***And***, in conformance with the mode of fruitional Secret Mantra, I also prostrate to ***the*** special deity by prostrating to the emptiness actuality ***vajra*** not at all degraded by elaborated concept and to its unstopped compassionate activity, that is, to the Owner of the Secret[43] appearing as the ***dharma*** speech personified.

---

[42] The Tibetan translation of the term "bhagavat" is literally "defeated, possessing, transcendent". An exceptionally complete explanation of the term can be found in PKTC's publication *Unending Auspiciousness, The Sutra of the Recollection of the Noble Three Jewels, with commentaries by Ju Mipham, Tāranātha, and the Author* by Tony Duff, ISBN 978-9937-838-61-0.

[43] Sanskrit "guhyapati" meaning "Owner of the Secret" is a title originally given to the bodhisatva Vajrapāṇi. The Buddha proclaimed to his followers that he could not be the teacher for the "secret", meaning the Vajra Vehicle teachings, because it would interfere with his being the teacher of monks. Therefore, he formally entrusted the responsibility to one of his eight heart sons, the bodhisatva Vajrapāṇi, and officially gave him this title. "Owner" means that he owns and oversees the secret level teaching. You will sometimes see this translated as "Secret Lord", but that is mistaken.

2. The Main Part

This has two parts: explanations of the particulars of view and the particulars of yogic conduct.

2.a. Explanation of the Particulars of View

This has two parts: explanations of the views of outsiders[44] and the views of the followers of this dharma[45].

2.a.i. Explanation of the views of outsiders

This has two parts: synopsis and explanation.

2.a.i.i. Synopsis

The worldly realm comprised of transitory phenomena with its levels is the outer container. The ***sentient beings*** or persons contained in it are imputations made on the continua of the five aggregates by rational mind without the slightest investigation of the situation. These sentient beings are the same in being productions of ignorance, so all of them have prajñā which, ***mistaken***, has strayed from the meaning of the authentic. Following on from that, they have their own beliefs, the details of which result in their having ***countless views*** because of their limitless mistaken ways of thought. Nevertheless, their countless views ***collect into four basic types: Phyal ba, Chārvāka, Paryanta, and Tīrthika.*** The term "basic types" has the sense "specific causes" or "conditions for appearance" and it is their count which is used to make the count here.

---

[44] "Outsiders" are those who are not Buddhists, "insiders" are those who are Buddhists.

[45] Followers of this dharma refers to insiders, meaning Buddhists.

Due to not having any tenet or vehicle and not having any higher goals towards which they aspire, there is Phyal ba[46].

Not taking the next world into account because of being occupied with scheming for this life, there is the Chārvāka or *Tossing Far* away thoughts of future lives. Alternatively, it is called *Benefiting Far* because beings with this view say "this world is all there is" then stay focussed on the appearances of this life coming one after another far into the distance and work at benefiting this life alone, so have no connection to anything of greater meaning.[47]

The name Tīrthika refers to *having arrived on a step at the edge of a river* that flows down into the ocean of nirvana. It is explained to mean "having a basis".[48]
When "Benefiting Far" is not being used as a specific selector, it refers to all outsider non-Buddhists in common, as seen in the *Mahāparinirvāna Sutra* when it says:

> Is it so according to the Bhagavat or according to the ones Benefiting Far in the world?

---

[46] See the explanation of "Phyal ba" in the introduction.

[47] These two names Tossing Far (Tib. rgyangs 'phen) and Benefiting Far (Tib. rgyangs phan) are variations on how the Sanskrit name "Chārvāka" was understood by Tibetan translators. The first one, which is the official Tibetan translation equivalent for "Chārvāka", concerns putting aside or *tossing far* away thoughts of future lives and thinking only of this life. The second one concerns believing that there is nothing more than this life so having an eye only to improving or *benefiting* the progression of this life as *far* as its reaches into the future; with it, there is such pre-occupation with this life and where it can be taken that there is no connection to higher aims of any kind.

[48] Tīrthika actually includes nihilist Paryanta and eternalist Tīrthika, so he has not mentioned Paryanta here. See the introduction and also the glossary for more explanation of "Tīrthika".

Nevertheless, it has to be understood that it is being used here in the teaching on views to select one of four types of view and is not being used as a general term. In other words, it is being used here specifically to refer to one of the views under discussion.

Going further with this, "Tossing Far", when used to refer to those with a view of nihilism following Bṛihaspati's system is not wrong understanding as in the Paryantika, it is not understanding[49]. Tossing Far and Phyal ba are similar in that they do not investigate the things of cause and effect, but different in that Tossing Far exhibits a small amount of intelligence concerning the affairs of this life whereas Phyal ba does not. Tossing Far, which is a step further along than Phyal ba, is mostly found in the good migrations. That being so, it is necessary to understand the term "Benefiting Far" in the world as it is used; if it is taken to mean a specific case only such as followers of Bṛihaspata, or something else like that, then the intent of Padmasambhava's text will not be understood. In other words, as with the term "senāṅga", to accept a specific understanding that does not appear anywhere in the explanations of a treatise would not be all right.[50]

---

[49] "Bṛihaspati" is mentioned in the Hindu scripture as a person who followed a nihilist approach. However, his philosophy is counted as one of not understanding, not a deliberate wrong understanding. Thus his view and the followers of it are counted as Chārvāka view, not as Paryanta. This is explained at length in the introduction.

[50] "Senāṅga" is a Sanskrit word. What does it mean here? We cannot guess because it is not used or explained anywhere in Padmasambhava's text. Thus, we have no choice but to use the dictionary definition meaning "an army with its divisions". Likewise, we cannot assume meanings for terms such as Chārvāka which are used in the text if such meanings are not discussed anywhere in the text. Chārvāka is not used in this text to indicate specific views such as Bṛihaspatika, and so on. It is only used in the sense of "Tossed Far" and "Benefiting Far" as explained above. Another way to say it is that it is only used in Padma-

(continued ...)

Similarly with Paryanta, the use of which is explained in the *Sutra Petitioned by Kāśhyapa* to have the sense of "outsiders" in common:

> Kāśhyapa, my teaching cannot be destroyed by the ninety-six Paryanta; the destroyer of it will be one of my monks like me.

And the same is true for Tīrthika, which is used as a general term for outsiders advocating permanence or nihilism, though if it is understood here as a general name for the advocates of nihilism and permanence in that order, that meets nicely with the meaning of the term and is the intent of this text of Padmasambhava.

In relation to those moreover, the basis for the path holds a single precious gem. Some people do not see it, some see it as a small matter, some see it as something great within the ordinary run of things, and some see it for what it is[51]. The ones who do not see it, the Phyal ba and Chārvāka, are put into one category together in accordance with the way they see it, which is that they have no understanding of the ultimate actuality of the authentic. They are migrators who have gone primarily into the three bad migrations and, not understanding in the slightest that they should give consideration to past and future lives, are stupid as cattle. Theirs is the lowest of views, one lower than that not being possible.

---

[50] (... continued)
sambhava's text as a selector of one of the four views currently under discussion.

[51] The single precious gem is buddha-nature. Some people do not see its presence as a basis of being at all, some see it as of little account, some see it as important but do so while clinging to things as real, and some see it for what it really is. Of those, the first is described below, the second is the Paryantika and Tīrthika, the third is the Buddhist vehicles of characteristics, and the fourth is the Buddhist vehicles of the tantras.

You might think, "They have not entered a path, so it makes no sense to speak of a view for them". It is true that theirs is a case of ignorant mind not understanding a view and that they will need to determine a view before they can know what to abandon. However, they, the majority of sentient beings, already cling to conceived things and dwell in the view of the perishing collection[52], yet due to their weak concepts and prajñā they apprehend the things of cause and effect through concept labels[53], then are oppressed by the dullness of a view that does not discriminate specifics.

2.A.I.2. Explanation

This has two parts.

2.A.I.2.A. Explanation of both Phyal ba and Charvaka

What is ***Phyal ba***? It ***is not understanding in relation to the existence or non-existence of the causes*** from which ***all*** of these outer and inner ***dharmas*** arise ***and*** the ***effects*** that arise from those causes, and is simply living in ignorance that is ***a total stupidity*** in regard to cause and effect.

Chārvāka or Tossing Far and also Benefiting Far ***is not understanding in relation to the existence or non-existence of past and future lives and is*** making efforts at various methods for ***accomplishing rulership, wealth, and power for this life alone***. The latter is ***done*** on the basis of things that are explained in the system of the world and do not become doorways to complete liberation. They are things done by oneself or by others at one's instigation, such as accomplishing worldly works, planning attacks, plotting to gain rulership and so on, and also evil spells for killing, divinations, shamanism, exorcism

---

[52] This is the name for a whole set of wrong views that all sentient beings have because of their ignorance. It is a set of views that arise in regard to the five aggregates, which are known in this case as the "perishing collection". The views are of permanence, and so forth.

[53] For concept labels, see the glossary.

of harmful spirits, worshipping locale owners[54], rituals for prosperity, and so forth, ***in reliance on the words privy to the world.***[55]

2.A.I.2.B. EXPLANATION OF THE TENETS OF THE PARYANTIKA AND THE TIRTHIKA

Paryanta takes the view that cause and effect for all dharmas—the observable objects that can be known—***does not exist and*** moreover ***that all dharmas produced in one life are***, rather than having been propelled by actions of a past life, ***adventitiously-produced dharmas*** like a deer in a meadow[56] or bubbles on water ***that are finally annihilated***[57] like the flame of an oil-lamp that has been extinguished.

Tīrthika takes the view that an eternal self which while being non-existent ***is conceived of in all dharmas***—the things of cause and effect—***exists***[58]. ***And, as well as that***, one school ***takes a view of*** a

---

[54] "Locale owners" are spirits who have taken a location, a piece of territory, for themselves. Some people make offerings to them to appease them and get their abilities onside. For example, Hindu villagers often make offerings to tree spirits to keep them from harming the worshippers and to get them to help their lives.

[55] "Privy to the world" means that which is known exclusively to the world. These are things not spoken of in the paths leading beyond the world.

[56] Deer, who are very nervous creatures, can suddenly be there in the middle of a field and then equally suddenly be gone, without trace.

[57] The words here "taking the view" and "annihilated" come down to "having a view of annihilation or nihilism".

[58] The explanation of Tīrthika starts with the presentation of the belief in an eternal self in dharmas which is true for all Tīrthika. Following that the views of three of the major orthodox Hindu schools are presented. The first is the school called Sāṃkhya or Enumerators. The second could refer to at least two schools which believe in Iśhvara,

(continued ...)

causeless, conditionless nature[59] within whose entity all dharmas have come about, so it asserts a nature whose superficies are not different from it, and due to that assertion calls it "a self alone apprehended as a whole". It takes the view that appearing things are primordially established and have no other cause that creates them. That is what is referred to by "a view of ***the existence of effects without a cause***". Going further, if you ask, "How does it posit an effect if it does not relate to a cause?", the answer is that existence itself is the effect or what is established, like saying "space is primally established", and that statement is the school's only reference. "***And a wrong view of cause and effect***" is the school which asserts a being called "Iśhvara" who, having existed primally is permanent, who "has control over and manifests all things, animate and inanimate" and that for the purpose of pleasing Iśhvara many ritual offerings of sacrificed living creatures, etcetera, must be made. This has two references, contained in their statement that "Iśhvara is permanent, his manifestations are impermanent". The school says that "non-virtuous karmas produce higher existences and that permanent causes create impermanent effects". "***And a view of cause existing without an effect***" refers to viewing a creator as the cause, in which it is asserted that a mere thumb of an eternal self, and so on, flies away like a little bird when its terracotta cage has been broken. This school has three references: the assertion of a permanent self that only performs the function of causation; the assertion of effects created thereby, the entities of the aggregates, which are impermanent, changeable dharmins; and those effects, moreover, are merely once-off effects, they are not causes that

---

[58] (... continued)
meaning an almighty god, to whom animal sacrifices should be offered. The third is a specific Hindu school called Vaiśheṣhika. In the explanation of the third school, "a mere thumb" means just a little thing, said to distinguish their idea of self from the all-encompassing atman or self spoken of in other major Hindu schools.

[59] The nature, called "prakṛti" in Sanskrit, is a central tenet of this Hindu Sāṃkhya school.

create other aggregates, their continuity at that time having been cut.[60]

All types without exception of the views of nihilism and eternalism held by outsiders are included within those two views of annihilation and permanence.

Those four views shown above ***are views*** that are not conducive to knowledge[61], views that are equivalent to ***ignorance***.

When presenting the views of the world, Padmasambhava teaches only the views; he does not teach the paths and fruitions because of considering it meaningless to do so.

2.A.II. Explanation of the views of the followers of this dharma

This has two parts: synopsis and explanation.

2.A.II.I. Synopsis

In relation to the path without outflows[62], ***there are two types of path that transcend the world: the vehicle of characteristics*** which shows the characteristics without mixing in one with another of dharmas—those which are self- and generally-characterized dharmas and which are total affliction and complete purification—and shows which are

---

[60] For dharmin, see the glossary. Here, the point is that they are conceptually known items and not the dharmatā of reality known by wisdom.

[61] Knowledge here is the opposite of ignorance; the knowing of enlightenment.

[62] Outflows are what happens when wisdom, the enlightened state, loses its footing and starts to have outflows or discharges of dualistic muck. Thus, these words mean, "Now that we have finished talking about the views which are not connected with wisdom, the ones that are connected with paths leading to wisdom are as follows".

to be discarded and which to be adopted, ***and the vehicle of the vajra*** which shows that the two—total affliction and complete purification—are an indivisible entity that never falls away from being so, the maṇḍala of enlightened body, speech, and mind.[63]

2.A.II.2. Explanation

This has two parts: the presentations of the vehicle of characteristics and the mantra vehicle.

2.A.II.2.A. Presentation of the Vehicle of Characteristics

This has two parts: synopsis and explanation.

2.A.II.2.A.I. Synopsis

The vehicle of characteristics is of three types corresponding to how strongly people cling or do not cling to those characteristics due to the influence of their karmic fortunes, interests, and faculties. They are: ***the śhrāvaka vehicle***, whose followers *śhrā* hear the verbal instructions from someone then *vaka* speak of it to others so that they hear it; ***the pratyekabuddha vehicle***, whose followers at the time of their last existence in rebirths by themselves embody a fruition of the truth; ***and the bodhisatva vehicle***, whose followers have a steadfast mind for enlightenment or have both enlightenment and sentient beings in mind.

2.A.II.2.A.II. Explanation

This has three parts: explanations of the śhrāvaka, pratyekabuddha, and bodhisatva vehicles.

2.A.II.2.A.II.I. Explanation of the Shravaka Vehicle

The view of those people ***who have entered the vehicle of*** the path that causes them to attain the fruition of a ***śhrāvaka is*** a tenet

[63] For total affliction and complete purification, see the glossary.

ascertained through their orientation towards what is determined by prajñā. Here it is shown in three parts: view, meditation, and fruition.

In their view, the view of non-existence from the outset or of absolute non-existence—*nihilism, and the view of existence of permanence and so on which the* outsider *Tīrthikas and their like conceive of in all* the *dharmas* contained in the aggregates, dhātus, and āyatanas *through* conceiving the *over*-statement of permanence in what is non-existent *and* the *under-statement* of non-existence in what is existent *are non-existent like a rope seen as a snake. For them, the* personage of the *aggregates, dhātus, and āyatanas, and so on* which are like the rope that is the basis of appearance—the matter of external form and so on, *the atoms of the four great elements* which are the cause of coarse appearance—*and* the moments of internal *consciousness are viewed as superfactually* or truly *existent.*

In regards to that view of theirs, there are two schools: the Particularists and the Followers of Sutra[64]. The two have some differences, with the former asserting the permanence of un-compounded phenomena and the latter asserting that they absolutely do not exist, like a barren women's son, and so on, and even within the Particularists there are many individual assertions that are subtly different, but they are basically the same in proclaiming that atoms and moments of consciousness are superfactual, so are classed as one.

Their meditation is *meditative cultivation of* the stages of meditative absorption[65], and *the four truths of the noble ones*—suffering, origin, cessation, and the path. The four are exactly what is, so, being

---

[64] Skt. vaibhāṣhika and sautrāntika respectively.

[65] Skt. dhyāna.

non-mistaken, are true and they are realized in mind by the noble ones or can be said to be noble in nature[66].

Those truths, having been understood as four truths of the three realms, are then cultivated until, one day, the path of seeing wisdom, a path having the nature of the sixteen moments of knowledge and forbearance, is produced. Then, gradually, the afflictions of the nine levels of the three realms, which are to be discarded through meditative cultivation, are discarded in four steps as follows. Someone who has become liberated from the first three of the nine afflictions—the three of the desire realm—is a stream-enterer; someone who has discarded through the sixth is a once-returner; someone who has discarded through the ninth is a non-returner; and someone who has abandoned the afflictions without exception through to the peak rebirth in samsara is an arhat. Thus, ***the four types of fruition are gradually accomplished.***

2.A.II.2.A.II.2. Explanation of the Pratyekabuddha Vehicle

The view of those who have entered the vehicle of the path that results in the attainment of the fruition of a ***pratyekabuddha***, a fruition having the characteristic of being uncompounded ***is as follows. They are in accord with the śhrāvakas in viewing that the permanent self that the Tīrthikas and their like conceive of through over- and under-statement for all dharmas is non-existent. However, they have the distinction of realizing absence of self in one part*** consisting of non-revelatory form and the ten items having form in the āyatanas and dhātus ***of dharmadhātu, the form aggregate***, in short, of the dharmas included in the form aggregate.

---

[66] The Buddha explained in a sutra that the name "four truths" means "the four truths of the noble ones" because the truths are fully comprehended only by noble ones. However, it is also possible to say that they are noble truths, in which case they could be called "the four noble truths".

And moreover, by habituation[67] to that, one day ***when*** at the end of rebirth they attain the fruition of a self-enlightenment, ***it will not have been through relating to a spiritual friend as the śhrāvakas do but*** will have used a style of meditation in which, ***by the force of past habituation***—having apprenticed to the buddhas and trained themselves on the levels of seeing the wholesome[68], and so—***they realize the profound meaning of the dharmatā by way of the twelve links of interdependent origination*** having the nature of the four truths of the noble ones. The seven sufferings are the truth of suffering, the three afflictions and the two karmas are the truth of its origin, being divorced from those afflictions is the truth of cessation, and understanding the meaning of interdependent origination and habituating oneself with that is the path that takes a person there.

In one approach, each of the twelve links also has its own four truths: their attainment, each one, is the truth of suffering; their being conditioned one by another is the truth of origination; their being stopped one by another is the truth of cessation; and their being meditated on correctly to make them cease is the truth of the path. In accordance with that, the sixteen moments of wisdom regarding the four truths occurs for each of the links, making one hundred and ninety-two moments of wisdom, and when these are produced in one sitting, the fruition of self-enlightenment has been attained. That is the way in which they realize the profound meaning of illusion-like dharmatā. They stay in a samādhi of extreme cessation, not expressible by speech, though the idea "this is inexpressible" does not occur to them, because they have abandoned conceptual thinking.

---

[67] For habituation, see the glossary.

[68] There are eight levels of accomplishment in the Lesser Vehicle: 1) the level of family line; 2) the level of continuing; 3) the level of seeing; 4) the level of diminishment; 5) the level of being free of desire; 6) the level of realizing it has been done; 7) the śhrāvaka level; 8) the pratyekabuddha level.

Going further, interdependent origination is a path common to all Buddhists. Śhrāvakas, through their strong clinging to the characteristics of causes and effects, dispel outsiders' misunderstanding of cause and result. Pratyekabuddhas have the deeper understanding that there are no facts[69] even of the grasped-at entities[70] of cause and effect. Yogacharins have the even deeper understanding that there is not even a self which is the grasper of the things of cause and effect[71]. Madhyamikas or Middle Way Followers understanding that the things of cause and effect do not exist even in the personage of self-knowing[72], reach a level of very fine pacification of elaboration.

Having shown that as their way of doing the path meditation, the fruition is that they ***then attain the fruition of a self-enlightenment*** either while practising together or being a loner, like a rhinoceros.

❁ ❁ ❁

2.A.II.2.A.II.3. Explanation of the Bodhisatva Vehicle

The "bodhisatva vehicle" refers to a causal vehicle and there is the Mantra Vehicle as a whole which is a fruitional vehicle. Both of these

---

[69] "Fact" here is Mind Only style talk in which there are no objects external to mind but mind assumes the form of what appears to be an external object. Such objects are called "facts" in the Mind Only system. The tantras use a Mind Only way of talking about dualistic mind, which is why this way of talking is seen here and elsewhere in the commentary.

[70] Grasped-at entities are the "facts" which are one half of dualistic grasped-grasping, the production of what seem to be external objects but which are actually mind.

[71] The previous sentence dealt with the external half of the dualistic process and this sentence deals with the internal half, the mind itself as the thing which knows the externally grasped facts.

[72] Self-knowing is the ultimate perspective of the Mind Only school.

pāramitā and mantra vehicles are the same in being Great Vehicle vehicles, but the bodhisatva or pāramitā vehicle is, when specified according to path, one of the vehicles of characteristics. Accordingly, ***the view of those who have entered the bodhisatva vehicle*** of characteristics ***is as follows.***

They assert that all of the dharmas of total affliction—those of samsara with its causes and effects—***and complete purification***—those of nirvana with its causes and effects—***in superfact are without*** any established true ***nature.*** They make what superfact actually is, its entity, to be freedom from elaboration. The wording "superfact" is used because of its etymology of *super*ior wisdom's *fact* or object and its more general meaning that it is the superior of all attainments possible[73]. When they classify superfact, they present two kinds: "assessed superfact" involving a one-sided elimination of elaboration and "unassessed superfact" involving the pacification of elaboration in its entirety.

... ***and in the fictional ...*** The "fictional" is confused consciousness together with its appearances. "Fictional" is used because it is classed as something which obscures the fact of the authentic or which is a fiction, a concept, made up by the adventitious confusion of the

[73] What he is saying is that the Sanskrit term "paramārtha" etymologically means *parama* a superior mind and *artha* a fact known to that mind. The *parama* part comes down to meaning wisdom that knows and the *artha* to meaning the fact or object known to it. In a more general way, Indian religions all use this term to mean the *parama* highest or superior *artha* fact or truth that could be attained by following their system. This term has been mis-translated for many years now, using the term "absolute". If the term is translated into English according to its etymology and its meaning, we end up with "superfact", a very accurate translation which, because of its accuracy can be used to translate discussions of superfact, like the one here, without any loss of meaning.

rational mind[74]. When classified, there are two kinds of fictional: correct and incorrect. Under the influence of that fiction, truthless appearances appear ***as mere illusions***, where the term "mere" excludes their being authentically existent.

Faced with those mere appearances, it would not be all right to understate them saying, "They are incapable of performing their respective functions, and so on", for they ***are existent***, with ***their individual characteristics***—such as being wholly pure or impure domains—***unmixed with that of the others*** which is so because they are established in the face of a conventional valid cognizer that performs a self-evaluation[75].

In that way, non-ultimately they are to be ascertained in the faces of the two types of valid cognizer[76] and ultimately to be nicely determined as the mode of the great unified appearance-emptiness,

---

[74] "Fiction" stands in contrast to superfact. Fiction is a deliberate cover-up of superfact made by the confused rational or dualistic mind. It engages in the coverup by seeing superfact through a filter of concept. This term also has been mis-translated for many years now, using the term "relative". The original Sanskrit term "saṃvṛitti" is a common word in Sanskrit which simply means "deliberate coverup", "deception", and according to the Indian scholars means exactly "fiction". This again is a very accurate translation which, because of its accuracy, can be used to translate discussions of superfact and fiction, like the one here, without any loss of meaning. I suggest that you try reading this section substituting "absolute" for "superfact" and "relative" for "fiction"; you will see a vast difference in meaning and you will also see that the meaning contained in Mipham's explanation cannot be understood or explained if "absolute" and "relative" are used instead.

[75] This is a type of validating consciousness which looks at the thing itself and says, "Do you exist conventionally?" The answer for all of these fictional dharmas is that they do.

[76] ... those of direct perception and inference ...

inseparable two truths, elaboration-free equality. Having been ascertained and determined that way by prajñā, the path for cultivating them through meditation is shown. Among all kinds of prajñā, the one which is superior, which has been taken to its end, is the wisdom of non-duality, so, in order to show the path, the text mentions the ten virtuous dharmas of generosity and the others gripped by that non-dual wisdom, which are then called the "ten pāramitās". The term "pāramitā" or "gone to the other shore" refers to something beyond prajñā—something which does not become its object—the dharmatā free of elaboration. Because this dharmatā is the other shore gone to and because it is the other shore of the ocean of samsara to which one will go, it is described with that phrase[77]. Those are the two ways in which the non-dual wisdom pāramitās are connected with the path.

They assert that the ultimate ***fruition*** which comes ***at the end of*** the temporary fruitions of ***coursing in the ten pāramitās and gradually traversing the ten levels is the accomplishment of an unsurpassed enlightenment*** characterized by having complete all the accumulations of good qualities—the strengths, fearlessnesses, and so on which are distinguished compared to those of the śhrāvakas and pratyekabuddhas.

❁ ❁ ❁

2.A.II.2.B. Presentation of the Vajra Vehicle

This has two parts: synopsis and explanation.

---

[77] Pāramitā means both the self-existing reality to which one will go and the version of that reality that one takes up on the path. In other words, pāramitā has both fruition and path meanings.

2.A.II.2.B.I. Synopsis

The vehicle of the vajra when classified ***has three types: the vehicle of Action or Krīya Tantra*** which asserts that while inner samādhi is indeed the principal cause of accomplishment, accomplishment cannot be attained without relating to external *actions* of ritual cleanliness, austerities, and so forth; ***the vehicle of*** both correspondingly named "Half Each" or "***Ubhaya Tantra***", which asserts accomplishment using both external actions and inner samādhi; ***and the vehicle of Yoga Tantra***, which asserts accomplishment not through relating to external actions but through inner samādhi alone.

2.A.II.2.B.II. Explanation

This has three parts: the Krīyatanta, Charyātantra, and Yogatantra presentations.

2.A.II.2.B.II.I. Presentation of Kriyatantra

The view of those who have entered the Krīyatantra vehicle is as follows. From superfact in which there is no birth and cessation of an entity of any of all the dharmas ***in the fictional one meditates on the body of the deity's form.*** That is saying that someone who has enlightenment mind[78] and the three suchnesses is a vessel for accomplishment. The three suchnesses are the suchness of oneself, the suchness of the deity, and the suchness of mantra recitation. The three respectively subsume the nature of samsaric phenomena, the characteristics of nirvana, and the characteristics of the method—or sadhana—by which the latter is realized.

For "the suchness of oneself", the mere unanalyzed fact of the five aggregates is the "self" and its suchness is asserted in three different ways. In keeping with the śhrāvakas, it is empty of the "I", "mine", "permanent and annihilate", and so forth conceived by the Tīrthikas, yet it would not be all right to understate that by saying that the mere dharmas of the aggregates and so on are non-existent. For the Yoga-

---

[78] Skt. bodhichitta. See the glossary.

charins, it is empty of the conceived grasped-grasping that the śhrāvakas conceive of, yet it would not be all right to make the understatement that the mere self-knowing of mind and mental factors are non-existent. For the Madhyamikas, it is empty even of the Yogacharins not-discursively-thinking wisdom conceived of as being existent in superfact; the Madhyamikas assert a complete pacification of all of concept labels' elaborations.

The "suchness of the deity" refers to the ingredients of secret mantra—dharmatā, sound, and so forth—known as the "six deities". Moreover, they maintain that dressing the suchness of oneself, which is like a gold bar, in the suchness of the deity, which is like refined mercury, is meditating on the deity.[79]

The "suchness of recitation" consists of three suchnesses: three great images, three visualizations, and having four limbs. Those three suchnesses are those of wisdom, name, and form. That is, one realizes that in superfact the pure dharmatā of the deity and the impure dharmatā of oneself are not of two different natures, and then, meditating accordingly, knows that the pure self-knowing wisdom of the deity and the impure self-knowing consciousness of oneself are inseparable in nature, and likewise that the distinguished appearance of the deity's body and speech and the non-distinguished appearance of one's own body and speech are also without difference. Based on that understanding, their view is that even in the fictional one creates oneself as and transforms into a deity and that by cultivating that in meditation, confusion, which is purity itself, is accomplished as the deity whose entity is the fruition.

When meditating in accord with that mode just described, the three great images are: first, the enlightened body image that is the enlightened body with its marks and signs; second, the enlightened mind

---

[79] The point here is that gold naturally amalgamates with mercury. This is explained in the next paragraph.

image that is meditation on the moon disk, the symbol of enlightenment mind, at the deity's heart centre; and third, the enlightened speech that is the essence-mantra displayed on that moon-disc. And, the three visualizations are that, at the time of reciting the mantra, the jñānasattva is visualized in front and, with all three of the images for it, there are three visualizations to be done. And having four limbs is that there is one limb of recitation for each of the four components—the three visualizations plus oneself who is the samayasattva doing the recitation. The approaches of two visualizations, three limbs, and so forth are included within the approach just explained.

Thus, although the practitioner is not the deity now, one day when, due to causes and conditions, a transformation takes place, the practitioner's mindstream will be seen as the deity.

And, to assist with that, they assert that ***accomplishment happens primarily through bringing together the devices of body-images, mind-symbols, mantra-recitation, ritual cleanliness, set times, planets and stars of the zodiac, and so on, and through causes and conditions.*** In other words, to gain accomplishment, they rely on the use primarily of the following devices.

First are the drawn or moulded body images of which of the three families[80] one is interested in and the images or symbols of the mind of the three families. For the latter, of the three samayamudras of binding, holding, and contemplating, the last consists of three things to be meditated on: vajra and bell because of being a yogin; lotus, vajra, sword, and so on, the mind symbols of the jñānasattva; and the mind symbols of samayasattva and jñānasattva.

Next is the image of speech, mantra recitation, which has the three points of certainty, uninterruptedness, and completion. They are

---

[80] In Krīyatantra, three of the five buddha families are considered: the three families of tathāgata, vajra, and padma families.

respectively: keeping to what one has committed; avoidance of faults such as yawning, coughing, human talk, and so on while reciting the mantra; and completing the required number of recitations.

Next is their outer behaviour of practising ritual cleanliness in order to keep the domain pure through activities such as cleaning the surroundings and washing themselves, and so on. Next, they observe the set times for activities and undertakings and observe all the astrological omens involving the planets such as Jupiter and the others and the stars of the zodiac such as Puṣhya and the others[81]. Relying primarily on those devices, they also rely on other devices such as the causes and their conditions, outer and inner, of attainment.

Here, Padmasambhava has simply shown the two modes of absence of birth and cessation in superfact and meditation on the deity in the fictional, so he has not mentioned how the fictional domain might be viewed as either pure or impure or the particulars of the fruition. His intention here is that by having said, "They meditate on the deity in the fictional", there is no need to make the statement "They view the deity as the fictional". The point is that they do their habituation using a samādhi determined by the view. The reasoning involved is that view and meditation could not be contradictory because of the need for rigpa together with feet and because the texts of secret mantra reference the domain of complete purity.[82] [83]

---

[81] There are twenty-eight constellations in the Indian astrological zodiac—Puṣhya is one of them. It is the star Delta Cancri.

[82] "Complete purity" is the nirvana side. On that side, there is none at all of the impurity of the samsara side. Tantras as a whole look at the nirvana side; for them, even samsara is nirvana, so to speak.

[83] "Rigpa with feet" is a quality of the buddha, and one which is also mentioned in relation to the path. It means that knowledge is supported by method, with the knowledge being the eyes that tell the feet, the

(continued ...)

The fruition accomplished is not consistent with common karmic and worldly attainments, but is consistent with the supreme attainment, unsurpassed enlightenment, so has not been separately mentioned.

2.A.II.2.B.II.2. Presentation of Ubhayatantra

The view of those who have entered the vehicle of Ubhayatantra is as follows. From superfact in which there is no birth and cessation, in the fictional one meditates on the body of the deity's form and accomplishment happens through reliance on the samādhi of meditation possessing the four suchnesses of oneself, the deity, samādhi, and recitation. The first is creation of oneself as the samayasattva. The second is to invite the jñānasattva which comes to sit directly ahead of the point between the brows. The third is to arrange, in the heart-centre ahead of you, the moon, seed-syllable, and mantra for reading. The fourth is to recite, with the ten faults discarded, the mantra and to join the recitation to the breathing, such that it goes out with the thought of urging on experience and comes in with the thought of requesting attainments.

They assert accomplishment of the ordinary and supreme attainments at the level of the fourth family, Vajradhara, which happens in reliance on both the internal samādhi just described ***and on*** external ***devices and*** assembling ***causes and conditions*** and not corrupting samaya, ***and so on***.

❁ ❁ ❁

---

[83] (... continued)
method, where to go.

2.A.II.2.B.II.3. Presentation of Yogatantra

This has two parts: synopsis and explanation

2.A.II.2.B.II.3.A. Synopsis

The view of those who have entered the vehicle of Yogatantra, a vehicle which directly knows the fact of dharmatā, ***is of two types***. The one which, in the fictional, does not view oneself and the buddha as equal and does not admire the yogic conducts of equality conduct[84] is ***that of the outer yoga vehicle***. It cannot be influenced by anything inimical to it because, although it is at a level where the higher samayas are not kept and so cannot be practised, it does not cause the practitioner to discard the ordinary vows[85] and because it has meditation on the three places as the three secrets[86]. Therefore, it is called the vehicle of ***the tantra of capability***[87]. The other side to that is ***the inner yoga vehicle*** of ***the tantra of method***, where method means having the skilful means to turn whatever appears into great bliss.

❁ ❁ ❁

---

[84] The two items mentioned here are features of inner Yogatantra; outer Yogatantra has not progressed that far.

[85] It does not make a practitioner discard the śhrāvaka vows or the bodhisatva vows, and therefore it has a great capacity for withstanding opposing forces.

[86] It also has meditations on the three places of enlightened body, speech, and mind, which bless the practitioner's being, giving it the power to withstand opposing forces.

[87] In other words, it does not have the great capacity to withstand opposing forces found in the Unsurpassed Yogatantra level because of the more potent way of keeping samayas and the various other features found in that level. However, it is still capable of withstanding opposing forces, something which in general is described with the term "capability", therefore it is called "the tantra of capability" to indicate its relative position amongst all the yogatantra levels.

2.A.II.2.B.II.3.B. EXPLANATION

This consists of two parts: outer Yogatantra and Anuttara or Unsurpassed Tantra's presentations.

2.A.II.2.B.II.3.B.I. PRESENTATION OF OUTER YOGATANTRA

The view of those who have entered the vehicle of outer yoga, the tantra of capability, is as follows. They assert that ***accomplishment*** of the ordinary and supreme attainments ***does not come through primarily holding to external devices*** as Krīyatantra does, ***but through primarily doing the*** inner ***yoga of meditation. The meditation is done using a samādhi on male and female deities without birth and cessation in superfact***, that is, male and female deities that are the nature of superfact shining forth into the factor of appearance ***and on a totally pure mindstream having a similarity to that*** sort of meditation view. That samādhi of two aspects is used ***to meditate on a noble one's form body.***

That describes two deities, one that is superfactual and one that is a detail of mind, which are the two deities, one of superfact and the other a factor of appearance of the fictional. Meditation on a deity consistent with a cause that has both factors included is the deity that is designated as the samaya being. Doing the habituation in that way, a deity having the nature of the two truths is produced and, moreover, in terms of the samādhi used to produce it, the deity's creation is done via the five manifest enlightenments and the four great miracles, and done ***having the four seals.***

The great seal—mahāmudrā—of the buddha-body is the actual body and its causal syllable, and its sceptres, and so on. The dharma seal—dharmamudrā—of buddha-speech is the meditation of a five-pointed vajra and so forth on the tongue. The commitment seal—samayamudrā—consists of holder and held; the holder is the appearance of a five-pointed vajra, and so forth, the sign of mastery of the five wisdoms, and that which is held is the vajra and bell. The action seal—

karmamudrā—of enlightened activity is the crossed vajra on top of a moon-disk in the heart-centre, emitting and absorbing light-rays to invite the noble ones and perform the sakes of migrators, and so on. By those seals, the deity does not depart from the body, speech, mind, and enlightened activity of great beings, and effort is made towards accomplishing that; alternatively, application of those seals is to seal the deity into one entity.

❁ ❁ ❁

2.A.II.2.B.II.3.B.II. Presentation of the Unsurpassed or Anuttara Tantras

This consists of two parts: synopsis and explanation.

2.A.II.2.B.II.3.B.II.1. Synopsis

The view of those who have entered the vehicle of inner yoga, the tantra of method, is of three types: that of Mahāyoga, ***the mode of creation,*** which primarily teaches method, creation stage; that of Anuyoga, ***the mode of completion,*** which predominantly[88] teaches prajñā completion stage; ***and*** that of Atiyoga, ***the mode of great completion***, which primarily teaches non-dual unification.

2.A.II.2.B.II.3.B.II.2. Explanation

This has two parts: a general explanation of the three modes and a detailed explanation of the entrance to great completion.

---

[88] "Predominantly" here rather than "primarily" has the particular meaning that it teaches both creation and completion, with completion predominating.

2.A.II.2.B.II.3.B.II.2.A. General explanation of the three modes

This has three parts: the modes of creation, completion, and great completion.

2.A.II.2.B.II.3.B.II.2.A.I. The mode of creation

The mode of creation is as follows. The three inner tantras do not view that one is a deity when the creation of a deity is done and not a deity when it is not done, because they share the view that the deities exist in a maṇḍala of indivisible cause and effect spontaneous existence. Nevertheless, samādhi has to be used to train one's ability at being the deity, though that ends up being no more than gradually training in the spontaneously-existing deity.

In regard to that process of training, all dharmas are viewed as being buddha in a maṇḍala of mere images, and within that, buddhas are of the three types: nature, realized, and accomplished. The first of the three refers to sentient beings, and among them there are buddhas whose life is cause, basis, and accomplishment—the first referring to semen, blood, and mind, the three causes that produce the body; the second to the totality of body and mind constituents come from both parents; and the third to the time when the body has fully developed[89]—with the set of three making the point that we sentient beings are buddhas by nature. The second of the three, realized buddhas, are those who abide on the vidyādhara levels. The third of the three,

---

[89] In other words, there are these three main steps in the birth of a human: the moment of conception when the semen of the father, blood of the mother, and consciousness of the new being come together; the period following that when the embryo, consisting of the materials come from both parents, is developing; and the time when it has fully developed. Semen of the father and blood of the mother is how the ancient systems speak of the contributions of the parents. All of this is to the point that a sentient being, no matter what its stage of life, is always a buddha by nature.

accomplished buddhas, are those who see suchness directly and these moreover are asserted to be of both nature and non-ultimate types.[90]

Thus it is that there is no referring to dharmas that are not buddhahood, but, in order to realize what has not been realized and habituate to what has not been habituated to, the inner tantras assert the training of rational mind on three buddha-levels. For training the rational mind on the level Total Light there is the meditation on the no-discursive-thinking samādhi of suchness; for habituation on the level Having Lotuses there is conjoining prajñā and compassion in the samādhi of total appearance; and for habituation on the level of The Great Assembly of Letter Wheels, there is cultivation of the causal samādhi of syllable letters. Thus, ***it asserts creation in steps by the three types of samādhi and*** then, if the habituation is done, ***accomplishment by displaying the maṇḍala*** of support and supported ***in steps and meditating on it.***

2.A.II.2.B.II.3.B.II.2.A.2. THE MODE OF COMPLETION

The mode of completion—Anuyoga—***is as follows.*** It speaks of the ability to meditate such that any of the meanings to be cultivated and practised that are expounded in the texts of Yogatantra are complete in a single moment of enlightenment mind's nature, rigpa, and clearly evident. In other words, while not wavering from two, the meaning is evident in one, and while indivisible in one, it is unmixed in three; it is like the planets and constellations of stars shining forth in a single ocean or the four miraculous behaviours on show at the same time.

---

[90] In essence, he is explaining the view of this vehicle that all dharmas are, primordially, buddhahood. That being so, there are beings who have that only as their nature, ones who have some realization of it, and ones who have fully manifested it. Tathāgatagarbha theory as taught in the third turning of the wheel of dharma says that the garbha is of two types: one which is there by nature and one which has been to a greater or lesser extent developed. Those two are the nature and non-ultimate types respectively.

There are "the two non-waverings". One is ***not wavering from*** the intended meaning of all appearance and rebirths—whose nature is ***the male and female deities*** of the maṇḍala of images that is spontaneously existing in the nature of being ***without birth and cessation in superfact***—being buddhahood. Two is ***and*** also ***not wavering from the dharmadhātu central channel, the fact of not thinking discursively*** in any of the extremes.[91]

While not wavering from either one of them, ***in the fictional,*** using higher samādhi[92], ***one meditates on*** all the aggregates, dhātus, and āyatanas ***clearly evident*** as the maṇḍala, the ***bodily form of a noble one***, which is called "one clearly evident", ***and on*** all of whatever appears, whatever is being meditated on, ***being equality*** in the dhātu of dharmatā enlightenment, which is called "indivisible in one". ***And,*** with the ***unmixed*** three—the meditation on everything as a spontaneously-existing maṇḍala not being mixed with another samādhi; the body-colours, sceptres, and other details in the maṇḍala of higher samādhi clearly evident yet not mixed with one another; and the principal dhāraṇī together with the retinue-maṇḍala individually there and not mixed with one another—enlightenment mind's nature is evident in one moment of rigpa. ***And by that meditation*** done in that way ***there is accomplishment.***

---

[91] In Anuyoga one meditates on the form body of a deity but also meditates on the channels, winds, and drops within it. The central channel ultimately speaking is the dharmadhātu, no-thought wisdom in fact, or you could say in superfact.

[92] "Higher samādhi" has two meanings here. Firstly and generally speaking, the Buddha taught three main trainings—śhīla, samādhi, and prajñā—which he called "higher trainings" to distinguish them from the trainings of similar names proclaimed in Tīrthika teachings. Secondly, in this particular context, it is not the lesser samādhi on the aggregates, and so on, of the vehicles below, but the higher samādhi of seeing them as part of a maṇḍala of primordial buddhahood.

If that could be done such that it was existing without concept-based endeavour, spontaneously, and if it could be done equally at all times and places, then it would be no different from great completion. However, here in the mode of completion, application is laden with conceived of effort and rigpa is only partially joined. It is understood as a moment in time—as an instant in which everything is complete.

In addition to that, in this context of twofold creation and completion, apart from merely showing the path meditation, their general views and the specific fruition have not been discussed. Padmasambhava's intention here, like that shown earlier, is "Given the view of the maṇḍala of deities being without birth and cessation in superfact and being the illusions of total purity in fiction, and the view of the two truths as inseparable, and the fruition of unsurpassed enlightenment which is not different between all the great vehicles, there is no need to discuss those matters separately".

❁ ❁ ❁

2.A.II.2.B.II.3.B.II.2.A.3. The mode of great completion

The mode of great completion is as follows. In regard to this, great completion has both meaning and mode. Its meaning is that all dharmas are shown to be self-arising wisdom, the nature of enlightenment. Its mode is the method and doorway for entering into that meaning.

Intending to give a synopsis of both meaning and mode, Padmasambhava says that the superficies of ***all*** the differentiations of ***dharmas*** into "this" and "that" as many as there are—***worldly and beyond worldly***, superfact and fiction, self-characterized and generally characterized, white and black[93], etcetera—are inseparable. Where does their ***being inseparable*** happen? ***They are primordially*** inseparable in ***the nature of the maṇḍala of enlightened body, speech, and mind***, which, for example, is like teaching that all the conventional characteristics posited in the presentations of ordinary worldlings and Tīrthika outsiders, and all the characteristics of all persons, are contained within the buddha-type dharmas.

In what way are they inseparable? He gives a synopsis by saying, "***That***, which is their nature primordially, ***is realized then*** is to be ***meditated on***. Then he continues by saying, ***going further***, the *Guhyagarbha Tantra*, showing this using vajra words[94], ***says*** that they are the nature of the vajras of enlightened body, speech, and mind:

> ***The limbs of the vajra aggregate are***
> ***Known as the five complete buddhas.***
> ***All of the many āyatanas and dhātus***
> ***Are the maṇḍala itself of bodhisatvas.***
> ***Earth and water are Lochanā and Māmakī,***
> ***Fire and wind are Pāṇḍurā and Tārā,***
> ***And space is Dhātvīṣhvarī;***
> ***The three rebirths are primordially the complete purity.***

Master Padmasambhava combines that with his teaching like this. ***All of the dharmas of samsara and nirvana*** are the nature of rigpa, enlightenment mind, so are ***primordially unborn, and*** while remaining in great, birthless emptiness, their appearing aspects of earth and the rest of the elements are shining forth unstopped, ***illusions capable of performing*** their own ***functions***. They, having ***the nature of the ten male and female sugatas***, the male and female bodhisatvas, and so forth are not like contrivances and transformations made by the path,

---

[93] Why white and black? This phrase refers to what is good and bad, to be adopted and rejected, which is a major theme of the teaching of the vehicles below this one, vehicles in which there is no unification.

[94] ... Vajra Vehicle words ...

rather, they are *primordially so. Therefore, all dharmas are by nature nirvana. The five great ones*—the elements of earth, and so forth—*are in nature the five female* sugatas: earth is Buddhalochanā, water is Māmakī, fire is Pāṇḍurā, wind is Samayatārā, and space is Dhātvīṣhvarī. Likewise, *the five aggregates are the buddhas of the five families*: consciousness is Akṣhobhya, feeling is Ratnasaṃbhava, perception is Amitābha, intention is Amoghasiddhi, and form is Vairochana. *The four consciousnesses are in nature four bodhisatvas*: eye-consciousness is Kṣhitigarbha, ear-consciousness is Vajrapāṇi, nose-consciousness is Ākāśhagarbha, and tongue-consciousness is Avalokiteśhvara. *The four objects are in nature the four goddesses of beauty* who arouse delight in the consciousnesses: visible form is Āsyā or Grace, sound is Gīti or Song, smell is Mālā or Garland, and taste is Nṛiti or Dance. *The four faculties are in nature four bodhisatvas*: the eye-faculty is Maitreya, the ear-faculty is Nivāraṇaviṣhkambhin, the nose-faculty is Samantabhadra, and the tongue-faculty is Mañjuśhrī. *The four times are in nature the four offering goddesses*: past time is Dhūpā or Fragrance, the present is Puṣhpā or Flower, the future is Ālokā or Lamp, and unspecified occurrence is Gandhā or Perfume. *The body faculty, its consciousness, its object* of touch, *and the* great bliss *enlightenment mind arisen from them*—from their contact—*are in nature the four wrathful ones*: the reason why they are defined as four very strong "wrathful ones" is that the secret vajra of the body faculty coming in contact with an object defeats other sense-consciousnesses, causing them not to be present. Touch is Amṛitakuṇḍalin, the body faculty that does the touching is Hayagrīva, the object of touch is Mahābalī, and the touch consciousness is Yamāntaka. *The four bounds of permanence and nihilism are in nature the four female wrathful ones*: the purity of the abidings in the view of permanence is Aṅkuśhā or Iron Hook, similarly for the view of nihilism it is Pāśhā or Noose, for the view of self it is Sphotā or Iron Shackles, and for the view of concept labels it is Ghaṇṭā or Bell. *The mental consciousness is in nature the enlightenment mind*—the undeclining mind having the nature of enlightenment that is indestructible like a *vajra, Samantabhadra* who does not reject any dharma of all the dharmas, *and its objects*—the objects of that mind—

compounded and uncompounded dharmas, are in nature the female maker of dharmas, Samantabhadri. Moreover, their nature is primordially manifest complete buddhahood, it is not that they are newly ***made by the path.***

Now, having quoted the tantra itself, other scripture in agreement with it will be quoted. Teaching ***like that*** that all the dharmas appear in the three maṇḍalas and also are the root, the single unique sphere of enlightenment mind, self-arising wisdom, ***all compounded and uncompounded dharmas in the ten directions, three times, three realms, and so on are never split off from one's own mind, which has been said like this*** in *Realization Victorious Over the Three Realms*:

> ***One's own mind discriminated*** correctly or properly
> ***Is itself buddha, bodhisatva,*** and so on.
> When that is realized it is buddha, when not realized it appears as samsara's containers and contents, so ***is itself the three worlds;***
> ***Is itself the great elements.***

It has been said like this in the *Guhyasamāja:*

> ***All dharmas reside in mind*** meaning that whatever appears is no more than the appearance of one's own mind.
> ***Mind resides in space*** meaning that mind's nature is unborn, similar to space.
> ***Space*** because it is free of all characteristics ***does not reside anywhere.***

And, in another scripture:

> ***All dharmas***, being devoid of establishment as the superficies of dharmin and dharmatā, are devoid of presentations like "this is empty of this", so ***are empty of entitiness.***
> ***All dharmas***, primordially never having known the stains themselves of the afflictions, ***are primally complete purity.***

All dharmas, having primordially never had the darkness of obscuration established, ***are universal luminosity.***
All dharmas, because they are without the duality of what is inimical and antidotes to it ***are by nature nirvana.***
All dharmas, because they are free from the two obscurations having to be diminished and the two accumulations needing to be accumulated ***are manifest complete buddhahood.***

This is the great completion. Here there is an ancient ***note in*** the ***text: The mode of great completion is the accumulations of method and wisdom being complete in this mode of the fruition dharmas existing spontaneously, the factual situation entered.***[95]

2.A.II.2.B.II.3.B.II.2.B. Detailed explanation of the entrance to great completion

This is explained in four modes: four realizations, three characteristics, having four limbs, and order of entry into the maṇḍala.

The four realizations are the object mode, defined as the basis of its characterization. The three characteristics are the method mode, defined as its characteristics. Having the four limbs of approach and attainment is the fruition mode, defined as foremost instruction on crossing over[96]. The mode of entry into the spontaneously-existing maṇḍala is defined as the steps of entry.

To explain them further: realization in the two modes of single cause and seed-syllables are the object mode; realization in having been

---

[95] "Factual situation entered" means that this is not conceptual in any way at all, this is happening in superfact, reality as it actually is, without a trace of dualistic mind.

[96] "Crossing over" is Great Completion path terminology; see also cross over in the glossary.

blessed is the method mode; and realization in direct perception is the fruition mode. Likewise, for the three characteristics: the characteristic of awareness is the object mode; the characteristic of entrance is the method mode; and the characteristic of fruition is the fruition mode. For having the four limbs of approach and attainment: approach is the object mode; close approach and attainment are the method mode; and great attainment is the fruition mode. Likewise, for the three stages of entry: to open the eyes through hearing is the object mode; to have entered the maṇḍala through doing the habituation to it is the method mode; and to gain great attainments by having manifested it by the power of that habituation is the fruition mode.

Having ascertained it that way, the four modes of entrance have been individually explained.

2.A.II.2.B.II.3.B.II.2.B.I. The four realizations

The two accumulations are completed so it is "completion". However, their completion does not happen through a journey of training in them as is done in the vehicles below, rather, it happens through their primal, spontaneous existence as the fruitional dharmas of enlightened body, speech, and mind, so it is "great". The method for or door to entry into that factual situation is called its "mode". It is necessary to develop ***conviction***[97] ***in that mode of great completion***, which is done or ***happens via the path of the four types of realization. The four types of realization are*** as stated in the eleventh chapter of the root tantra[98]:

---

[97] This is usually translated as "trust". There is a progression of increasing certainty that happens as one treads the great completion path. The final level of that is a deep-seated conviction born of direct personal experience of the truths being discussed here. Alternatively, you could say a deep-seated trust in that.

[98] The root tantra means the *Guhyagarbha Tantra*, which is the root

(continued ...)

The modes of a single cause and of syllables,
Of blessing and of direct perception;
By these four types of thorough realizations,
All is the manifest completion Great King!

In other words, they are: ***realization of single cause, realization through the mode of syllables, realization through blessing, and realization in direct perception.***

Two approaches have been explained for these four realizations: gradual and sudden. However, great completion is being determined here as a single unique sphere of self-arising wisdom, so they will be explained according to the sudden approach.

Realization of single cause—where cause means nature or basis—*is as follows.* ***All dharmas in the superfactual are unborn so*** in their unborn nature ***are not individualized,***[99] ***and in the fictional have the characteristic of illusion***—appearances empty of truth—***so are not individualized.*** This much is known in the common Great Vehicle. ***And the unborn-ness*** while remaining unborn ***appears as various illusions like moons in water, able to perform*** their respective ***functions. And the illusoriness*** as it appears also being ***without entity is unborn, so all these dharmas are inseparable fictional and superfactual and are thus realized to be of a single cause***, that is, their union, self-arising wisdom. The above in this paragraph is an uncommon teaching known from profound scripture.

To sum it up, self-arising wisdom, the entity of enlightenment mind, is the nature of inseparable appearance-emptiness. Nothing in all of

---

[98] (... continued)
tantra of all the Mahāyoga tantras.

[99] "Individualized" means that they have not been made into dharmins, that is, individually conceived-of items produced in dualistic mind.

samsara and nirvana goes beyond that single mode, so that is their single cause.

Realization through the mode of syllables is as follows. This shows that that nature of inseparable appearance-emptiness primally has been buddhahood as the fruitional dharmas of enlightened body, speech, and mind. ***The unborn-ness of all dharmas is realized to be*** symbolized by ***A*, *the nature of enlightened speech. Their unborn-ness appearing as illusions able to perform functions is realized to be*** symbolized by ***O*, *the nature of enlightened body. The rigpa realizing such, the wisdom of illusion without edge and centre, is realized to be*** symbolized by ***OṂ*, *the nature of enlightened mind.*** Taking that further, through the mode of syllables one realizes that the wisdom of primally unified appearance-emptiness never has the decrease and increase that comes with removal and addition[100] and has a nature of complete purity, so samsara is "the great primally cleared situation"[101] and its play primally remains part of the three maṇḍalas.

Realization through blessing is as follows. It is awareness of the power and blessing of the previous two realizations. ***It is*** becoming aware of, ***realizing that, as for example the power to bless white cotton cloth into red exists in the dye, so the power to bless all dharmas into*** primally being ***buddhahood comes through being blessed by the power of the modes of single cause and syllables.***

All dharmas are indeed primally buddhahood, yet that will not help those who do not have the above two realizations. It will be seen to

---

[100] "Removal and addition" is the process of adding to something or removing something from it in order to fix it and make it right. Primordial buddhahood needs none of this "fixing" in order to make it right; it is primordially already complete and finalized.

[101] "Cleared" refers to clearing away dirt and the like. Primally, samsara is already cleared of all the dirt of confusion and obscuration, so is already nirvana.

help those who do have them—the power of the two realizations will be seen to bless all dharmas into primordially being buddha, so this is called "realization through blessing".

Realization in direct perception is as follows. Generally speaking there are sense-faculty direct perceptions, and so on, but what is meant here is direct perception by the faculty of prajñā, which in this case should be understood to be discriminating prajñā. ***Knowing that all dharmas primordially residing as buddhahood is not contradictory to*** trustworthy ***authoritative statement and*** the ***foremost instruction*** of the gurus of the lineage, one uses them.

Melting, cutting, and rubbing allows one to know whether something is gold or not, and if it is gold, whether it is faulty or faultless, good or bad. As with that example, authoritative statement stops all confusion concerning the general conceptual understanding and foremost instruction then clears any misunderstandings that might arise regarding the provisional and definitive meanings and various covert intents of the authoritative statement, bringing conviction with it. One might have authoritative statement and foremost instruction, but it is also possible that one does not have a deep-seated conviction because of having merely pursued the words involved and not having practised to gain direct experience. Thus, ***rather than relying on the mere words of authoritative statement and foremost instruction, this is realization entailing a deep-seated conviction in rational mind, through*** discriminating prajñā or ***one's own rigpa in direct perception.***

The words here are to the point that: authoritative statement leads to the conceptual meaning being understood without error; foremost instruction prevents misinterpretation of the intent of the authoritative statement; and realization in direct perception by prajñā clears and prevents the weakness of such knowledge obtained merely through hearing, and so on.

Conviction by the path of that sort ***is as follows***. Knowing ***the meaning of the four types of realization, rigpa itself, is a yogin's path. Moreover, it is not the kind*** of path found in the vehicle of characteristics ***that looks forward to the time*** in the future ***of a fruition of*** buddhahood of ***a cause deliberately made*** in the past. ***Rather, it is one of realizing it by oneself in direct perception*** in the present by the faculty of prajñā ***and gaining conviction in it.***

2.A.II.2.B.II.3.B.II.2.B.II. THE THREE CHARACTERISTICS

For that, the three characteristics—knowing, engaging, and made manifest—***will finalize the meaning*** of great completion as it is to be realized. Moreover, ***the mode of the four realizations, rigpa,*** which what is to be determined, ***has the characteristic of knowing*** the cause. ***Doing the habituation to it again and again has the characteristic of engaging*** the conditions for it. ***The power of habituation to it having made*** the meaning just as ***it*** is, ***manifest has the characteristic of the*** finalized ***fruition.***

The characteristic of knowing the cause is view, the characteristic of engaging the conditions is meditation, and having been made manifest is fruition. This set of three modes causes the meaning to be finalized so it is not all right not to have it. Thus, ***the three characteristics reveal the relationship, need, and core need***[102]. ***The relationship is as***

---

[102] Buddhist masters of ancient India came up with a system to prove that a treatise was a valid treatise, one that correctly explained the Buddha-word or related matters. The *Illuminator Tibetan-English Dictionary* says: "A valid treatise has four aspects present. They are: 1) that which is to be expressed or the specific meaning to be transmitted by the written expressions in the treatise; 2) the need or the purpose being addressed by the expressions of the treatise; 3) the core need, an extension of the need, or the real, inner purpose being addressed by the expressions of the treatise; and 4) the relationship which is that the previous three must be related to each other or the treatise does not fulfil its function." The explanation here assumes the first and then explains

(continued ...)

follows. Everything designated as the dharmas of total affliction and complete purification is because of the mode of syllables *primordially the personage of enlightened body, speech, and mind* [103] *and* is *by nature the realm of buddhahood,*[104] *and*—because of the meaning realized in blessing and realized in direct perception—*the meaning of blessing is realized,*[105] *which has the characteristic of knowing the cause, so* what is the relationship? *They are related in meaning because of being the cause of accomplishing unsurpassed buddhahood.*

The need is as follows. It has the characteristic of engaging. *Everything designated as the dharmas of total affliction and complete purification, and the five medicines, five nectars,* five antidotes, five poisons[106], *and so on,* whether clean or unclean, pure or impure *is taken without the use of adoption and rejection into the great equality* because of their nature *of primordial buddhahood, which has the characteristic of engaging.* Why do they need to be engaged like that? *That is a need because of being the* uncommon *cause of accomplishing unsurpassed buddhahood,* there being no method for becoming a buddha without realizing the equality of adopting and rejecting.

The core need is having the characteristic of fruition. *Because everything designated as the dharmas of total affliction and complete purification* in general *and in particular* as the things to be worked with, *the five medicines, five nectars, and so on is spontaneously*

---

[102] (... continued)
how the remaining three are present.

[103] That is the view.

[104] That is the meditation.

[105] That is the fruition.

[106] The "five medicines" and so on are substances used in the practices of tantra. As it says a little below "and in particular as the things to be worked with ..."

existing without adoption or rejection in the state of the great equality of primordial buddhahood, the samsara of rebirths itself the nature of unsurpassed buddhahood spontaneously exists in the characteristic of nirvana, so or because of that, ***it has the characteristic of fruition. It is the wheel***—the kind that enters disciples' minds and cuts through their obscurations—***of ornamentation of*** forever ***unending enlightened body, speech, and mind***—meaning the immeasurable play of wisdom filling the dharmadhātu, like a golden eye embellished with turquoise—now seen in direct perception, which is the core need.[107]

Is it not contradictory to posit the great completion, primordial buddhahood, as having a cause-and-condition produced fruition? The texts of the vehicles below it, Mahāyoga and so on, assert that fruition is accomplished by way of a path with the four limbs of approach and attainment, but in this case there is no need to do it like that. Here, the four types of approach and attainment are completed without the use of endeavour in a yoga of spontaneous existence. This is connected with a foremost instruction of crossing over: "Actually there are none of the conceived things of cause, condition, and fruition here".

That being so, threefold object of consciousness, engagement with it, and its being evident are not different in their nature of being dharmatā enlightenment mind, so this is the great spontaneous existence which in nature is ground and fruition inseparable.

---

[107] "Golden eye" refers to the Garuḍa bird which roams the vast heavens without restriction, seeing everything everywhere within that space. It is like wisdom which pervades the entire dharmadhātu and knows everything. The turquoise embellishment is the fact that the wisdom does not merely see everything but has the ornamentation of all the buddha qualities that benefit beings ceaselessly.

2.A.II.2.B.II.3.B.II.2.B.III. HAVING FOUR LIMBS

For that, one has to be diligent at a yoga in which the meanings of approach, close approach, accomplishment, and great accomplishment—that is, all four limbs of approach and accomplishment—*become* without endeavours, *spontaneously existing*. That is a synopsis, stating the manner in which the four limbs of approach and accomplishment of Mahāyoga are crossed over to[108] in Great Completion; that all appearances on the male and female sides that are based in cause and effect—the causally effective elements and aggregates, the three complete emancipations, method and prajñā in union, appearance-emptiness indivisible, and so on—must be joined with in a natural, endeavour-less, spontaneously-existing mode.

Approach is the *knowing* of *enlightenment mind* that is entering ground alpha-purity and spontaneous existence unified*; it is the realization of all dharmas* of total affliction and complete purification *being their nature of primordial buddhahood without* newly *accomplishing it by a path or contriving it by the use of antidotes.*

Close approach is, within the state of that view, *knowing oneself* whose nature is the five aggregates *as the deity; it is the realization that all dharmas being the nature of primordial buddhahood I also am the nature of the primordial deity, not that the deity is something now to be accomplished* as happens in the creation of oneself as the deity within the state of the view of Mahāyoga, and so on.

Accomplishment is the creation of the female consort, it is not like the creation of the female consort in Mahāyoga, and so on, rather, it is *the realization of a primordial female consort that comes from the great female consort, the realm of space, with that space itself appearing as and performing the functions of* providing opportunity,

[108] "Crossed over" is Great Completion path terminology meaning "resolved". Thus, it says, "That is how the four limbs ... of Mahāyoga are resolved as great completion". See also cross over in the glossary.

stability, cohesiveness, ripening, and movement respectively of the space great female consort itself and ***the four great female consorts—earth, water, fire, and air.***

Great accomplishment is the connection of method and prajñā. How is the connection done? ***From the prajñā of the*** nature-less ***five great*** elements, the ***female consorts and their emptiness*** complete emancipation ***space come the male consorts, the buddhas of the five aggregates*** of unstopped appearance, the method, and with the aspect of being ***in wishlessness***, the two are not intentionally connected together now by a path, rather, they are ***connected together by way of being primordially already unified. From them come*** through their nature of being inseparable together in ***enlightenment mind*** all the āyatanas as ***the*** child ***brother and sister manifestations whose nature*** is not like the child brothers and sisters emanated from the enlightenment mind of the deliberately connected male and female of Mahāyoga and so on, but ***is the fact of primordial buddhahood. Within that*** primordial ***fact, illusion***-like rigpa wisdom, the male consort, ***plays in*** the ***illusion***-like object, dharmadhātu, the female consort, ***and*** one practises in that, experiencing the music of the realization mind, the wisdom of the bliss of being unstopped, non-referencing, inseparable, free of all clinging to biasses shining forth however it does. That experiencing of it is without so much as a speck of dualistic attachment, so ***there is*** a joyful wisdom that is supreme bliss. This way of practising the experience and playing in ***a stream of great bliss illusion*** also comes with a stream of not being separated from the entity itself for a moment, like space.

The bliss illusion ***just as it happens is kept in equilibrium with the fact of*** being free of all elaboration, the complete emancipation of ***signlessness, not referencing*** any extremes at all, ***space***[109]. ***Thus***, not

[109] Note that he has included what are called the three complete emancipations in this. They are taught in the Prajñāpāramitā, which is fitting because "great female consort" is also a name for Prajñāpāramitā (often

(continued ...)

going outside the enclosure of great equanimity like that, it ***has turned into*** the ***inspace*** of a single encompassing dharmatā of self-arising wisdom and ***without endeavours for its production it is spontaneously existing***; the cause of outflows, grasped-grasping, has been purified into self-arising wisdom and the unceasing stream of the appearances of entitiness[110] are the accumulation of merit and the absence of the slightest of amount of clinging to grasping at the elaborations of concepts is the accumulation of wisdom.

By that sort of spontaneously-existing two accumulations, great self-arising wisdom, ***the four types of māra also are tamed then the fact of finalization is accomplished.***

The mode of taming the four māras is as follows. The approach, characterized by knowing enlightenment mind, using the samādhi of the unborn defeats the Lord of Death māra. The close approach, characterized by knowledge of oneself as the deity, using the samādhi which is illusion-like defeats the aggregates māra. The accomplishment, characterized by the creation of the female consort, using the samādhi of separating from matter defeats the afflictions māra. The great accomplishment, characterized by connecting together method and prajñā, using the samādhi of holding the equilibrium with non-referencing—space—defeats the māra of distraction, the obstacle of the son of the god's māra. That being so, the path which has the power

---

[109] (... continued)
translated as the great mother but if we do that here, we lose the male-female aspect, which is a primary meaning). The three are: emptiness, wishlessness, and signlessness. All three are named in this explanation. The three are taught in the Prajñāpāramitā sutras as the realizations that the bodhisatva has of mother Prajñāpāramitā, which is ultimate reality in that system, as he treads the bodhisatva levels.

[110] Entitiness here means the innermost nature, which is the empty, alpha purity having the nature in general of self-arising wisdom.

to tame the four types of māra is the path of complete purity, it is the great path of being without endeavour, spontaneously existing.

2.A.II.2.B.II.3.B.II.2.B.IV. The steps of entering the mandala of the great completion

Entering the primordial unsurpassed maṇḍala transcending all the representations and images of it made with coloured sand, and so on, ***whose sphere is the totally undelimited*** in direction and time ***immeasurable palace of the wish-fulfilling jewel*** that can be milked for the magical display of all desires ***of the primal complete purity of all dharmas moreover is to*** begin by using the prajñā of listening to ***hear*** from the guru ***the texts of the vehicle of method***—the thirteenth chapter of the *Guhyagarbha* expounding the meaning of primal buddhahood together with foremost instruction—and the texts of the other vehicles, great completion and so on, ***which opens the eyes. Understanding their meaning*** by the use of the prajñā of contemplation ***is to see the maṇḍala. Having understood it*** by the use of the prajñā of meditation, ***doing the habituation is to have entered it*** and gained the empowerment. ***Having entered it*** like that, ***its having become manifest is to have gained great attainment.***

❁ ❁ ❁

Now, in order to show that this mode of great completion is not common to all, he says "***That mode is*** equality ***great completion's final meaning*** which is beyond all the cause and effect vehicles in the sense one cannot go higher than it.

One spontaneously or without endeavour ***enters*** the fruition of this path, ***the level of the Great Assembly of Letter Wheels.*** To explain that, generally speaking in the vehicles of characteristics overall, the buddha level is called "Total Light", because many light rays are emitted to make the beings to be tamed into suitable vessels. In the Vajra Vehicles in general, three buddha levels are known as follows. Total Light, being the dharmakāya without concept labels, is naturally luminous, giving off light that pervades everywhere. Having Lotuses, which does not see any fact of dharmakāya when it looks with non-referencing prajñā, is the basis for undefiled[111] compassionate activity. The Great Assembly of Letter Wheels is, at that very time, wisdom and the personage of the symbolic maṇḍala that is without endeavour spontaneously existing; there are two types of letter—wisdom and symbolic—and symbolic ones are also of two types—words and forms—and forms are also of two types—those appearing totally complete and partially complete. That which is spontaneously existing as the great assembly of the maṇḍala of this kind of fruition is called "the level of the Great Assembly of Letter Wheels", also known as the "thirteenth buddha level".

Beings of the very best mental ability will get the meaning of primordial buddhahood in direct knowledge of primordial buddhahood then, without relating to the endeavour-filled activities of a path ***will*** in a moment, ***go on to have habituation to it in a flash*** or suddenly, ***but that is not the usual way*** that most beings contemplate and do their habituation. ***Most beings who hear this*** sort of thing ***will, no matter how*** assiduously ***they contemplate it, not develop the conviction of its truth and*** its great ***profundity. Due to the difficulty the minds of average people have developing conviction in it and understanding it and due to their not understanding its truth and profundity, when they try to experience it*** themselves, ***it comes out the same as everyone else's usual experience. Saying "they are false"*** about those who have realized Great Completion and to all dharmas being primordially buddha, ***they will denigrate the best type of beings and develop an attitude of rejecting*** the great vehicle. ***Because of that, it has to be*** something which is ***utterly secret, which is why the***

---

[111] ... like a lotus is a thing that pleases others and also has left behind the defilement of the filthy swamp in which it grew ...

instruction was given by the teacher himself ***that "It is the*** nature ***secret vehicle"***.[112]

That being so, until the mind that is capable of correctly ***realizing the meaning of all dharmas being primordial buddhahood has been produced, if the vehicles below this one***—the paths of gods and humans, śhrāvakas, pratyekabuddhas, and so on—***are to be used to work for the sake of migrators, so that those to be tamed*** do ***not*** have their mind-streams ***damaged, the master must be expert in*** explaining ***the faults of samsara*** for lesser minds, extolling ***the good qualities of nirvana, and the*** stages in their ***entirety*** of ***all the vehicles***, and should be someone who will gradually lead disciples through connecting those meanings with their own experience. ***Otherwise, if there are some areas*** of the vehicles that ***he does not know, it is widely stated*** in the sutras and tantras ***that he should not hold the position of master.***

❁ ❁ ❁

2.B. Explanation of the Particulars of Yogic Conduct

This has two parts: a synopsis and an explanation.

2.B.I. Synopsis

The particulars of view will also entail specific austerities of body and speech which will be done for the sake of obtaining desired good qualities ***and yogic conducts*** or yogic behaviours which will be done to transform one's previous state of being into another. That is so

---

[112] "It is the nature secret vehicle" as was taught in the first verse of the thirteenth chapter of the *Guhyagarbha Tantra* by Samantabhadra, the teacher of the tantra. Great Completion belongs to the secret Vajra Vehicle in general. It is further known as Nature Great Completion, which is what the "nature secret" refers to.

because what is decided by the view, which is like the eyes, will be followed by austerities and yogic conducts, which are like the feet.

In accordance with the particulars of view, there are two possibilities for austerities: views that have them and do not have them. *The ones that do not have austerities are* twofold: *the worldly Phyal ba* and the outsider *Paryantikas* do not have austerities due to not having anything to accomplish in relation to a view. *There are four types in relation to those who do have them* due to their having something to be accomplished in relation to a view*: the worldly austerities*—not related to the path of liberation—*of the* worldly *Chārvāka and* the outsider *Tīrthika*, and the austerities that become the path to transcending the world—*the austerities of śhrāvakas, the austerities of bodhisatvas, and the austerities of the unsurpassed ones.*

2.B.II. EXPLANATION

The worldly *Phyal ba*—who were mentioned above, in the section on views—*because of their stupidity regarding cause and effect* have no knowledge of the subject of adoption and rejection, so *have no austerities*. The outsider *Paryantikas because of having the view of nihilism* in which there is no cause and effect do not seek benefit for their future lives so *have no austerities.*

Those two do not have austerities; now for the side that does have them, the worldly *Chārvākas have the austerities of* cleanliness, *and so on in order to make this life better* than that of others by obtaining power, wealth, and so on that is superior to that of others. Outsider *Tīrthikas perform the austerities of rejecting the body* by subjecting it to heat and cold, and so on, *relying on the five fires*—one on each of the four sides and the sun above—*and so on, and have wrong* or low-grade, tiring, and meaningless *yogic conduct* like the behaviour of dogs, pigs, and so forth *in order to purify the eternal self they believe to exist.*

The śhrāvaka austerities are, as it says in the Vinaya in a summary of the three trainings:

Do not do the slightest evil deed and
Carry out a perfection of virtue,
And tame one's own mind entirely—
This is the teaching of the Buddha.

The first line is from the standpoint of the training in discipline. It means to turn away from the path of the ten non-virtuous actions which are not to be done, especially the heaviest ones like killing, taking what is not given, sexual conduct, and telling lies, which are the four defeats.

The second line is from the standpoint of training in prajñā. It means all dharmas of the path and fruition of the noble ones that are to be practised and attained are included in prajñā which correctly realizes the meaning of the four truths.

The third line is from the standpoint of the training of mind. It refers to the training of mind; it is the training in meditative absorption in which one turns mind away from being distracted to externals then sets it in one-pointed equipoise.[113]

The fourth line consists of words that validate the first three lines. The words in this verse are not like the statements of one of the outsiders' gods like Īśhvara. This is the teaching of the Buddha which, because it is valid, can be relied on by everyone; it is the holy dharma of the Vinaya that has been well-spoken.[114]

---

[113] "Training of mind" is another way in the sutras of saying "training in samādhi". He has explained these three lines as being one each for the three higher trainings of śhīla, samādhi, and prajñā.

[114] "The dharma of the Vinaya that has been well-spoken" is one of the attributes of the Buddha's dharma mentioned in the *Sutra of the Recollection of Dharma*. It is explained to mean that the dharma taught by the Buddha was taught in an excellent way, such that beings could success-

(continued ...)

Thus, ***with the view that all the dharmas of virtue and non-virtue are individually existing both in fiction and superfact*** means that those dharmas that appear to a fictional awareness also appear to a superfactual awareness, and that is why they are said to "exist in both". Thus, ***they carry out*** through body and speech ***the austerities and yogic conducts of living in virtue and abandoning non-virtue.***

Pratyekabuddhas were discussed separately in the section above on view, but their austerities are not stated here because they are the same as those of the śhrāvakas.

The bodhisatva austerities are as follows. Arousing the mind of all-knowing wisdom in order to save all sentient beings from the ocean of samsara is the actual taking of the vow. Without the attainment of all-knowing wisdom, it is not possible to act for the sake of sentient beings, so there are these three things: the cause, which is enlightenment mind; the root, which is great compassion; and the finalization, which is skilful means. None of these three can be missing.

What is inimical to that is what are wrongdoings by nature[115], four things that defeat enlightenment mind. To give up enlightenment mind is inimical to fully taking on enlightenment mind; the two things of not protecting sentient beings due to avarice and harming them with harmful intent are inimical to compassion; and to abandon the holy dharma is inimical to skilful means.

---

[114] (... continued)
fully follow it. By implication it means that the dharma taught by others, such as the Tīrthikas, was not well taught and could not be successfully used to gain enlightenment.

[115] There are two types of what are literally called "unmentionables", meaning wrongdoings, which in the society of bodhisatvas would be embarrassing to mention. The first is "by nature", meaning without a vow, and the second is "with a vow" meaning that something has been done which corrupts or defeats a vow.

When you are not in the grip of those four, but are held by compassion, it is necessary to carry out even physical and verbal eliminations. ***As it says in the Twenty Verses on Bodhisatva Vows:***

> If a bodhisatva could through an act of elimination ***create a suitable condition*** for taming beings but ***does not act for*** migrators' ***sakes*** by doing the elimination, his vow will be corrupted.
> If he could tame beings through such unholy acts as conning, reviling, ***menacing*** them, ***and so on by*** a show of ***magic***, but ***does not engage*** in that, then again it will be corrupted.
> Why is that? ***Because*** if he is motivated by ***having compassion and loving-kindness***
> ***And*** his ***mind*** is ***not going wrong*** even if the application is rough ***in regard to virtue ...***

If you are held by a motivation of ***great compassion, any dharma that you do whether virtuous or*** seemingly ***unvirtuous will not corrupt the*** bodhisatva's ***vows. The bodhisatva vow in brief is to set great compassion as the basis then act.***

The secret ***unsurpassed ones' austerities are, as it says in the Sutra of Great Samaya:***

> ***If*** his mind ***is utterly certain*** or has complete assurance ***of the*** great equalness of method and prajñā, the unsurpassed ***buddha vehicle, then***
> ***He might act in the five afflictions and desirables,***
> ***But like mud*** does not contaminate ***a lotus,***
> ***For*** that supreme person, all ***the*** śhrāvaka ***disciplines*** and vows of a bodhisatva ***will be perfect.***

Because of the primordial equality of all dharmas that person primordially possesses compassion, thus it cannot be lost, so ***there is no attending to compassion and*** anger is without self-characterization, so there is ***no abandoning of anger.*** When that primordial equality or sameness is known by a mind with that attitude of equality, the realized mind knows "There is no contradiction at all".

In short, the śhrāvaka vow is to refrain from inflicting harm on sentient beings. The bodhisatva vow is, on top of that, to engage in aiding them. The vow of secret mantra is, on top of those two, to practise carrying out the activities of a tathāgata.

Furthermore, the śhrāvaka vow is, from both perceived and actual points of view, primarily concerned with action; in the bodhisatva vehicle compassion is the primary concern; and in secret mantra prajñā is the primary concern.

Further still, śhrāvakas train by following after the noble arhats of the past, bodhisatvas train following after the noble bodhisatvas abiding on great levels, and followers of secret mantra train following after the tathāgata himself. Now the equality of dharmas might in that way have been manifested, but ***for those who*** in the eight vehicles either absolutely or partially ***do not understand such, it is not that compassionate activity does not arise;*** reference-less compassionate activity arises as the entitiness spontaneously coming into existence.

In short, in secret mantra, for every one of all actions carried out within the samaya of the great equality, there is no not being complete purity—***as primordial complete purity has been known through the view, so austerities and yogic conduct will be carried out as complete purity.*** With those concluding words about secret mantra's samaya of great equality, he has shown how secret mantra's austerities and yogic conducts are distinguished over those of the vehicles below.

3. Conclusion

This consists of two parts: the vessel to whom this foremost instruction is entrusted and the colophon appended at the end of the composition.

3.A. The Vessel

The specifics of views high and low have been condensed down to what was needed and arranged into a continuous string, like a garland, so it has been called "A Garland of Views".

This garland of views is secret: given that it condenses into a few words the meanings of the vehicles in their entirety then gives foremost instructions which are to be borne in mind and given that its few words that cause the realization of many meanings make it a lamp, it has been determined that, like a precious gem, it is to be kept hidden. Alternatively, given that the meaning of Great Completion, the most uncommon meaning of all, is present here in one place, this should be kept secret as a means of great compassionate activity.

Next, Padmasaṃbhava makes a prayer for this profound dharma. ***Like a blind man who*** cannot see, one day, by his own merit finds a precious gem or ***naturally opens and regains his eyes***, a being who has been blinded by ignorance since time without beginning and never caught sight of the fact of the authentic, one day, due to merit from the past comes into contact with a virtuous spiritual friend and through that regains his eyes of the three prajñās. ***If there is a supreme being who*** like that finds or ***has the capabilities of prajñā shine forth*** and so becomes a vessel of Nature Great Completion, ***may he come into contact with this*** precious oral instruction that will become meaningful for him, this ***secret garland of views!*** This has been expressed in the form of a prayer.

3.B. The Colophon

This ***Foremost Instruction*** called ***"A Garland of Views"*** which was given by the great master Padmasambhava when he was about to return from the country of Tibet having spent three winters in the meadows at Red Rock Trembling Lake, at the time of his parting from the son of the gods Trisong Deutsen and his subjects, ***is*** now ***complete***. Virtue!

❁ ❁ ❁

May I, through the merit of writing this, in all my
lifetimes,
Enter the vajra essence of the soft Padma lotus and
Having realized all the profound key points of the
authentic view,
Illuminate for migrators the excellent path of the
conqueror!

This was written by Mipham in between sessions. Maṅgalaṃ!

❁ ❁ ❁

The foregoing has been the un-retouched annotations of Jamgon Mraway Senge, Mipham Ösel Dorje, embellished with topic headings to the commentary composed by Owner of the Secret, Lodro Thayay. With the great preceptor Lama Kunzang Palden, a great holder of the piṭakas, acting as the chief editor, it was corrected and edited then finalized in the earth-female-sheep year of the fifteenth rabjung called "Dondrup", in the wilderness of Zhechen Monastery.

This is the juice, the foremost instructions of the
conqueror and vidyādhara lineages,
That had trickled down into the mind-lake of the leading
conqueror Padma
And from there been offered as instruction to the
karmically connected king, ministers, and retinue.
It is the gem treasured by the holders of the conqueror's
teaching,
The most cherished part even now at the end of time,
Its arousing of mind, an aspiration sent in a straight line,
hits the mark

Then the nectar having the blessings of the close lineage
Is enjoyed; what could not be good about this fortune?

On account of that, this text containing Guru Jamgon's annotations,
Has been respectfully compiled and I think not tainted by my own mind,
Nevertheless, I ask those who have the dharma eye to be tolerant
Of any mistakes that might have been made, faults of my own mind.

By the stainless, supreme virtue derived from the work,
May the lotus grove of the supreme vehicle's teaching spread,
And may I become Padma's servant in all my births,
Illuminating the good path of the authentic view!

This too was written by Jamyang Lodro Gyatso. Virtue!

GLOSSARY OF TERMS

Actuality, Tib. gnas lugs: A key term in both sutra and tantra and one of a pair of terms, the other being "apparent reality" (Tib. snang lugs). The two terms are used when determining the reality of a situation. The actuality of any given situation is how (lugs) the situation actuality sits or is present (gnas); the apparent reality is how (lugs) any given situation appears (snang) to an observer. Something could appear in many different ways, depending on the circumstances at the time and on the being perceiving it but, regardless of those circumstances, it will always have its own actuality of how it really is. This term is frequently used in the tantras to mean the fundamental reality of any given phenomenon or situation before any deluded mind alters it and makes it appear differently.

Adventitious, Tib. glo bur: This term has the connotations of popping up on the surface of something and of not being part of that thing. Therefore, even though it is often translated as "sudden", that only conveys half of the meaning. In Buddhist literature, something adventitious comes up as a surface event and disappears again precisely because it is not actually part of the thing on whose surface it appeared. It is frequently used in relation to the afflictions because they pop up on the surface of the mind of buddha-nature but are not part of the buddha-nature itself.

Affliction, Skt. kleśha, Tib. nyon mongs: This term is often translated as emotion or disturbing emotion and the like but the Buddha was very specific about the meaning of this word. When the Buddha referred to the emotions, meaning a movement of mind, he did not refer to them as such but called them "kleśha" in Sanskrit, meaning exactly "affliction". It is a basic part of the Buddhist teaching that emotions afflict beings, giving them problems at the time and causing more problems in the future.

Aggregates, dhatus, and ayatanas, Skt. skandha dhātu āyatana, Tib. phung po khams skyed mched: The Buddha taught this set of three in the Lesser Vehicle teachings where they were an essential part of the teaching on how samsara is constructed and how it perpetuates itself. Skandhas are the "aggregates" that make up a samsaric being. Dhātus are the items within a samsaric being's makeup that are the "bases" of all samsaric minds; they are a detailed listing of the things that allow dualistic mind to occur with all of its attendant problems. Āyatanas are those specific members of the dhātus which cause samsaric consciousness to ignite. A very complete presentation of the skandhas, dhātus, and āyatanas can be found in the book *The Six Topics that All Buddhists Learn* by Tony Duff, published by Padma Karpo Translation Committee, 2012, ISBN: 978-9937-572-13-2.

Alpha purity, Tib. ka dag: A Great Completion term meaning purity that is there from the first, that is, primordial purity. There are many terms in Buddhism that express the notion of "primordial purity" but this one is unique to the Great Completion teaching. The term "alpha purity" matches the Tibetan term both literally and in meaning.

Animate and inanimate, Tib. brtan g-yo. This is a stock phrase used to sum up the entirety of cyclic existence.

Appearance and rebirths, Tib. snang srid: This is a stock phrase usually meaning all of samsara and nirvana, though occasionally meaning all of samsara. Appearance refers to the worlds and rebirth refers to the beings in those worlds. It is equivalent to another stock phrase "containers and contents" and the two are sometimes put together.

Arousing the mind, Tib. sems bskyed: This is a technical term nearly always used to mean "arousing the enlightenment mind", although it can be used to refer to the deliberate production of other types of mind, for example renunciation. There are two types of arousing the enlightenment mind—fictional and superfactual; see under fictional enlightenment mind and superfactual enlightenment mind.

Assurance, Tib. gdeng: Although often translated as confidence, this term means assurance with all of the extra meaning conveyed by that term. A bird might be confident of its ability to fly but, more than that, it has the assurance that it will not fall to the ground because it knows it has wings and it has the training to use them. Similarly, a person might be confident that he could liberate the afflictions but not be assured of doing so because of lack of training or other causes. However, a person who has accumulated the causes to be able to liberate afflictions is assured of the ability to do so.

Authoritative statement, Skt. āgama, Tib. lung: This means statement made by someone who has the knowledge needed to make fully reliable statements about a subject; it can refer to verbal statement or scripture. It is often used to indicate dharma taught by the Buddha or his disciples which is authoritative because of its source. It is also used in the pair "authoritative statement and realization" which, the Buddha explained, summed up the ways of transmitting his realization.

Bliss, Skt. sukha, Tib. bde: The Sanskrit term and its Tibetan translation are usually translated into English as "bliss" but refer to the whole range of possibilities of everything on the side of good as opposed to bad. Thus, the term will mean pleasant, happy, good, nice, easy, comfortable, blissful, and so on, depending on context.

Bodhichitta, Tib. byang chub sems: See under enlightenment mind.

Bodhisatva, Tib. byang chub sems dpa': A bodhisatva is a person who has engendered the bodhichitta, enlightenment mind, and with that as a basis has undertaken the path to the enlightenment of a truly complete buddha specifically for the welfare of other beings. Note that, despite the common appearance of "bodhisattva" in Western books on Buddhism, the Tibetan tradition has steadfastly maintained since the time of the earliest translations that the correct spelling is bodhisatva; see under satva and sattva.

Clinging, Tib. zhen pa: In Buddhism, this term refers specifically to the twofold process of dualistic mind mis-taking things that are not true, not pure, etcetera as true, pure, etcetera and then, because of seeing them as highly desirable even though they are not, attaching itself to or clinging to those things. This type of clinging acts as a kind of glue that keeps a person joined to the unsatisfactory things of cyclic existence because of mistakenly seeing them as desirable.

Compassionate activity, Tib. thugs rje: This does not mean compassionate activity in general. It refers to the fact that wisdom spontaneously does whatever needs to be done, throughout all reaches of time and space, for all beings. Although it includes the word "compassion" in its name, it is more primordial than that. It is the dynamic quality of enlightenment which choicelessly, ceaselessly, spontaneously, and pervasively acts to benefit others. The term is often used in discussions of Great Completion.

Complete purity, rnam dag: This term refers to the quality of a buddha's mind, which is completely pure compared to a sentient being's mind. The mind of a being in samsara has its primordially pure nature covered over by the muck of dualistic mind. If the being practises correctly, the impurity can be removed and mind can be returned to its original state of complete purity.

Concept label, Tib. mtshan ma: This is the technical name for the structures or concepts which function as the words of conceptual mind's language. They are the very basis of operation of the third aggregate and hence of the way that dualistic mind communicates with its world. For example, a table seen in direct visual perception will have no concept labels involved with knowing it. However, when thought becomes involved and there is the thought "table" in an inferential or conceptual perception of the table, the name-tag "table" will be used to reference the table and that name tag is the concept label.

Although we usually reference phenomena via these concepts, the phenomena are not the dualistically referenced things we think of them as being. The actual fact of the phenomena is quite different from the concept labels used to discursively think about them and is known by wisdom rather than concept-based mind. Therefore, this term is often used in Buddhist literature to signify that dualistic samsaric mind is involved rather than non-dualistic wisdom.

Confusion, Tib. 'khrul pa: In Buddhism, this term mostly refers to the fundamental confusion of taking things the wrong way that happens because of fundamental ignorance, although it can also have the more general meaning of having lots of thoughts and being confused about it. In the first case, it is defined like this: "confusion is the appearance to rational mind of something being present when it is not", and it refers, for example, to seeing an object, such as a table, as being truly present, when in fact it is present only as mere, interdependent appearance.

Consciousness, Skt. vijñāna, Tib. rnam shes: The term literally means "awareness of superficies". A consciousness is a dualistic (jñā) awareness which simply registers a certain type of (vi) superfice, for example, an eye consciousness by definition registers only the superficies of visual form. A very important point is that the addition of the "vi" to the basic term (jñā) for awareness conveys the sense of a less than perfect way of being aware. This is not a wisdom awareness which knows every superfice in an utterly uncomplicated way but a limited type of awareness which is restricted to knowing one kind of superfice or another and which is part of the complicated—and highly unsatisfactory process—called (dualistic) mind. Note that this definition, which is a crucial part of understanding the role of consciousness in samsaric being, is fully conveyed by the Sanskrit and Tibetan terms but not at all by the English term.

Containers and contents, Tib. snod bcud: Containers are the outer worlds and environment and their contents are the beings living in them. This phrase is sometimes extended to "outer and inner, containers and contents" with the same meaning. It usually means "the entirety of samsara", though sometimes means "the entirety of samsara and nirvana".

Contrivance, contrived, Tib. bcos pa: A term meaning that something has been altered from its native state.

Cross Over, Tib. la zla ba: This is a special term of Great Completion. It means to resolve in direct experience that a certain situation is that way. First you learn about the view, then you resolve or cross over into it, then you meditate on the view that has been resolved in order to fully manifest it.

When discussing conduct (of view, meditation, and conduct), the tantras differentiate two types: conventional conduct such as that taught in the sutras in which there is a specific type of activity to be done in order to achieve a specific goal and a non-conventional type of conduct taught in Mahāmudrā and Great Completion which simply bypasses all the activities of such conduct designed to achieve a specific goal and crosses over into the meditation.

Cyclic existence: See under samsara.

Dharmadhatu, Skt. dharmadhātu, Tib. chos kyi dbyings: A *dhātu* is a place or basis from or within which something can come into being. In the case of a dharma dhātu, it is the place or space which is a basis from and in which all dharmas or phenomena, can and do come into being. If a flower bed is the place where flowers grow and are found, the dharmadhātu is the dharma or phenomena bed in which all phenomena come into being and are found. The term is used in all levels of Buddhist teaching with that general meaning but the explanation of it becomes more profound as the teaching becomes more profound. For example, in Great Completion, it is the all-pervading sphere of luminosity-wisdom, given that luminosity is where phenomena arise and luminosity is none other than wisdom.

Dharmadhatu, Skt. dharmadhātu, Tib. chos kyi khams: This is the name for one of the eighteen elements. It is the element of that which is known by mental faculty and mental consciousness. The Sanskrit name is the same as the entry above but the meaning is different.

Dharmata, Skt. dharmatā, Tib. chos nyid: This is a general term meaning the inherent property or properties of any given dharma or phenomenon. It can be applied to anything at all. For example, the dharmatā of water is its wetness, liquidity, and so on. Dharmatā is used frequently in Tibetan Buddhism to mean the most fundamental property of dharmas or phenomena which is their emptiness because of which it is not commonly thought of as meaning "reality". However, that is not correct. To read texts which use this term successfully, one has to understand that the term has a general meaning and then see how that applies in context.

Dharmin, Tib. chos can: A dharmin is defined as an awareness having, meaning knowing, a dharma or phenomenon. The awareness can either be a dualistic or a non-dualistic awareness, that is, it can either be a samsaric consciousness or wisdom knower, though it is mostly used to indicate a samsaric awareness of a phenomenon.

Discursive thought, Skt. vikalpa, Tib. rnam rtog: This means more than just the superficial thought that is heard as a voice in the head. It includes the entirety of conceptual process that arises due to mind contacting any object of any of the senses. The Sanskrit and Tibetan literally mean "(dualistic) thought (that arises from the mind wandering among the) various (superficies *q.v.* perceived in the doors of the senses)".

Endeavour, Tib. rtsol ba: In Buddhism, this term means efforts made to accomplish something with concept involved. It has the sense of using a conceptually driven technique to accomplish something. Thus it implies the presence of dualistic mind.

Elaboration, Skt. prapañca, Tib. spro ba: This is a general name for what is given off by dualistic mind as it goes about its conceptual business. The term is pejorative in that it implies that a story has been made up, un-necessarily, about something which is actually nothing, which is empty. Elaborations, because of what they are, prevent a person from seeing emptiness directly.

Freedom from elaboration or being elaboration-free implies direct sight of emptiness. It is important to understand that these words are used in a theoretical or philosophical way in the second turning sutra teachings but are used in an experiential way in the final teachings of the third turning sutras and in the tantras of Great Completion and Mahāmudrā. In the former, being free of elaborations is a definition of what could happen according to the tenets of the Middle Way, and so on; in the latter it is a description of a state of being, one which, because it is empty of all the elaborations of dualistic being, is the actual sphere of emptiness.

Enlightenment mind, Skt. bodhichitta, Tib. byang chub sems: This is a key term of the Great Vehicle. It is the type of mind that is connected not with the lesser enlightenment of an arhat but with the enlightenment of a truly complete buddha. As such, it is a mind which is connected with the aim of bringing all sentient beings to that same level of buddhahood. A person who has engendered this mind has by definition entered the Great Vehicle and is either a bodhisatva or a buddha.

It is important to understand that "enlightenment mind" is used to refer equally to the minds of all levels of bodhisatva on the path to buddhahood and to the mind of a buddha who has completed the path. Therefore, it is not "mind striving for enlightenment" as is so often translated, but "enlightenment mind", meaning that kind of mind which is connected with the full enlightenment of a truly complete buddha and which is present in all those who belong to the Great Vehicle.

Entity, Tib. ngo bo: The entity of something is just exactly what that thing is. In English we would often simply say "thing" rather than entity. However, in Buddhism, "thing" has a very specific meaning rather than the general meaning that it has in English. It has become common to translate this term as "essence" *q.v.* However, in most cases "entity", meaning what a thing is rather than an essence of that thing, is the correct translation for this term.

Evil, evil deed, Skt. papaṃ, Tib. sdig pa: The original Sanskrit means something which someone has done which is truly bad, rotten. Anyone who has done such a thing is looked down upon. The Tibetan for it relates to the idea of a scorpion, a nasty creature that will sting you and injure you. In Buddhism, the term does not have the Christian sense of evil but simply means action done that, being done under the influence of an affliction, degrades you now in other's eyes, degrades you now because of the bad karmic seeds that you have planted by doing it, and degrades you in the future because of the ripening of the bad karmas into unpleasant results.

Fact, Skt. artha, Tib. don: "Fact" is that knowledge of an object that occurs to the surface of mind or wisdom. It is not the object but what the mind or wisdom understands as the object. Thus there are two usages of "fact": fact known to dualistic and non-dualistic minds. The higher tantras especially use "fact" to refer to the actual fact known in direct perception of actuality. Thus, there are phrases such as "in fact" which do not mean that the author is speaking truly about something but that whatever is about to be said is referring to actual fact as known to wisdom. A further complexity is that phrases such as "in fact" in those contexts are often abbreviations of "in superfact" *q.v.* This brings a further difficulty for the reader because "superfact" can be used in a general way to indicate directly perceived non-samsaric fact or can be used according to its specific definition (for which see superfact). In Buddhist tradition, problems like this are solved by having the text explained by one's teacher. That might not be possible for some readers, so uses of the word "fact" should be looked at carefully to see whether they are indicating fact in general or the factual situation of knowing reality in direct perception.

Habituation, Tib. goms pa: This is similar to but not the same as meditation (Tib. sgom pa). Where meditation is the process of creating then cultivating a certain quality which was not there before, habituation is the process of familiarizing yourself with a quality that is already present, even if it has become temporarily unavailable due to being covered over.

Fictional, Skt. saṃvṛtti, Tib. kun rdzob: This term is paired with the term "superfactual" *q.v.* In the past, these terms have been translated as "relative" and "absolute" respectively, but those translations are nothing like the original terms. These terms are extremely important in the Buddhist teaching so it is very important that they be corrected, but more than that, if the actual meaning of these terms is not presented, then the teaching connected with them cannot be understood.

The Sanskrit term saṃvṛtti means a deliberate invention, a fiction, a hoax. It refers to the mind of ignorance which, because of being obscured and so not seeing suchness, is not true but a fiction. The things that appear to that ignorance are therefore fictional. Nonetheless, the beings who live in this ignorance believe that the things that appear to them through the filter of ignorance are true, are real. Therefore, these beings live in fictional truth.

Fictional truth, Skt. saṃvṛtisatya, Tib. kun rdzob bden pa: See under fictional.

Grasped-grasping, Tib. gzung 'dzin: When mind is turned outwardly as it is in the normal operation of dualistic mind, it has developed two faces that appear simultaneously. Special names are given to these two faces: mind appearing in the form of the external object being referenced is called "that which is grasped" and mind appearing in the form of the consciousness that is registering it is called the "grasper" or "grasping" of it. Thus, there is the pair of terms "grasped-grasper" or "grasped-grasping". When these two terms are used, it alerts one to the fact that a Mind Only style of presentation is being discussed. This pair of terms pervades Mind Only, Middle Way, and tantric writings and is exceptionally important in all of them.

Note that one could substitute the word "apprehended" for "grasped" and "apprehender" for "grasper" or "grasping" and that would reflect one connotation of the original Sanskrit terminology. The solidified duality of grasped and grasper is nothing but an invention of dualistic thought; it has that kind of character or characteristic.

Great Bliss, Skt. mahāsukha, Tib. bde ba chen po: Great bliss is a standard but inexact translation of this key term. The phrase actually means "the great state of satisfactoriness" that comes with entering an enlightened kind of existence. It is blissful in that it is totally satisfactory, a condition of perfect ease, in comparison to samsaric existence which is totally unsatisfactory and always with some kind of dis-ease. As Thrangu Rinpoche once observed, if samsara is thought of as "great suffering" then this is better thought of as the "great ease". Similarly, if samsara is "total unsatisfactoriness" then this is the "great satisfactoriness".

Great Vehicle, Skt. mahāyāna, Tib. theg pa chen po: The Buddha's teachings as a whole can be summed up into three vehicles where a vehicle is defined as that which can carry a person to a certain destination. The first vehicle, called the Lesser Vehicle, contains the teachings designed to get an individual moving on the spiritual path through showing the unsatisfactory state of cyclic existence and an emancipation from that. However, that path is only concerned with personal emancipation and fails to take account of all of the beings that there are in existence. There used to be eighteen schools of Lesser Vehicle in India but the only one surviving nowadays is the Theravāda of south-east Asia. The Greater Vehicle is a step up from that. The Buddha explained that it was great in comparison to the Lesser Vehicle for seven reasons. The first of those is that it is concerned with attaining the truly complete enlightenment of a truly complete buddha for the sake of every sentient being where the Lesser Vehicle is concerned only with a personal liberation that is not truly complete enlightenment and which is achieved only for the sake of that practitioner. The Great Vehicle has two divisions: a conventional form in which the path is taught in a logical, conventional way, and an unconventional form in which the path is taught in a very direct way. This latter vehicle is called the Vajra Vehicle because it takes the innermost, indestructible (vajra) fact of reality of one's own mind as the vehicle to enlightenment.

Intent, Tib. dgongs pa: This is the honorific form of (Tib. sems pa) meaning "to think, to comprehend", so is used to refer to an enlightened person's understanding, though the Gelugpa school is even more restrictive and uses it only for wisdom understanding of the Buddha. In some places "intent" meaning the intended meaning based on an enlightened person's understanding and in other places simply "understanding" should be understood for this term.

Kaya, Skt. kāya, Tib. sku: The Sanskrit term means a functional or coherent collection of parts, similar to the French "corps", and hence also comes to mean "a body". It is used in Tibetan Buddhist texts specifically to distinguish bodies belonging to the enlightened side from ones belonging to the samsaric side.

Enlightened being in Buddhism is said to be comprised of one or more kāyas. It is most commonly explained to consist of one, two, three, four, or five kāyas, though it is pointed out that there are infinite aspects to enlightened being and therefore it can also be said to consist of an infinite number of kāyas. In fact, these descriptions of enlightened being consisting of one or more kāyas are given for the sake of understanding what is beyond conceptual understanding so should not be taken as absolute statements.

The most common description of enlightened being is that it is comprised of three kāyas: dharma, saṃbhoga, and nirmāṇakāyas. Briefly stated, the dharmakāya is the body of truth, the saṃbhogakāya is the body replete with the good qualities of enlightenment, and the nirmāṇakāya is the body manifested into the worlds of samsara and nirvana to benefit beings.

Dharmakāya refers to that aspect of enlightened being in which the being sees the truth for himself and, in doing so, fulfils his own needs for enlightenment. The dharmakāya is purely mind, without form. The remaining two bodies are summed up under the heading of rūpakāyas or form bodies manifested specifically to fulfil the needs of all un-enlightened beings. "Saṃbhogakāya" has been mostly translated as "body of enjoyment" or "body of rapture" but it is clearly stated in Buddhist texts on the subject that the name refers to a situation replete with what is useful, that is, to the fact that the saṃbhogakāya contains all of the good qualities of enlightenment as needed to benefit sentient beings. The saṃbhogakāya is extremely subtle and not accessible by most sentient beings; the nirmāṇakāya is a coarser manifestation which can reach sentient beings in many ways. Nirmāṇakāya should not be thought of as a physical body but as the capability to express enlightened being in whatever way is needed throughout all the different worlds of sentient beings. Thus, as much as it appears as a supreme buddha who shows the dharma to beings, it also appears as anything needed within sentient beings' worlds to give them assistance.

The three kāyas of enlightened being is taught in all levels of Buddhist teaching. It is especially important in Great Completion and is taught there in a unique and very profound way.

Kayas and wisdoms, Tib. sku dang ye shes: Enlightened being might be empty of samsaric phenomena but it does have enlightened content. "Kāyas and wisdoms" or "bodies and wisdoms" is a stock phrase used to indicate either the content of enlightenment or to imply that it does have content.

Latency, Skt. vāsanā, Tib. bag chags: The original Sanskrit has the meaning exactly of "latency". The Tibetan term translates that inexactly with "something sitting there (Tib. chags) within the environment of mind (Tib. bag)". Although it has become popular to translate this term into English with "habitual pattern", that is not its meaning. The term refers to a karmic seed that has been imprinted on the mindstream and is present there as a latency, ready and waiting to come into manifestation.

Lesser Vehicle, Skt. hīnayāna, Tib. theg pa dman pa: See under Great Vehicle.

Luminosity, Skt. prabhāsvara, Tib. 'od gsal ba: The core of mind has two aspects: an emptiness factor and a knowing factor. The Buddha and many Indian religious teachers used "luminosity" as a metaphor for the knowing quality of the core of mind. If in English we would say "Mind has a knowing quality", the teachers of ancient India would say, "Mind has an illuminative quality; it is like a source of light which illuminates what it knows".

This term has been translated as "clear light" but that is a mistake that comes from not understanding the etymology of the word. It does not refer to a light that has the quality of clearness (something that makes no sense, actually!) but to the illuminative property which is the nature of the empty mind.

Note also that in both Sanskrit and Tibetan Buddhist literature, this term is frequently abbreviated just to Skt. "vara" and Tib. "gsal ba" with no change of meaning. Unfortunately, this has been thought to be another word and it has then been translated with "clarity", when in fact it is just this term in abbreviation.

Mara, Skt. māra, Tib. bdud: The Sanskrit term is closely related to the word "death". Buddha spoke of four classes of extremely negative influences that have the capacity to drag a sentient being deep into samsara. They are the "māras" or "kiss of death" of: having a samsaric set of five skandhas; having afflictions; death itself; and the son of gods, which means being seduced and taken in totally by sensuality.

Migrator, Tib. 'gro ba: Migrator is one of several terms that were commonly used by the Buddha to mean "sentient being". It shows sentient beings from the perspective of their constantly being forced to go here and there from one rebirth to another by the power of karma. They are like flies caught in a jar, constantly buzzing back and forth. The term is often translated using "beings" which is another general term for sentient beings, but doing so loses the meaning entirely. Buddhist authors who know the tradition do not use the word loosely but use it specifically to give the sense of beings who are constantly and helplessly going from one birth to another, and that is how the term should be read. The term "six migrators" refers to the six types of migrators within samsaric existence—hell-beings, pretas, animals, humans, demi-gods, and gods.

Mind, Skt. chitta, Tib. sems: There are several terms for mind in the Buddhist tradition, each with its own, specific meaning. This term is the most general term for the samsaric type of mind. It refers to the type of mind that is produced because of fundamental ignorance of enlightened mind. Whereas the wisdom of enlightened mind lacks all complexity and knows in a non-dualistic way, this mind of un-enlightenment is a very complicated apparatus that only ever knows in a dualistic way.

Nature Great Completion, Tib. rang bzhin rdzogs pa chen po: This is one of several names for Great Completion that emphasizes the path aspect of Great Completion. It is not "natural great completion" nor is it "the true nature Great Completion" as commonly seen. In terms of grammar, the first term is the noun "nature" not the adjective "natural". In terms of meaning, the noun nature is used because it refers to the nature aspect in particular of the three characteristics of the essence of mind—entity, nature, and un-stopped compassionate activity—used to describe Great Completion as experienced by the practitioner. Thus, this name refers to the approach taken by Great Completion and does not refer at all to Great Completion being a "natural" practice or its being connected with a "natural reality" or any of the many other, incorrect meanings that arise from the mistaken translation "natural Great Completion".

Noble one, Skt. ārya, Tib. 'phags pa: In Buddhism, a noble one is a being who has become spiritually advanced to the point that he has passed beyond cyclic existence. According to the Buddha, the beings in cyclic existence were ordinary beings, spiritual commoners, and the beings who had passed beyond it were special, the nobility.

Outflow, Skt. āsrāva, Tib. zag pa: The Sanskrit term means a bad discharge, like pus coming out of a wound. Outflows occur when wisdom loses its footing and falls into the elaborations of dualistic mind. Therefore, anything with duality also has outflows. This is sometimes translated as "defiled" or "conditioned" but these fail to capture the meaning. The idea is that wisdom can remain self-contained in its own unique sphere but, when it loses its ability to stay within itself, it starts to have leakages into dualism that are defilements on the wisdom. See also under un-outflowed.

Prajna, Skt. prajñā, Tib. shes rab: The Sanskrit term, literally meaning "best type of mind" is defined as that which makes correct distinctions between this and that and hence which arrives at correct understanding. It has been translated as "wisdom" but that is not correct because it is, generally speaking, a mental event belonging to dualistic mind where "wisdom" is used to refer to the non-dualistic knower of a buddha. Moreover, the main feature of prajñā is its ability to distinguish correctly between one thing and another and hence to arrive at a correct understanding.

Rational mind, Tib. blo: Rational mind is one of several terms for mind in Buddhist terminology. It specifically refers to a mind that judges this against that. It is mainly used to refer to samsaric mind, given that samsaric mind only works in the dualistic mode of comparing this versus that. Because of this, the term is mainly used in a pejorative sense to point out samsaric mind as opposed to a non-dualistic enlightened type of mind. However, it is occasionally used to refer to the discriminating wisdom aspect of non-dualistic mind, for example, in the case of a buddha. In that case it is a mind making distinctions between this and that but within the context of non-dualistic wisdom.

This term has been commonly translated simply as "mind" but that fails to identify it properly and leaves it confused with the many other words that are also translated simply as "mind". It is not just another mind but is specifically the sort of mind that creates the situation of this and that (*ratio* in Latin). Therefore, the term "rational mind" fits perfectly. This is a key term which must be understood as a specific term with a specific meaning and should not be just glossed over as "mind".

Realization, Tib. rtogs pa: Realization has a very specific meaning: it refers to correct knowledge that has been gained in such a way that the knowledge does not abate. There are two important points here. Firstly, realization is not absolute. It refers to the removal of obscurations, one at a time. Each time that a practitioner removes an obscuration, he gains a realization because of it. Therefore, there are as many levels of realization as there are obscurations. Maitreya, in the *Ornament of Manifest Realizations*, shows how the removal of the various obscurations that go with each of the three realms of samsaric existence produces realization.

Secondly, realization is stable or, as the Tibetan wording says, "unchanging". As Guru Rinpoche pointed out, "Intellectual knowledge is like a patch, it drops away; experiences on the path are temporary, they evaporate like mist; realization is unchanging".

Reference and Referencing, Tib. dmigs pa: Referencing is the name for the process in which dualistic mind references an actual object by using a conceptual label instead of the actual object. Whatever is referenced is then called a reference. Note that these terms imply the presence of dualistic mind and their opposites, non-referencing and being without reference, imply the presence of non-dualistic wisdom.

Rigpa, Tib. rig pa: This is the singularly most important term in the whole of Great Completion and Mahāmudrā. In particular, it is the key word of all words in the Great Completion system of the Thorough Cut. Rigpa literally means to know in the sense of "I see!" To translate it as "awareness", which is common practice today, is a poor practice; there are many kinds of awareness but there is only one rigpa and besides, rigpa is substantially more than just awareness. Since this is such an important term and since it lacks an equivalent in English, I choose not to translate it.

Samsara, Skt. saṃsāra, Tib. 'khor ba: This is the most general name for the type of existence in which sentient beings live. It refers to the fact that they continue on from one existence to another, always within the enclosure of births that are produced by ignorance and experienced as unsatisfactory. The original Sanskrit means to be constantly going about, here and there. The Tibetan term literally means "cycling", because of which it is frequently translated into English with "cyclic existence" though that is not exactly the meaning of the original Sanskrit term.

Satva and sattva: According to the Tibetan tradition established at the time of the great translation work done at Samye under the watch of Padmasambhava not to mention one hundred and sixty-three of the greatest Buddhist scholars of Sanskrit-speaking India, there is a difference of meaning between the Sanskrit terms "satva" and "sattva", with satva meaning "an heroic kind of being" and "sattva" meaning simply "a being". According to the Tibetan tradition established under the advice of the Indian scholars mentioned above, satva is correct for the words Vajrasatva and bodhisatva, whereas sattva is correct for the words samayasattva, samādhisattva, and jñānasattva, and is also used alone to refer to any or all of these three sattvas.

All Tibetan texts produced since the time of the great translations conform to this system and all Tibetan experts agree that this is correct, but Western translators of Tibetan texts have for the last few hundred years claimed that they know better and have changed "satva" to "sattva" in every case, causing confusion amongst Westerners confronted by the correct spellings. Recently, publications by Western Sanskrit scholars have been appearing in which these great experts finally admit that they were wrong and that the Tibetan system is and always has been correct!

Secret, Skt. guhya, Tib. sang ba: This term is used in Buddhist texts in a specific way. It does not mean that someone has made something secret but that something has a nature which is hidden from the view of ordinary sentient beings, that it is not obvious to them.

With that meaning, it is used in this text in two ways. Firstly, it is used to refer to the tantric or Vajra Vehicle level of teaching; this teaching is about profound subjects that are not immediately understood by ordinary beings and so are called secret. Secondly, it is used to refer to enlightenment; for example, "the three secrets" mentioned in the book are the enlightened body, speech, and mind of a buddha; see under three secrets for more.

Self-arising wisdom, Tib. rang byung ye shes: The words "self-arising" are added to wisdom *q.v.* to indicate that it is not caused, that it is outside the samsaric process of cause and effect. As the vidyādhara Chogyam Trungpa said, it is self-existing.

Spontaneous existence, Tib. lhun grub: Spontaneous existence is a key term in Great Completion. The term "grub" refers to something coming into existence. The term "lhun" means that it is happening spontaneously, though note that spontaneous here has the specific meaning of being without karmic cause and effect. Thus, spontaneous existence in these teachings has two, equally important connotations: presence as opposed to absence and a type of existence occurring of itself, outside the process of karmic cause and effect.

It is not correct to call this "spontaneous presence". Presence merely indicates that something is present as opposed to absent. The original term includes that sense but has as its main connotation a process of coming into existence, and that process is one which is not the karmic cause and effect process. Moreover, there is the issue that this term has both noun and verb forms. While one can talk about "spontaneously existing"or "spontaneously coming to exist" one cannot talk of "spontaneous presencing", and the like. Many translations of the texts using these terms have simply conflated the noun and verb forms into the noun form "spontaneous presence". In the process, most of the shades of meaning in this term—all of which are crucial to understanding this material— have been lost.

Sugata, Tib. bde bar gshegs pa: This term is one of many names for a buddha. It has the twofold meaning of someone who has gone on a good, pleasant, easy journey and someone who has arrived at a place which is good, pleasant, and full of ease. The meaning in relation to buddhahood is explained at length in *Unending Auspiciousness, the Sutra of the Recollection of the Noble Three Jewels* by Tony Duff, published by Padma Karpo Translation Committee, 2010, ISBN: 978-9937-8386-1-0.

Superfactual, Skt. paramārtha,Tib. don dam: This term is paired with the term "fictional" *q.v.* In the past, these two terms have been translated as "relative" and "absolute", but those translations are nothing like the original terms. These terms are extremely important in the Buddhist teaching so it is very important that their translations be corrected but, more than that, if the actual meaning of these terms is not presented, the teaching connected with them cannot be understood.

The Sanskrit term paramārtha literally means "the fact for that which is above all others, special, superior" and refers to what is known to the wisdom mind possessed by those who have developed themselves spiritually to the point of having transcended samsara. That wisdom is *superior* to an ordinary, un-developed person's consciousness and the *facts* that appear on its surface are superior compared to the facts that appear on the ordinary person's consciousness. Therefore, it is superfact or, more colloquially, the highest thing that could be known. What this wisdom knows is true for the beings who have it, therefore what the wisdom sees is superfactual truth.

Superfactual truth, Skt. paramārthasatya, Tib. don dam bden pa: See under superfactual.

Superfice, superficies, Tib. rnam pa: In discussions of mind, a distinction is made between the entity of mind which is a mere knower and the superficial things that appear on its surface and which are known by it. In other words, the superficies are the various things which pass over the surface of mind but which are not mind. Superficies are all the specifics that constitute appearance—for example, the colour white within a moment of visual consciousness, the sound heard within an ear consciousness, and so on.

The authentic, Skt. bhūta, Tib. yang dag: This is a term commonly used in the sutras as a synonym for reality. For example "view of the authentic" means "view of reality". The sutras also often have the Sanskrit term "bhūtakoṭi" literally meaning "limit of the authentic" referring to the meaning final or utmost reality, that is, nirvāṇa.

Three secrets, Tib. gsang ba: This term is usually defined as a path term which refers to the body, speech, and mind of a person who is on the way to buddhahood. When a person becomes a buddha, he has reached his full state of enlightenment and at that point the three secrets have become unchanging so are now referred to with what is defined as a fruition term, "the three vajras" of a tathāgata.

Tirthika, Skt. tīrthika, Tib. mu stegs pa: This is a very kind name adopted by the Buddha for those who did not follow him but who, because they followed some other spiritual path, had at least arrived at the brink of the true path back to enlightenment. The Sanskrit name means "those who have arrived at the steps at the edge of the pool" and comes to mean those on the brink of actually crossing the river of samsara. A lengthy explanation is given in the *Illuminator Tibetan-English Dictionary* by Tony Duff and published by Padma Karpo Translation Committee.

Total affliction and complete purification, Tib. kun nas nyon rmongs pa dang rnam par byang ba: The Buddha divided all types of existence into two: enlightened existence and un-enlightened existence. He taught his disciples that their unenlightened existence was total (through and through) affliction, but if they followed the path to enlightenment, they would arrive, through the practice of purification of that affliction, at the state of enlightened existence, which he then referred to as "complete purification". In this way, he made the character of these two types of existence clear and at the same time goaded his disciples to get on the path and reach the point of complete purification. Note that "complete purification" refers to the result of having followed the path and is only used in relation to "total affliction"; it is not the same as complete purity.

Valid cognizer, valid cognition, Skt. pramāṇa, Tib. tshad ma: The Sanskrit term "pramāṇa" literally means "best type of mentality" and comes to mean "a valid cognizer". Its value is that is can be used to validate anything that can be known. The Tibetans translated this term with "tshad ma" meaning an "evaluator"—something which can be used to evaluate the truth or not of whatever it is given to know. It is the term used in logic to indicate a mind which is knowing validly and which therefore can be used to validate the object it is knowing.

Valid cognizers are named according to the kind of test they are employed to do. A valid cognizer of the conventional or a valid cognizer of the fictional tests within conventions, within the realm of rational, dualistic mind. A valid cognizer of the ultimate or valid cognizer of superfact tests for the superfactual level, beyond dualistic mind.

Wheel of ornamentation of unending enlightened body, speech, and mind, Tib. sku sung thugs mi zad pa'i rgyan gyi 'khor lo: This phrase is used to express final enlightenment as it actually functions. All three vajras of the tathāgatas perpetually engage in a limitless expression of enlightenment which is expressed throughout the entirety of the dharmadhātu. It is the single unique sphere of wisdom bursting at the seams with the display of enlightened activity. "Wheel" can be understood to mean "ongoing".

Wisdom, Skt. jñāna, Tib. ye shes: This is a fruition term that refers to the kind of mind—the kind of knower—possessed by a buddha. Sentient beings do have this kind of knower but it is covered over by a very complex apparatus for knowing, that is, dualistic mind. If they practise the path to buddhahood, they will leave behind their obscuration and return to having this kind of knower.

The Sanskrit term has the sense of knowing in the most simple and immediate way. This sort of knowing is present at the core of every being's mind. Therefore, the Tibetans called it "the particular type of awareness which is there primordially". Because of the Tibetan wording it has often been called "primordial wisdom" in English translations, but that goes too far; it is just "wisdom" in the sense of the most fundamental knowing possible.

Wisdom does not operate in the same way as samsaric mind; it comes about in and of itself without depending on cause and effect. Therefore it is frequently referred to as "self-arising wisdom" *q.v.*

About the Author, Padma Karpo Translation Committee, and Their Supports for Study

I have been encouraged over the years by all of my teachers to pass on the knowledge I have accumulated in a lifetime dedicated to study and practice, primarily in the Tibetan tradition of Buddhism. On the one hand, they have encouraged me to teach. On the other, they are concerned that, while many general books on Buddhism have been and are being published, there are few books that present the actual texts of the tradition. Therefore they, together with a number of major figures in the Buddhist book publishing world, have also encouraged me to translate and publish high quality translations of individual texts of the tradition.

My teachers always remark with great appreciation on the extraordinary amount of teaching that I have heard in this life. It allows for highly informed, accurate translations of a sort not usually seen. Briefly, I spent the 1970's studying, practising, then teaching the Gelugpa system at Chenrezig Institute, Australia, where I was a founding member and also the first Australian to be ordained as a monk in the Tibetan Buddhist tradition. In 1980, I moved to the United States to study at the feet of the Vidyadhara Chogyam Trungpa Rinpoche. I stayed in his Vajradhatu community, now called Shambhala, where I studied and practised all the Karma Kagyu, Nyingma, and Shambhala teachings being presented there and was a senior member of the Nalanda Translation Committee. After the vidyadhara's nirvana, I moved in 1992 to Nepal, where I have been continuously involved with the study, practise, translation, and teaching of the Kagyu system and especially of the Nyingma system of Great Completion. In recent years, I have spent extended times in Tibet with the greatest living Tibetan masters of Great Completion, receiving very pure transmissions of the ultimate levels of this teaching directly in Tibetan and practising them there in retreat. In that way, I have studied and practised extensively not in one Tibetan tradition as is usually done, but in three of the four Tibetan traditions—Gelug, Kagyu, and Nyingma—and also in the Theravada tradition, too.

With that as a basis, I have taken a comprehensive and long term approach to the work of translation. For any language, one first must have the lettering needed to write the language. Therefore, as a member of the Nalanda Translation Committee, I spent some years in the 1980's making Tibetan word-processing software and high-quality Tibetan fonts. After that, reliable lexical works are needed. Therefore, during the 1990's I spent some years writing the *Illuminator Tibetan-English Dictionary* and a set of treatises on Tibetan grammar, preparing a variety of key Tibetan reference works needed for the study and translation of Tibetan Buddhist texts, and giving our Tibetan software the tools needed to translate and research Tibetan texts. During this time, I also translated full-time for various Tibetan gurus and ran the Drukpa Kagyu Heritage Project—at the time the largest project in Asia for the preservation of Tibetan Buddhist texts. With the dictionaries, grammar texts, and specialized software in place, and a wealth of knowledge, I turned my attention in the year 2000 to the translation and publication of important texts of Tibetan Buddhist literature.

Padma Karpo Translation Committee (PKTC) was set up to provide a home for the translation and publication work. The committee focusses on producing books containing the best of Tibetan literature, and, especially, books that meet the needs of practitioners. At the time of writing, PKTC has published a wide range of books that, collectively, make a complete program of study for those practising Tibetan Buddhism, and especially for those interested in the higher tantras. All in all, you will find many books both free and for sale on the PKTC web-site. Most are available both as paper editions and e-books. It would take up too much space here to present an extensive guide to our books and how they can be used as the basis for a study program. However, a guide of that sort is available on the PKTC web-site, whose address is on the copyright page of this book and we recommend that you read it to see how this book fits into the overall scheme of PKTC publications.

This book presents the views of the Nyingma path of the nine vehicles and especially of great completion. We have published a wide range of titles on these subjects. However, one which will be particularly useful as a support for the material in this book is the forthcoming :

- *The Dzogchen Resting Up Trilogy by Longchen Rabjam, in several volumes.*

We make a point of including, where possible, the relevant Tibetan texts in Tibetan script in our books. We also make them available in electronic editions that can be downloaded free from our web-site, as discussed below. The main Tibetan texts for this book are included at the back of the book. All the Tibetan texts for this book are available for download from the PKTC web-site.

Electronic Resources

PKTC has developed a complete range of electronic tools to facilitate the study and translation of Tibetan texts. For many years now, this software has been a prime resource for Tibetan Buddhist centres throughout the world, including in Tibet itself. It is available through the PKTC web-site.

The wordprocessor TibetDoc has the only complete set of tools for creating, correcting, and formatting Tibetan text according to the norms of the Tibetan language. It can also be used to make texts with mixed Tibetan and English or other languages. Extremely high quality Tibetan fonts, based on the forms of Tibetan calligraphy learned from old masters from pre-Communist Chinese Tibet, are also available. Because of their excellence, these typefaces have achieved a legendary status amongst Tibetans.

TibetDoc is used to prepare electronic editions of Tibetan texts in the PKTC text input office in Asia. Tibetan texts are often corrupt so the input texts are carefully corrected prior to distribution. After that, they are made available through the PKTC web-site. These electronic texts are not careless productions like so many of the Tibetan texts found on the web, but are highly reliable editions useful to non-scholars and scholars alike. Some of the larger collections of these texts are for purchase, but most are available for free download.

The electronic texts can be read, searched, and even made into an electronic library using either TibetDoc or our other software, TibetD Reader. Like TibetDoc, TibetD Reader is advanced software with many capabilities made specifically to meet the needs of reading and researching Tibetan texts. PKTC software is for purchase but we make a free version of TibetD Reader available for free download on the PKTC web-site.

A key feature of TibetDoc and Tibet Reader is that Tibetan terms in texts can be looked up on the spot using PKTC's electronic dictionaries. PKTC also has several electronic dictionaries—some Tibetan-Tibetan and some Tibetan-English—and a number of other reference works. The *Illuminator Tibetan-English Dictionary* is renowned for its completeness and accuracy.

This combination of software, texts, reference works, and dictionaries that work together seamlessly has become famous over the years and has been the basis for many, large publishing projects within the Tibetan Buddhist community around the world.

TIBETAN TEXTS

༄༅། །སློབ་དཔོན་པདྨ་མཛད་པའི་མན་ངག་ལྟ་བའི་ཕྲེང་བ་

ཞེས་བྱ་བ་བཞུགས་སོ།།

༄༅། །ལྟ་བ་དང་ཐེག་པ་ལ་སོགས་པའི་ཁྱད་པར་བསྡུས་པའི་བརྗོད་བྱང་། བཅོམ་ལྡན་འདས་འཇམ་དཔལ་གཞོན་ནུ་དང་། རྡོ་རྗེ་ཆོས་ལ་ཕྱག་འཚལ་ལོ། ། འཇིག་རྟེན་གྱི་ཁམས་ན་སེམས་ཅན་ཕྱིན་ཅི་ལོག་གི་ལྟ་བ་གྲངས་མེད་པ་མདོར་རྣམ་པ་བཞིར་འདུས་ཏེ། ཕྱལ་བ་དང་། རྒྱང་འཕེན་དང་། མུར་ཐུག་དང་། མུ་སྟེགས་པའོ། །དེ་ལ་ཕྱལ་བ་ནི་ཆོས་ཐམས་ཅད་རྒྱུ་དང་འབྲས་བུ་ཡོད་མེད་དུ་མ་རྟོགས་ཏེ། ཀུན་ཏུ་རྨོངས་པའོ། །རྒྱང་འཕེན་ནི་ཚེ་སྔ་ཕྱི་ཡོད་མེད་དུ་མ་རྟོགས་ཤིང་། ཚེ་གཅིག་ལ་བཙན་ཕྱུག་དང་མཐུ་སྟོབས་སྒྲུབ་པ་སྟེ། འཇིག་རྟེན་གྱི་གསང་ཚིག་ལ་བརྟེན་པའོ། །མུར་ཐུག་པ་ནི་ཆོས་ཐམས་ཅད་རྒྱུ་དང་འབྲས་བུ་མེད་པ་སྟེ། ཚེ་གཅིག་ལ་སྐྱེས་པའི་ཆོས་ཐམས་ཅད་གློ་བུར་དུ་སྐྱེས་ལ་མཐའ་ཆད་པར་ལྟ་བའོ། །མུ་སྟེགས་པ་ནི་ཆོས་ཐམས་ཅད་ལ་ཀུན་ཏུ་བརྟགས་པས་བདག་རྟག་པ་ཞིག་ཡོད་པར་ལྟ་བ་སྟེ། དེ་ལ་ཡང་རྒྱུ་མེད་ལ་འབྲས་བུ་ཡོད་པར་ལྟ་བ་དང་། རྒྱུ་འབྲས་ལོག་པར་ལྟ་བ་དང་། རྒྱུ་ཡོད་པ་ལ་འབྲས་བུ་མེད་པར་ལྟ་བ་དང་། འདི་

དག་ནི་མ་རིག་པའི་ལྟ་བའོ། །འཇིག་རྟེན་ལས་འདས་པའི་ལམ་ལ་ཡང་རྣམ་པ་
གཉིས་ཏེ། མཚན་ཉིད་ཀྱི་ཐེག་པ་དང་། རྡོ་རྗེའི་ཐེག་པའོ། །མཚན་ཉིད་ཀྱི་
ཐེག་པ་ལ་ཡང་རྣམ་པ་གསུམ་སྟེ། ཉན་ཐོས་ཀྱི་ཐེག་པ་དང་། རང་སངས་རྒྱས་
ཀྱི་ཐེག་པ་དང་། བྱང་ཆུབ་སེམས་དཔའི་ཐེག་པའོ། །དེ་ལ་ཉན་ཐོས་ཀྱི་ཐེག་པ་ལ་
ཞུགས་པ་རྣམས་ཀྱི་ལྟ་བ་ནི། ཆོས་ཐམས་ཅད་ལ་མུ་སྟེགས་པ་ལ་སོགས་པས་སྒྲོ་
དང་སྐུར་བས་ཀུན་ཏུ་བརྟགས་པས། ཡེ་མེད་པ་ཆད་པའི་ལྟ་བ་དང་། རྟག་པ་ལ་
སོགས་པའི་ཡོད་པར་ལྟ་བ་ནི། ཐག་པ་ལ་སྦྲུལ་དུ་མཐོང་བ་བཞིན་དུ་མེད་དེ།
ཕུང་པོ་ཁམས་དང་སྐྱེ་མཆེད་ལ་སོགས་པའི་འབྱུང་བ་ཆེན་པོ་བཞིའི་རྡུལ་ཕྲ་རབ་དང་།
རྣམ་པར་ཤེས་པ་ནི་དོན་དམ་པར་ཡོད་པར་ལྟ་ཞིང་། འཕགས་པའི་བདེན་པ་བཞི་
བསྒོམས་པས་རིམ་གྱིས་འབྲས་བུ་རྣམ་པ་བཞི་འགྲུབ་པ་ཡིན་ནོ། །རང་སངས་རྒྱས་
ཀྱི་ཐེག་པ་ལ་ཞུགས་པ་རྣམས་ཀྱི་ལྟ་བ་ནི། ཆོས་ཐམས་ཅད་ལ་མུ་སྟེགས་ལ་སོགས་
པས་སྒྲོ་དང་སྐུར་བས་ཀུན་ཏུ་བརྟགས་པའི་བདག་རྟག་པ་ལ་སོགས་པ་མེད་པར་ལྟ་བ་
ཉན་ཐོས་དང་མཐུན། དེ་ལས་ཁྱད་པར་དུ་གཟུགས་ཀྱི་ཕུང་པོའི་ཆོས་ཁམས་ཀྱི་
ཕྱོགས་གཅིག་ལ་བདག་མེད་པར་རྟོགས་ཤིང་། རང་བྱང་ཆུབ་ཀྱི་འབྲས་བུ་ཐོབ་པའི་
དུས་ནའང་། ཉན་ཐོས་ལྟར་དགེ་བའི་བཤེས་གཉེན་ལ་མི་ལྟོས་པར་སྔོན་གོམས་པའི་
ཤུགས་ཀྱིས་རྟེན་ཅིང་འབྲེལ་བར་འབྱུང་བ་ཡན་ལག་བཅུ་གཉིས་ཀྱི་སྒོ་ནས་ཆོས་ཉིད་ཟབ་
མོའི་དོན་རྟོགས་ནས། རང་བྱང་ཆུབ་ཀྱི་འབྲས་བུ་ཐོབ་པ་ཡིན་ནོ། ༄ བྱང་
ཆུབ་སེམས་དཔའི་ཐེག་པ་ལ་ཞུགས་པ་རྣམས་ཀྱི་ལྟ་བ་ནི། ཀུན་ནས་ཉོན་མོངས་པ་
དང་རྣམ་པར་བྱང་བའི་ཆོས་ཐམས་ཅད་དོན་དམ་པར་ནི་རང་བཞིན་མེད་པ་ཡིན་ལ།
ཀུན་རྫོབ་ཏུ་ནི་སྒྱུ་མ་ཙམ་དུ་སོ་སོའི་མཚན་ཉིད་མ་འདྲེས་པར་ཡོད་དེ། ཕ་རོལ་ཏུ་ཕྱིན་
པ་བཅུ་སྤྱོད་པའི་འབྲས་བུ་ས་བཅུ་རིམ་གྱིས་བགྲོད་པའི་མཐར་བླ་ན་མེད་པའི་བྱང་ཆུབ་ཏུ་
འགྲུབ་པར་འདོད་པ་ཡིན་ནོ། ༄ རྡོ་རྗེ་ཐེག་པ་ལ་ཡང་རྣམ་པ་གསུམ་སྟེ། བྱ་
བའི་རྒྱུད་ཀྱི་ཐེག་པ་དང་། གཉིས་ཀ་རྒྱུད་ཀྱི་ཐེག་པ་དང་། རྣལ་འབྱོར་རྒྱུད་ཀྱི་
ཐེག་པའོ། །དེ་ལ་བྱ་བའི་རྒྱུད་ཀྱི་ཐེག་པ་ལ་ཞུགས་པ་རྣམས་ཀྱི་ལྟ་བ་ནི། དོན་

དམ་པར་སྐྱེ་འགགས་མེད་པ་ལས། ཀུན་རྫོབ་ཏུ་ལྷའི་གཟུགས་ཀྱི་སྐུར་སྒོམ་ཞིང་སྐུ་གཟུགས་བརྙན་དང་། ཕྱག་མཚན་དང་། བཟླས་བརྗོད་དང་། གཙང་སྦྲ་དང་། དུས་ཚིག་དང་། གཟའ་དང་། རྒྱུ་སྐར་ལ་སོགས་པ་གཙོ་བོར་ཡོ་བྱད་དང་རྒྱུ་རྐྱེན་ཚོགས་པའི་མཐུ་ལས་འགྲུབ་པའོ། ༈ གཉིས་ཀའི་རྒྱུད་ཀྱི་ཐེག་པ་ལ་ཞུགས་པ་རྣམས་ཀྱི་ལྟ་བ་ནི། དོན་དམ་པར་སྐྱེ་འགགས་མེད་པ་ལས། ཀུན་རྫོབ་ཏུ་ལྷའི་གཟུགས་ཀྱི་སྐུ་བསྒོམ་ཞིང་། དེ་ཉིད་རྣམ་པ་བཞི་དང་ལྡན་པར་སྒོམ་པའི་ཏིང་ངེ་འཛིན་དང་། ཡོ་བྱད་དང་རྒྱུ་རྐྱེན་ལ་སོགས་པ་གཉིས་ཀ་ལ་བརྟེན་པ་ལས་འགྲུབ་པའོ། ༈ རྣལ་འབྱོར་རྒྱུད་ཀྱི་ཐེག་པ་ལ་ཞུགས་པ་རྣམས་ཀྱི་ལྟ་བ་ནི་རྣམ་པ་གཉིས་ཏེ། རྣལ་འབྱོར་ཕྱི་པ་ཐུབ་པའི་རྒྱུད་ཀྱི་ཐེག་པ་དང་། རྣལ་འབྱོར་ནང་པ་ཐབས་ཀྱི་རྒྱུད་ཀྱི་ཐེག་པའོ། །དེ་ལ་རྣལ་འབྱོར་ཕྱི་པ་ཐུབ་པའི་རྒྱུད་ཀྱི་ཐེག་པ་ལ་ཞུགས་པ་རྣམས་ཀྱི་ལྟ་བ་ནི། ཕྱི་ཡོ་བྱད་ལ་གཙོ་བོར་མི་འཛིན་པར་དོན་དམ་པར་སྐྱེ་འགག་མེད་པའི་ལྷ་དང་ལྷ་མོ་དང་། དེ་དང་འདྲ་བའི་རྒྱུད་ཡོངས་སུ་དག་པའི་ཏིང་ངེ་འཛིན་གྱིས་འཕགས་པའི་གཟུགས་ཀྱི་སྐུ་ཕྱག་རྒྱ་བཞི་ལྡན་པར་བསྒོམས་པའི་རྣལ་འབྱོར་གཙོ་བོར་བྱས་པ་ལས་གྲུབ་པའོ། །རྣལ་འབྱོར་ནང་པ་ཐབས་ཀྱི་རྒྱུད་ཀྱི་ཐེག་པ་ལ་ཞུགས་པ་རྣམས་ཀྱི་ལྟ་བ་ནི་རྣམ་པ་གསུམ་སྟེ། བསྐྱེད་པའི་ཚུལ་དང་། རྫོགས་པའི་ཚུལ་དང་། རྫོགས་པ་ཆེན་པོའི་ཚུལ་ལོ། །དེ་ལ་བསྐྱེད་པའི་ཚུལ་ནི། ཏིང་ངེ་འཛིན་རྣམ་པ་གསུམ་རིམ་གྱིས་བསྐྱེད་དེ་དཀྱིལ་འཁོར་རིམ་གྱིས་བཀོད་ཅིང་བསྒོམ་པས་འགྲུབ་པའོ། རྫོགས་པའི་ཚུལ་ནི། དོན་དམ་པར་སྐྱེ་འགགས་མེད་པའི་ལྷ་དང་ལྷ་མོ་དང་། རྣམ་པར་མི་རྟོག་པའི་དོན་དབུ་མ་ཆོས་ཀྱི་དབྱིངས་ལས་ཀྱང་མ་གཡོས་ལ། ཀུན་རྫོབ་ཏུ་འཕགས་པའི་གཟུགས་ཀྱི་སྐུ་ཡང་གསལ་བར་བསྒོམས་ཤིང་མཉམ་ལ་མ་འདྲེས་པར་བསྒོམ་པས་འགྲུབ་བོ། ༈ རྫོགས་པ་ཆེན་པོའི་ཚུལ་ནི། འཇིག་རྟེན་དང་འཇིག་རྟེན་ལས་འདས་པའི་ཆོས་ཐམས་ཅད་དབྱེར་མེད་པར་སྐུ་གསུང་ཐུགས་ཀྱི་དཀྱིལ་འཁོར་གྱི་རང་བཞིན་ཡེ་ནས་ཡིན་པར་རྟོགས་ནས་སྒོམ་པ་སྟེ། དེ་ཡང་རྒྱུད་ལས། རྡོ་རྗེ་ཕུང་པོའི་ཡན་ལག་ནི། །རྫོགས་པའི་སངས་རྒྱས་ལྔ་རུ་

གྲགས། །སྐྱེ་མཆེད་ཁམས་རྣམས་མང་པོ་ཀུན། །བྱང་ཆུབ་སེམས་དཔའི་དཀྱིལ་འཁོར་ཉིད། །ས་ཆུ་སྤྱན་དང་མཱ་མ་ཀཱི །མེ་རླུང་གོས་དཀར་སྒྲོལ་མ་སྟེ། །ནམ་མཁའ་དབྱིངས་ཀྱི་དབང་ཕྱུག་མ། །སྲིད་གསུམ་ཡེ་ནས་རྣམ་པར་དག །ཅེས་འབྱུང་སྟེ། འཁོར་བ་དང་མྱ་ངན་ལས་འདས་པའི་ཆོས་ཐམས་ཅད་ཡེ་ནས་མ་སྐྱེས་ལ། བྱ་བ་བྱེད་ནུས་པའི་སྒྱུ་མ་བདེ་བར་གཤེགས་པ་ཡབ་ཡུམ་བཅུ་ལ་སོགས་པའི་རང་བཞིན་ཡེ་ནས་ཡིན་པའི་ཕྱིར། ཆོས་ཐམས་ཅད་རང་བཞིན་གྱིས་མྱ་ངན་ལས་འདས་པ་སྟེ། ཆེན་པོ་ལྔ་ནི་ཡུམ་ལྔའི་རང་བཞིན། ཕུང་པོ་ལྔ་ནི་རིགས་ལྔའི་སངས་རྒྱས། རྣམ་པར་ཤེས་པ་བཞི་ནི་བྱང་ཆུབ་སེམས་དཔའ་བཞིའི་རང་བཞིན། ཡུལ་བཞི་ནི་མཛེས་པའི་ལྷ་མོ་བཞིའི་རང་བཞིན། དབང་པོ་བཞི་ནི་བྱང་ཆུབ་སེམས་དཔའི་རང་བཞིན། དུས་བཞི་ནི་མཆོད་པའི་ལྷ་མོ་བཞིའི་རང་བཞིན། ལུས་ཀྱི་དབང་པོ་དང་། རྣམ་པར་ཤེས་པ་དང་། ཡུལ་དང་དེ་ལས་བྱུང་བའི་བྱང་ཆུབ་ཀྱི་སེམས་ནི་ཁྲོ་བོ་བཞིའི་རང་བཞིན། རྟག་ཆད་མུ་བཞི་ནི་ཁྲོ་མོ་བཞིའི་རང་བཞིན། ཡིད་ཀྱི་རྣམ་པར་ཤེས་པ་ནི་བྱང་ཆུབ་ཀྱི་སེམས་རྡོ་རྗེ་ཀུན་ཏུ་བཟང་པོའི་རང་བཞིན། ཡུལ་ཆོས་འདུས་བྱས་དང་འདུས་མ་བྱས་ནི་ཆོས་བྱ་བ་མོ་ཀུན་ཏུ་བཟང་མོའི་རང་བཞིན་ཏེ། དེ་དག་ཀྱང་ཡེ་ནས་མངོན་པར་རྫོགས་པར་སངས་རྒྱས་པའི་རང་བཞིན་ཡིན་གྱི། དེ་ལམ་གྱིས་སྒྲུབ་པ་མ་ཡིན་ནོ། །དེ་ལྟར་ཕྱོགས་བཅུ་དུས་གསུམ་དང་། ཁམས་གསུམ་ལ་སོགས་པ་འདུས་བྱས་དང་འདུས་མ་བྱས་པའི་ཆོས་ཐམས་ཅད་རང་གི་སེམས་ལས་གུད་ན་མེད་དེ། ཇི་སྐད་དུ། རང་སེམས་སོ་སོར་རྟོགས་པ་ནི། །སངས་རྒྱས་བྱང་ཆུབ་དེ་ཉིད་དོ། །འཇིག་རྟེན་གསུམ་པོ་དེ་ཉིད་དོ། །འབྱུང་བ་ཆེ་རྣམས་དེ་ཉིད་དོ། །ཞེས་འབྱུང་ངོ་། །ཇི་སྐད་དུ། ཆོས་རྣམས་ཐམས་ཅད་ནི་སེམས་ལ་གནས་སོ། །སེམས་ནི་ནམ་མཁའ་ལ་གནས་སོ། །ནམ་མཁའ་ནི་ཅི་ལ་ཡང་མི་གནས་སོ། །ཞེས་འབྱུང་བ་དང་། ཆོས་ཐམས་ཅད་ནི་ངོ་བོ་ཉིད་ཀྱིས་སྟོང་པའོ། །ཆོས་ཐམས་ཅད་ནི་གདོད་མ་ནས་རྣམ་པར་དག་པའོ། །ཆོས་ཐམས་ཅད་ནི་ཡོངས་ཀྱིས་འོད་གསལ་བའོ། །ཆོས་ཐམས་ཅད་ནི་རང་བཞིན་གྱིས་མྱ་ངན་ལས་

འདས་པའོ། །ཆོས་ཐམས་ཅད་ནི་མངོན་པར་རྫོགས་པར་སངས་རྒྱས་པའོ། ། ཞེས་གསུངས་སོ། །འདི་ནི་རྫོགས་པ་ཆེན་པོའོ།...།རྫོགས་པ་ཆེན་པོའི་ཚུལ་ནི། བསོད་ནམས་དང་ཡེ་ཤེས་ཀྱི་ཚོགས་རྫོགས་པ། འབྲས་བུའི་ཆོས་ལྷུན་གྱིས་གྲུབ་པའི་ཚུལ་འདི་ནི་དོན་ལ་འཇུག་པའོ། །རྫོགས་པ་ཆེན་པོའི་ཚུལ་དེ་ནི། རྟོགས་པ་རྣམ་བཞིའི་ལམ་གྱིས་ཡིད་ཆེས་ཏེ། རྟོགས་པ་རྣམ་པ་བཞི་ནི། རྒྱུ་གཅིག་པར་རྟོགས་པ་དང་། ཡིག་འབྲུའི་ཚུལ་ཡིས་རྟོགས་པ་དང་། བྱིན་གྱིས་བརླབས་ཀྱིས་རྟོགས་པ་དང་། མངོན་སུམ་པར་རྟོགས་པའོ། །དེ་ལ་རྒྱུ་གཅིག་པར་རྟོགས་པ་ནི། ཆོས་ཐམས་ཅད་དོན་དམ་པར་མ་སྐྱེས་པས་སོ་སོ་མ་ཡིན་པ་དང་། ཀུན་རྫོགས་ཏུ་སྒྱུ་མའི་མཚན་ཉིད་དུ་སོ་སོ་མ་ཡིན་པ་དང་། མ་སྐྱེས་པ་ཉིད་ཆུ་ཟླ་ལྟར་སྒྱུ་མ་སྣ་ཚོགས་སུ་སྣང་ཞིང་བྱ་བ་བྱེད་ནུས་པ་དང་། སྒྱུ་མ་ཉིད་ངོ་བོ་མེད་དེ་མ་སྐྱེས་པས་ཀུན་རྫོབ་དང་དོན་དམ་པར་དབྱེར་མེད་པས་རྒྱུ་གཅིག་པར་རྟོགས་པའོ། །ཡིག་འབྲུའི་ཚུལ་གྱིས་རྟོགས་པ་ནི། ཆོས་ཐམས་ཅད་མ་སྐྱེས་པ་ནི་ཨ་སྟེ་གསུང་གི་རང་བཞིན། མ་སྐྱེས་པ་ཉིད་སྒྱུ་མར་སྣང་ཞིང་བྱ་བ་བྱེད་ནུས་པ་ནི་ཨོ་སྟེ་སྐུའི་རང་བཞིན། དེ་ལྟར་རྟོགས་པའི་རིག་པ་སྒྱུ་མའི་ཡེ་ཤེས་མཐའ་དབུས་མེད་པ་ནི་ཨོཾ་སྟེ་ཐུགས་ཀྱི་རང་བཞིན་དུ་རྟོགས་པའོ། །བྱིན་གྱིས་བརླབས་ཀྱིས་རྟོགས་པ་ནི་དཔེར་ན་རས་དཀར་པོ་ལ་དམར་པོར་བྱིན་གྱིས་རློབ་པའི་མཐུ་བཙོད་ལ་ཡོད་པ་བཞིན་དུ། ཆོས་ཐམས་ཅད་སངས་རྒྱས་པར་བྱིན་གྱིས་རློབ་པའི་མཐུ་ཡང་། རྒྱུ་གཅིག་པ་དང་ཡིག་འབྲུའི་ཚུལ་གྱི་མཐུས་བྱིན་གྱིས་བརླབས་པར་རྟོགས་པའོ། །མངོན་སུམ་པར་རྟོགས་པ་ནི། ཆོས་ཐམས་ཅད་ཡེ་ནས་སངས་རྒྱས་པར་གནས་པ་དེ་ཡང་ལུང་དང་མན་ངག་དང་འགལ་བ་ཡང་མ་ཡིན་ལ། ལུང་དང་མན་ངག་གི་ཚིག་ཙམ་ལ་བརྟེན་པ་ཡང་མ་ཡིན་པར། རང་གི་རིག་པས་བློའི་གཏིང་དུ་ཡིད་ཆེས་པས་མངོན་སུམ་དུ་རྟོགས་པའོ། །ལམ་གྱིས་ཡིད་ཆེས་པ་ནི། རྟོགས་པ་རྣམ་པ་བཞིའི་དོན་རིག་པ་ཉིད་རྣལ་འབྱོར་པའི་ལམ་སྟེ། དེ་ཡང་རྒྱུ་བསྒྲུབ་པའི་འབྲས་བུ་འབྱུང་བའི་དུས་ལ་ལྟོས་པ་ལྟ་བུ་མ་ཡིན་གྱི། རང་གིས་མངོན་སུམ་དུ་རྟོགས་ཤིང་ཡིད་ཆེས་པའོ། །དེ་ལ་མཚན་ཉིད་གསུམ་གྱིས་དོན་མཐར་

ཕྱིན་པར་འགྱུར་ཏེ། རྟོགས་པ་རྣམ་པ་བཞིའི་ཚུལ་རིག་པ་ནི་ཤེས་པའི་མཚན་ཉིད་དོ། །ཡང་ནས་ཡང་དུ་གོམས་པར་བྱེད་པ་ནི་འཇུག་པའི་མཚན་ཉིད་དོ། །གོམས་པའི་མཐུས་མངོན་དུ་གྱུར་པ་ནི་འབྲས་བུའི་མཚན་ཉིད་དོ། །མཚན་ཉིད་གསུམ་གྱིས་འབྲེལ་བ་དང་། དགོས་པ་དང་། དགོས་པའི་ཡང་དགོས་པ་སྟོན་ཏེ། དེ་ལ་འབྲེལ་བ་ནི། ཀུན་ནས་ཉོན་མོངས་པ་དང་། རྣམ་པར་བྱང་བའི་ཆོས་སུ་བཏགས་པ་ཐམས་ཅད། ཡེ་ནས་སྐུ་གསུང་ཐུགས་ཀྱི་བདག་ཉིད། རང་བཞིན་གྱིས་སངས་རྒྱས་པའི་དབྱིངས་དང་། བྱིན་རླབས་པའི་དོན་རྟོགས་པ་ནི། རྒྱུ་ཤེས་པའི་མཚན་ཉིད་དེ། དེ་ནི་བླ་ན་མེད་པའི་སངས་རྒྱས་སུ་གྲུབ་པའི་རྒྱུ་ཡིན་པའི་དོན་དུ་འབྲེལ་བའོ། །དགོས་པ་ནི་ཀུན་ནས་ཉོན་མོངས་པ་དང་། རྣམ་པར་བྱང་བའི་ཆོས་དང་། སྨན་ལྷ་དང་། བདུད་རྩི་ལྷ་ལ་སོགས་པར་བཏགས་པ་ཐམས་ཅད་ཡེ་ནས་སངས་རྒྱས་པའི་མཉམ་པ་ཆེན་པོ་ལ་བླང་དོར་མེད་པར་སྤྱོད་པ་ནི་འཇུག་པའི་མཚན་ཉིད་དོ། །དེ་ནི་བླ་ན་མེད་པའི་སངས་རྒྱས་སུ་གྲུབ་པའི་རྒྱུ་ཡིན་པའི་ཕྱིར་དགོས་པའོ། །དགོས་པའི་ཡང་དགོས་པ་ནི། ཀུན་ནས་ཉོན་མོངས་པ་དང་། རྣམ་པར་བྱང་བའི་ཆོས་དང་། སྨན་ལྷ་དང་། བདུད་རྩི་ལྷ་སོགས་ཁྱད་པར་དུ་བཏགས་པ་ཐམས་ཅད་ཡེ་ནས་སངས་རྒྱས་པའི་མཉམ་པ་ཆེན་པོའི་ངང་དུ་བླང་དོར་མེད་པར་ལྷུན་གྱིས་གྲུབ་པའི་ཕྱིར། སྲིད་པའི་འཁོར་བ་ཉིད་ཡེ་ནས་བླ་ན་མེད་པའི་སངས་རྒྱས་པའི་རང་བཞིན་མྱ་ངན་ལས་འདས་པའི་མཚན་ཉིད་དུ་ལྷུན་གྱིས་གྲུབ་པ་ཡིན་པས་འབྲས་བུའི་མཚན་ཉིད་དེ་སྐུ་གསུང་ཐུགས་མི་ཟད་པ་རྒྱན་གྱི་འཁོར་ལོ་མངོན་སུམ་དུ་གྱུར་པ་ནི་དགོས་པའི་ཡང་དགོས་པའོ། །དེ་ལ་བསྙེན་པ་དང་། ཉེ་བའི་བསྙེན་པ་དང་། སྒྲུབ་པ་ཆེན་པོའི་དོན་ལྷུན་གྱིས་གྲུབ་པར་གྱུར་པའི་རྣལ་འབྱོར་ལ་བརྩོན་པར་བྱའོ། །དེ་ལ་བསྙེན་པ་ནི་བྱང་ཆུབ་སེམས་ཤེས་པ་སྟེ། དེ་ཡང་ཆོས་ཐམས་ཅད་ཡེ་ནས་སངས་རྒྱས་པའི་རང་བཞིན་དུ་ལམ་གྱིས་བསྒྲུབ་ཅིང་གཉེན་པོས་བཅོས་སུ་མེད་པར་རྟོགས་པའོ། །ཉེ་བའི་བསྙེན་པ་ནི་བདག་ཉིད་ལྷར་ཤེས་པ་སྟེ། དེ་ཡང་ཆོས་ཐམས་ཅད་ཡེ་ནས་སངས་རྒྱས་པའི་རང་བཞིན་པས། བདག་ཉིད་ཀྱང་ཡེ་ནས་ལྷའི་

རང་བཞིན་ཡིན་གྱི་ད་ལྟ་སྒྲུབ་པ་ནི་མ་ཡིན་པར་རྟོགས་པའོ། །སྒྲུབ་པ་ནི་ལུས་བསྐྱེད་པ་སྟེ། །དེ་ཡང་ལུས་ཆེན་མོ་ནམ་མཁའི་དབྱིངས་ལས། ནམ་མཁའ་ཉིད་ལུས་ཆེན་མོ་ས་ཆུ་མེ་རླུང་བཞིར་སྣང་ཞིང་། བྱ་བ་བྱེད་པའི་ལུས་ཡེ་ནས་ཡིན་པར་རྟོགས་པའོ། །སྒྲུབ་པ་ཆེན་པོ་ནི། ཐབས་དང་ཤེས་རབ་འབྲེལ་བ་སྟེ། དེ་ཡང་ལུས་ཆེན་མོ་ལྔའི་ཤེས་རབ་དང་ལུས་ཀྱི་མཁའ་སྟོང་པ་ཉིད་ལས། ཕུང་པོ་ལྔ་སངས་རྒྱས་ཐམས་ཅད་ཀྱི་ཡབ་སྨོན་པ་མེད་པར་ཡེ་ནས་ཟུང་དུ་གྱུར་པས་འབྲེལ་བ་ལས། བྱང་ཆུབ་སེམས་སྤྲུལ་པ་ལྷུམ་དྲལ་དུ་གྱུར་པའི་རང་བཞིན་ནི། ཡེ་ནས་སངས་རྒྱས་པའི་དོན་ལ་སྒྱུ་མ་ལ་སྒྱུ་མ་རོལ་ཅིང་བདེ་མཆོག་སྒྱུ་མའི་རྒྱུན་ལ་བདེ་བའི་དུས་ཉིད་ན། མཚན་མ་མེད་པའི་དོན་མི་དམིགས་མཁའ་དང་སྙོམས་པ་ནི་ཀློང་དུ་བསྒྱུར་ནས་ལྷུན་གྱིས་གྲུབ་པ་སྟེ། བདུད་རྣམ་བཞི་ཡང་བཅུལ་ནས་མཐར་ཕྱིན་པའི་དོན་འགྲུབ་པའོ། །ཆོས་ཐམས་ཅད་གདོད་མ་ནས་རྣམ་པར་དག་པའི་ཡིད་བཞིན་གྱི་གཞལ་ཡས་ཁང་རྒྱ་ཡོངས་སུ་མ་ཆད་པའི་འཁོར་ལོ་ཡེ་ནས་བླ་ན་མེད་པའི་དཀྱིལ་འཁོར་དུ་འཇུག་པ་ཡང་ཐབས་ཀྱི་ཐེག་པའི་གཞུང་ཐོས་པ་ནི་མིག་ཕྱེ་བའོ། །དོན་རྟོགས་པ་ནི་དཀྱིལ་འཁོར་མཐོང་བའོ། །རྟོགས་ནས་གོམས་པར་བྱེད་པ་ནི་དཀྱིལ་འཁོར་དུ་ཞུགས་པའོ། །ཞུགས་ནས་མངོན་དུ་གྱུར་པ་ནི་དངོས་གྲུབ་ཆེན་པོ་ཐོབ་པའོ། ༔ དེ་ལྟར་ཚུལ་འདི་ནི་རྫོགས་པ་ཆེན་པོའི་མཐར་ཕྱིན་པའི་དོན་ནོ། །ཡི་གེ་འཁོར་ལོ་ཚོགས་ཆེན་གྱི་ས་ལ་ལྷུན་གྱིས་འཇུག་པ་སྟེ། སྐྱེས་བུ་བློ་རྩལ་རབ་ཀྱིས་ཡེ་ནས་སངས་རྒྱས་པའི་དོན་ལ་ཡེ་ནས་སངས་རྒྱས་པར་རིག་ནས། གོམས་པ་དྲག་རྩལ་དུ་འགྲོ་བ་ཡིན་གྱི་ཕལ་གྱི་བྱ་བ་ནི་མ་ཡིན་ནོ། །ཕལ་གྱིས་ཐོས་ཏེ་ཇི་ལྟར་བསམས་ཀྱང་བདེན་ཞིང་ཟབ་པར་ཡིད་ཆེས་པར་མི་འགྱུར་རོ། །ཡིད་ཆེས་པ་དང་ཕལ་གྱི་བློ་ལ་གོ་དཀའ་ཞིང་བདེན་པ་དང་ཟབ་པར་མ་ཤེས་པས་ཉམས་དང་སྒྱུར་ནས། ཀུན་ཀྱང་དེ་དང་འདྲ་སྙོམས་ནས་ཡོངས་བརྟུན་ཞེས་སྐྱེས་བུ་རབ་ལ་སྐུར་བ་འདེབས་ཤིང་སུན་འབྱིན་པའི་བློ་སྐྱེ་བར་འགྱུར་བས་རབ་ཏུ་གསང་བའི་ཕྱིར་ཡང་གསང་བའི་ཐེག་པ་ཞེས་བཀའ་སྩལ་ཏོ། དེ་བས་ན་ཆོས་ཐམས་ཅད་ཡེ་ནས་སངས་རྒྱས་པའི་དོན་ལ་རྟོགས་པའི་བློ

མ་སྐྱེས་བར་དུ་ཐེག་པ་འོག་མ་པས་འགྲོ་བའི་དོན་བྱས་ན་གདུལ་བྱ་ཆུད་མི་ཟ་བར་སློབ་དཔོན་གྱིས་འཁོར་བའི་སྐྱོན་དང་། མྱ་ངན་ལས་འདས་པའི་ཡོན་ཏན་དང་། ཐེག་པ་མཐའ་དག་ལ་མཁས་པར་བྱ་བ་ཡིན་གྱི། ཕྱོགས་འགའ་མི་ཤེས་པས་སློབ་དཔོན་གྱི་ས་བཟུང་དུ་མི་རུང་བར་རྒྱ་ཆེར་འབྱུང་ངོ་། ༄ ལྔ་བའི་ཁྱད་པར་གྱིས་དཀའ་ཐུབ་དང་བརྟུལ་ཞུགས་ཀྱང་བྱེ་བྲག་ཏུ་འགྱུར་ཏེ། དཀའ་ཐུབ་མེད་པ་ནི། འཇིག་རྟེན་ཕྱལ་བ་དང་མུར་ཐུག་གོ །དཀའ་ཐུབ་ཡོད་པ་ནི་རྣམ་པ་བཞི་སྟེ་རྒྱང་འཕེན་དང་། མུ་སྟེགས་པ་སྟེ། འཇིག་རྟེན་གྱི་དཀའ་ཐུབ་དང་། ཉན་ཐོས་ཀྱི་དཀའ་ཐུབ་དང་། བྱང་ཆུབ་སེམས་དཔའི་དཀའ་ཐུབ་དང་། བླ་ན་མེད་པའི་དཀའ་ཐུབ་བོ། །དེ་ལ་ཕྱལ་བ་ནི་རྒྱུ་འབྲས་ལ་རྨོངས་པའི་ཕྱིར་དཀའ་ཐུབ་མེད་པའོ། །མུར་ཐུག་པ་ནི་ཆད་པར་ལྟ་བའི་ཕྱིར་དཀའ་ཐུབ་མེད་པའོ། །རྒྱང་འཕེན་པ་ནི་ཚེ་འདིའི་ཁྱད་པར་སྒྲུབ་པའི་ཕྱིར་གཙང་སྦྲ་ལ་སོགས་པའི་དཀའ་ཐུབ་ཅན་ནོ། །མུ་སྟེགས་ནི་བདག་རྟག་པ་ཞིག་ཡོད་པ་དེ་དག་པར་བྱ་བའི་ཕྱིར། ལུས་སུན་འབྱིན་ཅིང་མེ་ལྔ་བརྟེན་པ་ལ་སོགས་པའི་དཀའ་ཐུབ་དང་། བརྟུལ་ཞུགས་ལོག་པར་སྤྱོད་པའོ། །ཉན་ཐོས་ཀྱི་དཀའ་ཐུབ་ནི། འདུལ་བ་ལས། སྡིག་པ་ཅི་ཡང་མི་བྱ་སྟེ། །དགེ་བ་ཕུན་སུམ་ཚོགས་པར་སྤྱོད། །རང་གི་སེམས་ནི་ཡོངས་སུ་འདུལ། །འདི་ནི་སངས་རྒྱས་བསྟན་པ་ཡིན། །ཞེས་འབྱུང་སྟེ། དགེ་བ་དང་མི་དགེ་བའི་ཆོས་ཐམས་ཅད་ཀུན་རྫོབ་དང་དོན་དམ་པར་གཉིས་ཀ་སོ་སོར་ཡོད་པར་ལྟ་བ་དང་། དགེ་བ་ནི་སྤྱོད་མི་དགེ་བ་ནི་སྤང་བའི་དཀའ་ཐུབ་དང་བརྟུལ་ཞུགས་སྤྱོད་པའོ། །བྱང་ཆུབ་སེམས་དཔའི་དཀའ་ཐུབ་ནི། བྱང་ཆུབ་སེམས་དཔའི་སྡོམ་པ་ལས། རྒྱུན་དུ་འཚམས་པར་དོན་མི་བྱེད། །རྫུ་འཕྲུལ་བསྡིགས་ལ་སོགས་མི་བྱེད། །སྙིང་རྗེར་ལྡན་ཞིང་བྱམས་ཕྱིར་དང་། སེམས་དགེ་བ་ལ་ཉེས་པ་མེད། །ཅེས་འབྱུང་སྟེ། སྙིང་རྗེ་ཆེན་པོས་ཟིན་ན་ཆོས་ཐམས་ཅད་དགེ་བ་དང་མི་དགེ་བ་གང་སྤྱོད་ཀྱང་སྡོམ་པ་ཉམས་པར་མི་འགྱུར་ཏེ། བྱང་ཆུབ་སེམས་དཔའི་སྡོམ་པ་ནི། མདོར་ན་སྙིང་རྗེ་ཆེན་པོས་གཞི་བཟུང་ནས་སྤྱོད་དོ། །བླ་ན་མེད་པའི་དཀའ་ཐུབ་ནི། དམ་ཚིག་ཆེན་པོའི་མདོ་ལས། སངས་

རྒྱས་ཐེག་པར་རབ་ངེས་ན། །ཉོན་མོངས་འདོད་ལྷ་ཀུན་སྤྱོད་ཀྱང་། །པདྨ་ལ་ནི་
འདམ་བཞིན་ཏེ། །དེ་ལ་ཚུལ་ཁྲིམས་ཕུན་སུམ་ཚོགས། །ཞེས་འབྱུང་སྟེ།
ཆོས་ཐམས་ཅད་ཡེ་ནས་མཉམ་པ་ཉིད་ཀྱི་ཕྱིར། སྙིང་རྗེ་ནི་བསྐྱེན་དུ་མེད་ལ། ཞེ་
སྡང་ནི་སྤང་དུ་མེད་དེ། དེ་ལྟར་མ་རྟོགས་པ་ལ་ཐུགས་རྗེ་མི་འབྱུང་བར་མ་ཡིན་ཏེ།
ཇི་ལྟར་བལྟས་པས་ཡེ་ནས་ ཇི་ལྟར་བལྟས་པས་ཡེ་ནས་རྣམ་པར་དག་པར་རྟོགས་པ་
བཞིན་དུ། དཀའ་ཐུབ་དང་བརྟུལ་ཞུགས་ཀྱང་དེ་ལྟར་རྣམ་པར་དག་པ་དང་མ་དག་པ་
སྤྱོད་དོ། །ལྟ་བའི་ཕྲེང་བ་གསང་བ་འདི། །དམུས་ལོང་རང་ཕྱེས་མིག་རྙེད་
ལྟར། །ཤེས་རབ་ཐབས་ཀྱི་རྒྱལ་འཆར་བའི། །སྐྱེས་མཆོག་ཡོད་ན་འཕྲད་གྱུར་
ཅིག །ལྟ་བའི་ཕྲེང་བ་ཞེས་བྱ་བའི་མན་ངག་རྫོགས་སོ།། །།དགེའོ།། །།

༄༅། །སློབ་དཔོན་ཆེན་པོ་པདྨ་འབྱུང་གནས་ཀྱིས་
མཛད་པའི་མན་ངག་ལྟ་བའི་ཕྲེང་བའི་མཆན་འགྲེལ་
ནོར་བུའི་བང་མཛོད་ཅེས་བྱ་བ་བཞུགས་སོ།།

༄༅། །ན་མོ་གུ་རུ་པདྨ་མཉྫུ་ཤྲཱི་ཡེ། དཔལ་ལྡན་སངས་རྒྱས་པདྨ་སྐྱེས། །
ཀུན་མཁྱེན་ཡེ་ཤེས་མཛོད་འཛིན་པ། །ཐེག་པ་སྣ་ཚོགས་སྟོན་པ་པོ། །ཨོ་རྒྱན་
དུས་གསུམ་མཁྱེན་པས་སྐྱོངས། །འདིར་སློབ་དཔོན་ཆེན་པོ་པདྨ་འབྱུང་གནས་ཀྱི་
ཞལ་སྔ་ནས་བསྐུལ་བའི་བསྟན་བཅོས་རྩོད་པ་དང་བྲལ་བ་མན་ངག་ལྟ་བའི་ཕྲེང་བ་ཉིད་
འཆད་པ་ལ་གསུམ། ཀླད་ཀྱི་དོན། གཞུང་གི་དོན། མཇུག་གི་དོན་ནོ།
དང་པོ་ལ་གཉིས། མཚན་བསྟན་པ་དང་། མཆོད་པར་བརྗོད་པའོ། །དང་པོ་ནི།
ཆོས་ཐམས་ཅད་ཡེ་ནས་རྫོགས་པ་ཆེན་པོར་ལྷུན་གྱིས་གྲུབ་པའི་ཚུལ་བསྟན་པ་རྒྱུད་དང་
ལུང་ཐམས་ཅད་ཀྱི་སྙིང་དཔལ་གསང་བའི་སྙིང་པོ་ལས། མ་རྟོགས་པ་དང་ལོག་པར་
རྟོགས། །ཕྱོགས་རྟོགས་ཡང་དག་ཉིད་མ་རྟོགས། །འདུལ་བ་དགོངས་པ་གསང་

བ་དང་། །རང་བཞིན་གསང་བའི་དོན་རྣམས་ནི། །ཡི་གེ་སྒྲས་བརྟགས་མིང་ཚོགས་ལ། །བརྟེན་པའི་ཚིག་གིས་རབ་མཚོན་ཏེ། །ཁོང་ནས་གབ་སྦས་དོན་འབྱིན་པ། །སྟོན་པ་རྡོ་རྗེའི་ཐུགས་ལ་གནས། །ཞེས་གསུངས་པ་ལྟར། གང་ཟག་གི་བློ་རིམ་དང་མཐུན་པར། །མ་རྟོགས་པ་འཇིག་རྟེན་ཕྱལ་པ་དང་རྒྱང་འཕེན་གཉིས། །ལོག་པར་རྟོགས་པ་ཕྱི་རོལ་མུར་རྟུག་པ་དང་མུ་སྟེགས་གཉིས། ཕྱོགས་ཙམ་རྟོགས་པ་ཉན་ཐོས་དང་རང་རྒྱལ་བ་གཉིས། ཡང་དག་ཉིད་མ་རྟོགས་པ་ཕ་རོལ་ཏུ་ཕྱིན་པའི་ཚུལ་ལ་གནས་པའི་བྱང་སེམས། འདུལ་བ་བྱ་བའི་རྒྱུད། དགོངས་པ་རྣལ་འབྱོར་གྱི་རྒྱུད། གསང་བ་རྣལ་འབྱོར་ཆེན་པོའི་ཚུལ་སྔགས་ནང་པ་བསྐྱེད་རྫོགས་གཉིས། རང་བཞིན་གསང་བ་རྫོགས་པ་ཆེན་པོའི་ཚུལ་ཏེ། འཇིག་རྟེན་ལས་འདས་མ་འདས་ཀྱི་**ལྟ་བ་དང་**།[116] ཁྱད་པར་དུ་ཉན་རང་བྱང་སེམས་ཏེ་མཚན་ཉིད་ཀྱི་ཐེག་པ་གསུམ་དང་། བྱ་སྤྱོད་རྣལ་འབྱོར་ཏེ་སྔགས་ཕྱི་པ་གསུམ་དང་། བསྐྱེད་རྫོགས་རྫོགས་ཆེན་ཏེ་ནང་པ་གསུམ་བཅས་རྣམ་གྲོལ་གྱི་ལམ། **ཐེག་པ་**རིམ་པ་དགུ་**ལ་སོགས་པ་**སྟེ་དེ་རྣམས་ཀྱི་འབྲས་བུའང་སྟོན་པའི། རྣམ་པ་མི་འདྲ་བའི་**ཁྱད་པར་**མཐའ་དག་གཞུང་ཉུང་ངུར་**བསྡུས་**ཏེ་སྔོན་གྱི་ལས་ཅན་རྒྱལ་འབངས་ཉེར་ལྔ་སོགས་ཀྱིས་བརྗོད་པར་དོགས་པའི་འཇིགས་ལ་སེལ་བའི་ཕྱིར་**བསྡུད་བྱང་**དུ་གུ་རུ་ཉིད་ཀྱིས་མཛད་པ་སྟེ་དོན་དང་མཐུན་པར་མཚན་བཏགས་པའོ། །གཉིས་པ་ནི། སྒྲིབ་པ་གཉིས་བག་ཆགས་དང་བཅས་པ་བཅོམ་ཤིང་རྒྱུ་འབྲས་ཕར་ཕྱིན་གྱི་ལེགས་པའི་ཡོན་ཏན་དྲུག་དང་ལྡན་པས་སྲིད་ཞིའི་མཐའ་གཉིས་ལས་འདས་པ་ཐུགས་ཆོས་ཉིད་སྤྲོས་པའི་ཟུག་རྔུ་དང་བྲལ་བས་འཛམ་ཞིང་དོན་གཉིས་ཀྱི་འབྱོར་པའི་དཔལ་དང་ལྡན་པ་རྒྱལ་སྲས་གཞོན་ནུ་ཡི་ཚུལ་ཅན་ཏེ་རྒྱུ་མཚན་ཉིད་ཀྱི་ཐེག་པ་དང་སྔོ་བསྟུན་པའི་ཤེས་རབ་ཀྱི་ལྷ་དང་།

116 The words of Padmasambhava's text in its entirety are inserted like this into the explanations given by Mipham. In the Tibetan text here, they are marked off using bold and, in publications where colour is supported, additionally marked off in colour.

གནས་ལུགས་སྟོང་པ་ཉིད་ཀྱི་རྡོ་རྗེ་སྤྲོས་མཚན་གང་གིས་ཀྱང་མི་ཕྱེད་ཅིང་ཐུགས་རྗེ་མ་
འགགས་པའམ་གསུང་ཆོས་ཀྱི་བདག་ཉིད་དུ་སྟོན་པ་གསང་བའི་བདག་པོ་དེ་ལ་ཕྱག་
འཚལ་ལོ་ཞེས་འབྲས་བུ་གསང་སྔགས་ཀྱི་ཚུལ་དང་སྒོ་མཐུན་པར་ལྷག་པའི་ལྷ་ལ་ཕྱག་
མཛད་པའོ། །གཉིས་པ་ལ། ལྟ་བའི་ཁྱད་པར་དང་། བརྟུལ་ཞུགས་ཀྱི་ཁྱད་
པར་བཤད་པ་གཉིས་ལས། དང་པོ་ལའང་། ཕྱི་རོལ་པ་དང་། ཆོས་འདི་པ་
རྣམས་ཀྱི་ལྟ་བ་བཤད་པ་གཉིས། དང་པོ་ལ་བསྟན་བཤད་གཉིས་ལས། དང་པོ་ནི།
འཇིག་པའི་ཆོས་དང་ལྡན་པའི་**འཇིག་རྟེན་གྱི་ཁམས**་སམ་ཕྱི་སྣོད་ཀྱི་རིས་**ན།** ནང་
ཕུང་ལྔའི་རྒྱུན་བློས་མ་ཕྱེ་ཙམ་ལ་བཏགས་པའི་**སེམས་ཅན**་ནམ་གང་ཟག་མ་རིག་པ་དང་
མཚུངས་པ་ལྡན་པས་ཡང་དག་པའི་དོན་ལས་གོལ་བ་**ཕྱིན་ཅི་ལོག་གི**་ཤེས་རབ་དང་མོས་
པའི་བྱེ་བྲག་གིས་**ལྟ་བ་གྲངས་མེད་པ**་ཡོད་དེ་ལོག་རྟོག་མཐའ་མེད་པའི་ཕྱིར་རོ། །
འོན་ཀྱང་དེའི་**མདོར་རྣམ་པ་བཞིར་འདུས་ཏེ**་དེ་ལ་རྣམ་པའི་སྒྲ་ནི་རྒྱུ་བྱེ་བྲག་འདྲ་བ་སྣང་བ་
གྲངས་རྐྱེན་རྣམས་ལ་འཇུག་པ་ལས་འདིར་གྲངས་ཉིད་བཟུང་བར་བྱའོ། །དེ་ཡང་
གྲུབ་མཐའ་དང་ཐེག་པ་མེད་པས་སམ། དོན་ལ་ཞེ་འདོད་ཀྱི་གཏད་སོ་མེད་པས་**ཕྱལ**
བ་དང་བསམ་སྦྱོར་གྱི་སྟེང་ནས་འཇིག་རྟེན་ཕ་རོལ་ལ་རྩིས་མི་འཛོག་པར་རྒྱང་རིང་དུ་
འཕེན་པ་ལྟར་བྱེད་པས་ན་**རྒྱང་འཕེན**་ནམ་ཡང་ན་འཇིག་རྟེན་ཇི་ཙམ་ཞེས་ཚེ་འདིར་སྣང་
རྒྱང་རྒྱང་ངམ་བྲེང་བྲེང་པོའི་ངོར་ཕན་པ་ཙམ་སྒྲུབ་པ་ལས་དོན་ཆེན་པོ་དང་བྲལ་བས་ན་
རྒྱང་ཕན་པ་དང་། མྱ་ངན་ལས་འདས་པའི་རྒྱ་མཚོའི་འབབ་པའི་ལམ་གྱི་ཆུ་རྒྱུན་གྱི་
མུ་ལ་སྟེགས་བཅས་ཤིང་རྟེན་པ་སྐད་དུ་འཆད་པས་མུ་སྟེགས་པའོ། །དེ་ཡང་རྒྱང་
ཕན་ཞེས་པ་སྒྲ་མ་འདོམ་བའི་ཚེ་སངས་རྒྱས་པ་མིན་པའི་ཕྱི་རོལ་པ་ཐུན་མོང་ལ་འཇུག་
སྟེ། མྱང་འདས་ལས། བཅོམ་ལྡན་འདས་ཀྱི་ལྟར་ན་ཞེའམ། འཇིག་རྟེན་རྒྱང་
ཕན་པའི་ལྟར་ན་ཞེས་གསུངས་པ་ལྟ་བུ་ཡིན་ལ། འདིར་ལྟ་བ་རྣམ་པ་བཞི་འདོམ་པའི་
སྐབས་སུ་སྤྱིའི་སྒྲ་བྱེ་བྲག་ལ་འཇུག་པར་སྦྱར་ཏེ། ཇི་སྐད་གསུངས་པའི་ལྟ་བ་ཕྱོགས་
གཅིག་ཏུ་སྦྱར་རོ། །ཡང་རྒྱན་འཕེན་ཞེས་ཕུར་བུའི་ལུགས་ཀྱི་རྗེས་འབྲང་ཆད་པར་ལྟ་
བ་རྣམས་ནི་ལོག་རྟོག་སྟེ། མུར་ཐུག་པ་ལྟ་བུ་མ་ཡིན་ལ། འདི་ནི་མ་རྟོགས་པ་སྟེ།

འདི་དང་ཕྲལ་བ་གཉིས་ཀྱིས་རྒྱུ་འབྲས་ཀྱི་དངོས་པོ་རྣམ་པར་མ་དཔྱད་པར་འདྲ་ཡང་། འདི་ལ་ཚེ་འདིའི་དོན་ལ་འཇུག་པའི་བློ་གྲོས་ཅུང་གསལ། ཅིག་ཤོས་མི་གསལ་བའི་ཁྱད་པར་ཡོད་དེ། ཕྱི་མ་ནི་བདེ་འགྲོ་ཕལ་ཆེ་བའོ། །དེས་ན་འཇིག་རྟེན་འདིར་ཕན་ཅེས་པའི་སྒྲ་སྐབས་ཀྱིས་གོ་བར་བྱ་དགོས་ཏེ་མཐའ་གཅིག་ཏུ་ཕུར་བུ་པ་སོགས་ལ་གཟུང་ན་གཞུང་གི་དགོངས་པ་མ་ཤེས་པ་སྟེ། དེས་ན་སེ་ན་ཧྲི་པའི་སྒྲ་བཞིན་དུ་ཚིག་ལ་གནས་སྐབས་ཀྱི་གོ་བ་ལེན་པ་ནི་བསྟན་བཅོས་ཐམས་ཅད་འཆད་པ་ལ་མེད་དུ་མི་རུང་ངོ་། །དེ་བཞིན་མུར་ཐུག་ཀྱང་འོད་སྲུང་གིས་ཞུས་པའི་མདོ་ལས། འོད་སྲུང་ངའི་བསྟན་པ་ནི་མུ་ཐུག་དགུ་པ་ཙུ་རྩ་དྲུག་གིས་ནི་འཇིག་པར་བྱེད་མི་ནུས་ཏེ། ངའི་དགེ་སློང་ང་དང་འདྲ་བས་འཇིག་པར་བྱེད་པར་འགྱུར་རོ། །ཞེས་ཕྱི་རོལ་པ་ཐུན་མོང་དུ་བཤད་པ་དང་། མུ་སྟེགས་ཀྱང་རྟག་ཆད་དུ་སྨྲ་བའི་ཕྱི་རོལ་པའི་སྤྱི་ལ་འཇུག་ཀྱང་། འདིར་དེ་གཉིས་རིམ་པ་ལྟར་ཆད་པ་དང་རྟག་པར་སྨྲ་བའི་ཕྱི་རོལ་པ་སྤྱི་མིང་དུ་སྦྱར་བར་བྱས་ན་སྒྲ་དོན་ལེགས་པར་འཁྲིད་ཅིང་གཞུང་འདིའི་དགོངས་པ་ཡིན་ནོ། །དེ་ལ་ཡང་ལམ་གྱི་གཞི་མདོར་ནོར་བུ་རིན་པོ་ཆེ་གཅིག་གནས་པ་ལ། ལ་ལས་གཞི་ནས་མ་མཐོང་། ཁ་ཅིག་གིས་འཆིང་བུར་མཐོང་། ཁ་ཅིག་གིས་ཆེན་པོ་ཆེ་ཕལ་པར་མཐོང་། ཁ་ཅིག་གིས་ཇི་ལྟ་བ་བཞིན་མཐོང་ན། གཞི་ནས་མ་མཐོང་བ་རྣམས་ཀྱང་། མཐོང་སྣངས་ཀྱི་མདོ་རིས་གཅིག་ཏུ་བྱེད་པ་དང་འདྲ་བར་རྒྱང་ཕྲལ་གཉིས་ཡང་དག་པའི་མཐར་ཐུག་གི་གནས་ལུགས་མ་རྟོགས་པས་གཅིག་ཏུ་བཞག་ལ། དེ་དག་ནི་ངན་སོང་གསུམ་གཙོ་བོར་གྱུར་པའི་འགྲོ་བ་སྐྱེ་བ་སྔ་ཕྱི་ལ་དཔྱོད་པ་ཙམ་ཡང་མི་ཤེས་པའི་རང་གར་བླུན་པ་ཕྱུགས་ལྟ་བུའོ། །དེ་ནི་ལྟ་བའི་དམའ་ཤོས་ཏེ་དེ་ལས་དམན་པ་མི་སྲིད་པས་སོ། །དེ་ལམ་ལ་མ་ཞུགས་པ་ཡིན་པས་ལྟ་བར་མི་རུང་སྙམ་ན་མ་རིག་མཚུངས་ལྡན་གྱི་སེམས་ཀྱིས་ལྟ་བ་མ་རྟོགས་པ་ཡིན་པས། ལྟ་བ་གཏན་ལ་ཕབ་པའི་སྐབས་སུ་སྤང་བྱར་ཤེས་དགོས་པའི་ཕྱིར་དུའོ། །དེ་ལ་སེམས་ཅན་ཕལ་མོ་ཆེ་དེ་དག །དངོས་པོ་ལ་ཞེན་ཅིང་འཇིགས་ཚོགས་ལ་ལྟ་བ་ལ་གནས་སུ་ཟིན་ཀྱང་འདུ་ཤེས་དང་ཤེས་རབ་ཀྱི་ཆ་ཞན་པས་རྒྱུ་འབྲས་ཀྱི་དངོས་པོ་རྣམས་ལ་མཚན་མར་བཟུང་

ནས་བྱེ་བྲག་མ་ཕྱེད་པའི་ལྟ་བའི་འཐིབ་པོས་ནོན་པའི་ཕྱིར་དེ་སྐད་ཅེས་བྱའོ། །གཉིས་པ་ལ་གཉིས་ལས། དང་པོ་ཕྱལ་རྒྱང་གཉིས་པ་བཤད་པ་ནི། དེ་ལ་ཕྱལ་བ་ནི་གང་ཞེ་ན། འདི་ལྟར་ཕྱི་ནང་གི་**ཆོས**་འདི་དག་**ཐམས་ཅད**་གང་འབྱུང་བའི་**རྒྱུ་དང**་གང་བྱུང་བའི་**འབྲས་བུ**་འདི་དག་**ཡོད**་པའམ་**མེད**་པ་དག་**ཏུ**་ཡང་**མ་རྟོགས་ཏེ**་རང་གར་གནས་པ་སྟེ་དེ་དག་ནི་རྒྱུ་འབྲས་ལ་**ཀུན་ཏུ་རྨོངས**་པའི་མ་རིག་པ་དང་མཚུངས་པར་ལྡན་**པའོ། །རྒྱང་འཕེན**་ནམ་རྒྱང་ཕན་པ་**ནི། ཚེ་སྔ་ཕྱི་ཡོད**་པའམ་**མེད**་པ་དག་**ཏུ་མ་རྟོགས་ཤིང་ཚེ་གཅིག་ལ་བཙན་ཕྱུགས་དང་མཐུ་སྟོབས་སྒྲུབ་པ**་ཡི་ཐབས་སྣ་ཚོགས་པ་ལ་འབད་པར་བྱེད་པ་**སྟེ**། དེ་ཡང་རྣམ་གྲོལ་གྱི་སྒོར་མ་གྱུར་པ་འཇིག་རྟེན་པས་བཤད་པ། འཇིག་རྟེན་གྱི་བྱ་བ་སྒྲུབ་པ་འཚོ་རྩིས་དང་སྲིད་སྐྱོང་དཔྱད་སོགས་དང་། གར་ཤེའི་ངན་སྔགས་དང་མོ་བོན་འདྲེ་མནན་ས་བདག་མཆོད་པ་གཡང་ལེན་སོགས་རང་ངམ་གཞན་ལ་བྱེད་དུ་འཇུག་པ་ལྟ་བུ་**འཇིག་རྟེན་པའི་གསང་ཚིག་ལ་བརྟེན་པའོ།** །གཉིས་པ་མུར་ཐུག་དང་མུ་སྟེགས་ཀྱི་གྲུབ་མཐའ་བཤད་པ་ནི། **མུར་ཐུག་པ་ནི**། ལྟ་ཡུལ་ཞེས་བྱའི་**ཆོས་ཐམས་ཅད་ལ་རྒྱུ་དང་འབྲས་བུ་མེད་པ་སྟེ**། དེ་ཡང་**ཚེ་གཅིག་ལ་སྐྱེས་པའི་ཆོས་ཐམས་ཅན**་ཚེ་སྔ་མའི་ལས་ཀྱིས་མ་འཕང་བར་སྐྱང་ལ་ཤྭ་མོ་དང་ཆུ་ལ་ཆུ་བུར་བཞིན་**གློ་བུར་དུ་སྐྱེས་ལ་མཐའ**་མར་མེ་རྒྱུན་ཆད་པ་ལྟར་**ཆད་པར་བལྟ་པའོ། །མུ་སྟེགས་པ་ནི**། རྒྱུ་འབྲས་ཀྱི་དངོས་པོའི་**ཆོས་ཐམས་ཅད་ལ**་མེད་བཞིན་དུ་**ཀུན་ཏུ་བརྟགས་པ**འི་**བདག**་ནི་**རྟག་པ་ཞིག་ཡོད་པར་ལྟ་བ་སྟེ**། **དེ་ལའང**་རང་བཞིན་རྒྱུར་ལྟ་བས། རང་བཞིན་རྒྱུ་རྐྱེན་མེད་པ་དེའི་ངོ་བོར་ཆོས་ཀུན་གྱུར་པས་རང་བཞིན་རྣམ་པ་ཐ་མི་དད་པར་འདོད་པས་བདག་གཅིག་པུ་རིལ་པོར་འཛིན་པ་ཞེས་བྱ་སྟེ། སྣང་བའི་དངོས་པོ་ཡེ་ནས་གྲུབ་པ་ཡིན་ལ། དེ་བསྐྱེད་པའི་རྒྱུ་གཞན་མེད་པར་བལྟ་བས་**རྒྱུ་མེད་པ་ལ་འབྲས་བུ་ཡོད་པར་ལྟ་བ་དང**་ཞེས་བྱ་སྟེ། དེ་ཡང་རྒྱུ་ལ་མ་ལྟོས་ན་འབྲས་བུ་ཇི་ལྟར་བཞག་ཅེ་ན་ཡོད་པ་ཉིད་འབྲས་བུའམ་གྲུབ་པ་སྟེ། ནམ་མཁའ་གདོད་ནས་གྲུབ་པ་ཞེས་བྱ་བ་བཞིན་ཏེ། འདི་ནི་དམིགས་པ་གཅིག་པུ་ཡིན་ནོ། །**རྒྱུ་འབྲས་ལོག་པར་ལྟ་བ་དང**་། **ཞེས་པ་ནི་དབང་ཕྱུག་ཞེས་བྱ་བའི་གང་ཟག་གདོད**

ནས་གྲུབ་པར། རྟག་པ་དེས། གཡོ་མི་གཡོའི་དངོས་པོ་ཐམས་ཅད་ལ་དབང་བསྒྱུར་ཞིང་རྣམ་པར་འཕྲུལ་ལོ་ཞེས་བྱ་ཞིང་། དབང་ཕྱུག་མཉེས་པའི་སླད་དུ་སྲོག་ཆགས་དུ་མའི་མཆོད་སྦྱིན་སོགས་བྱེད་ལ། འདི་ནི་དམིགས་པ་གཉིས་དང་ལྡན་ཏེ། དབང་ཕྱུག་རྟག་ལ་སྤྲུལ་པ་མི་རྟག་ཞེས་འདོད་པའོ། །འདིས་མི་དགེའི་ལས་ཀྱིས་མཐོ་རིས་སྒྲུབ་པས་སམ། རྒྱུ་རྟག་པས་འབྲས་བུ་མི་རྟག་པ་བསྐྱེད་པས་དེ་སྐད་ཅེས་བརྗོད་དོ། །རྒྱུ་ཡོད་ལ་འབྲས་བུ་མེད་པར་ལྟ་བ་སྟེ་ཞེས། འདིས་ནི་བྱེད་པ་པོ་རྒྱུར་ལྟ་བ་སྟེ། བདག་རྟག་པ་མཐེ་བོང་ཙམ་སོགས་རྫ་བཅག་བྱེའུ་འཕུར་བཞིན་དུ་འདོད་པ་སྟེ། འདི་ནི་དམིགས་པ་གསུམ་དང་ལྡན་ཏེ། བདག་རྟག་པ་རྒྱུའི་བྱ་བ་བོ་ན་བྱེད་འདོད་པ་དང་། དེས་བྱས་འབྲས་ཕུང་པོའི་ངོ་བོ་མི་རྟག་འགྱུར་བའི་ཆོས་ཅན་དུ་འདོད་པ་དང་། འབྲས་བུ་དེ་ཡང་ཐེབས་གཅིག་གི་འབྲས་བུ་ཙམ་སྟེ་དེས་ཕུང་པོ་གཞན་སྐྱེད་པའི་རྒྱུ་མེད་ཅིང་རྒྱུན་ཆད་པའོ། །རྟག་ཆད་ཀྱི་ལྟ་བ་དེ་གཉིས་ཀྱི་ཁོངས་སུ་ཕྱི་རོལ་པའི་འདོད་པའི་རྟག་ཆད་ཀྱི་རྣམ་པ་མ་ལུས་པ་ཟད་པར་འདུའོ། །གོང་བསྟན་བཞི་པོ་**འདི་དག་ནི་**རིག་པའི་མི་མཐུན་ཕྱོགས་སུ་གྱུར་པ་**མ་རིག་**པ་དང་མཚུངས་པར་ལྡན་**པའི་ལྟ་བའོ། །དེ་ལ་འཇིག་རྟེན་པའི་ལྟ་བའི་སྐབས་འདིར་ནི་ལྟ་བ་ཙམ་ཞིག་བསྟན་གྱི། ལམ་དང་འབྲས་བུ་མ་བསྟན་པ་ནི་དོན་མེད་པར་དགོངས་པར་ཟད་དོ། །གཉིས་པ་ལ་མདོར་བསྟན་པ་དང་། རྒྱས་པར་བཤད་པ་གཉིས། དང་པོ་ནི། ཟག་མེད་ཀྱི་ལམ་དང་རྗེས་སུ་འབྲེལ་པ་འཇིག་རྟེན་ལས་འདས་པའི་ལམ་ལའང་**དབྱེ་ན་**རྣམ་པ་གཉིས་ཏེ།** ཆོས་རྣམས་ཀྱི་རང་སྤྱི་དང་ཀུན་བྱང་གི་མཚན་ཉིད་རྣམས་སོ་སོར་མ་འདྲེས་པར་སྟོན་ཅིང་དེ་ལ་སྤང་བླང་དུ་སྟོན་པ་**མཚན་ཉིད་ཀྱི་ཐེག་པ་དང་། ཀུན་བྱང་གཉིས་ངོ་བོ་དབྱེར་མེད་སྐུ་གསུང་ཐུགས་ཀྱི་དཀྱིལ་འཁོར་དུ་མི་ཕྱེད་པར་སྟོན་པ་རྡོ་རྗེའི་ཐེག་པའོ།** །གཉིས་པ་མཚན་ཉིད་ཐེག་པ་དང་། སྔགས་ཀྱི་ཐེག་པའི་རྣམ་བཞག་གཉིས། དང་པོ་ལའང་གཉིས་ལས། མདོར་བསྟན་པ་ནི། **མཚན་ཉིད་ཀྱི་ཐེག་པ་ལའང་**སྐལ་པ་དང་མོས་པ་དབང་པོའི་བྱེ་བྲག་གིས་མཚན་ཉིད་དེ་ལ་མངོན་པར་ཞེན་མ་ཞེན་གྱི་དབང་གིས་**རྣམ་པ་གསུམ་སྟེ།** རང་ཉིད་ཀྱིས་གདམས་

ངག་གཞན་ལས་ཉན་ཅིང་གཞན་ལ་ཐོས་པར་བྱེད་པ་ཉན་ཐོས་ཀྱི་ཐེག་པ་དང་། སྲིད་པ་ཐ་མའི་དུས་སུ་རང་ཉིད་ཀྱི་བདེན་པའི་འབྲས་བུ་ཡོང་དུ་ཆུད་པ་རང་སངས་རྒྱས་ཀྱི་ཐེག་པ་དང་། བྱང་ཆུབ་ཀྱི་ཕྱིར་བསམ་པ་བརྟན་པའམ་བྱང་ཆུབ་དང་སེམས་ཅན་ལ་དམིགས་པ་ཡོད་པས་བྱང་ཆུབ་སེམས་དཔའི་ཐེག་པའོ། །གཉིས་པ་ལ། ཉན་ཐོས། རང་རྒྱལ། བྱང་སེམས་ཀྱི་ཐེག་པ་བཤད་པ་གསུམ་ལས། དང་པོ་ནི། དེ་ལ་ཉན་ཐོས་ཀྱི་འབྲས་བུ་ཐོབ་པར་བྱེད་པ་རང་ལམ་གྱི་ཐེག་པ་ལ་ཞུགས་པ་ཡི་གང་ཟག་རྣམས་ཀྱི་ལྟ་བ་ནི་གྲུབ་པའི་མཐའ་སྟེ་ཤེས་རབ་ཀྱིས་བཅད་པ་ལྟར་མོས་པས་ངེས་པའོ། །འདིར་ལྟ་སྒོམ་འབྲས་བུ་གསུམ་དུ་སྟོན་ཏེ། དེ་ལ་ལྟ་བ་ཡང་། ཕུང་ཁམས་སྐྱེ་མཆེད་ཀྱིས་བསྡུས་པའི་ཆོས་ཐམས་ཅད་ལ་ཕྱི་རོལ་མུ་སྟེགས་པ་ལ་སོགས་པས་མེད་པ་ལ་རྟག་པར་སྒྲོ་བཏགས་པ་དང་། ཡོད་པ་ལ་མེད་པར་སྐུར་བའི་རྣམ་པ་ཅན་གྱི་ཀུན་ཏུ་བརྟགས་པས་ཡེ་མེད་པའམ་གཏན་ནས་མེད་པ་ཆད་པའི་ལྟ་བ་དང་། རྟག་པ་ལ་སྒྱོགས་པའི་ཡོད་པར་ལྟ་བ་ནི་ཐག་པ་ལ་སྦྲུལ་དུ་མཐོང་བ་ཡི་སྦྲུལ་བཞིན་དུ་མེད་དེ། སྣང་གཞི་ཐག་པ་ལྟ་བུའི་ཕུང་པོ་དང་ཁམས་དང་སྐྱེ་མཆེད་ལ་སོགས་པའི་བདག་ཉིད་ནི་ཕྱི་རོལ་གྱི་གཟུགས་སོགས་བེམ་པོ་ནི་རགས་པར་སྣང་བའི་རྒྱུ་འབྱུང་བ་ཆེན་པོ་བཞིའི་རྡུལ་ཕྲ་རབ་དང་། ནང་གི་རྣམ་པར་ཤེས་པ་སྐད་ཅིག་མ་ནི་དོན་དམ་པར་རམ་བདེན་པར་ཡོད་པར་ལྟ་ཞིང་། འདི་ལ་བྱེ་སྨྲ་དང་མདོ་སྡེ་པ་གཉིས་པོ་སྨྲ་མས་འདུས་མ་བྱས་རྟག་པར་འདོད་པ་དང་། ཕྱི་མས་མོ་གཤམ་གྱི་བུ་བཞིན་གཏན་མེད་དུ་འདོད་པ་སོགས་ནང་ཚུང་མི་མཐུན་ཞིང་བྱེ་སྨྲ་ལའང་སོ་སོའི་འདོད་པ་ཕྲ་མོ་མི་མཐུན་པ་མང་ཡང་། དོན་དུ་རྡུལ་དང་སྐད་ཅིག་བདེན་པར་ཁས་ལེན་པ་འདྲ་བས་གཅིག་ཏུ་བཞག་གོ །བསྒོམ་པ་བསམ་གཏན་གྱི་རིམ་པ་དང་། སྡུག་ཀུན་འགོག་ལམ་སྟེ་འཕགས་པའི་བདེན་པ་བཞི་བསྒོམས་པ་སྟེ། དེ་ཡང་ངོ་བོ་ཇི་ལྟ་བ་ཡིན་པས་ཕྱིན་ཅི་ལོག་མེད་པས་བདེན་ལ། འཕགས་པ་རྣམས་ཀྱིས་ཐུགས་སུ་ཆུད་པའམ་འཕགས་པའི་རང་བཞིན་ཡིན་པས་ཀྱང་ངོ་། །བདེན་པ་དེ་དག་ཀྱང་ཁམས་གསུམ་གྱི་བདེན་བཞི་ལ་དམིགས་ནས་རྣམ་པ་བཅུ་དྲུག་གི་ཚུལ་ཅན་དུ་གོམས་པ་དང་། ནམ་

ཞིག་ཤེས་བཟོད་སྐད་ཅིག་མ་བཅུ་དྲུག་གི་རང་བཞིན་ཅན་གྱི་ཡེ་ཤེས་མཐོང་བའི་ལམ་སྐྱེ་ཞིང་། དེ་ནས་**རིམ་གྱིས་**ཁམས་གསུམ་ས་དགུའི་ཉོན་མོངས་པ་སྒོམ་སྤང་རྣམས་རིམ་པར་སྤང་སྟེ། དེ་ཡང་འདོད་ཉོན་དགུའི་རྣམ་པ་གསུམ་པ་བཞི་པ་ཡན་ཆད་ལས་གྲོལ་བ་རྒྱུན་ཞུགས། དྲུག་པ་སྤང་པ་ལན་གཅིག་ཕྱིར་འོང་། དགུ་པ་སྤང་པ་ཕྱིར་མི་འོང་། སྲིད་རྩེའི་ཉོན་མོངས་པ་མ་ལུས་པ་སྤང་བ་དགྲ་བཅོམ་སྟེ་**འབྲས་བུ་རྣམ་པ་བཞི་འགྲུབ་པ་ཡིན་ནོ། །གཉིས་པ་ནི་རང་སངས་རྒྱས་ཀྱི་**འབྲས་བུའི་ངོ་བོ་འདུས་མ་བྱས་པའི་མཚན་ཉིད་དེ་ཐོབ་པར་བྱེད་པའི་ལམ་གྱི་**ཐེག་པ་ལ་ཞུགས་པ་རྣམས་ཀྱི་ལྟ་བ་ནི། ཆོས་ཐམས་ཅད་ལ་སྨུ་སྨྱེགས་ལ་སོགས་པས་སྒྲོ་དང་སྐུར་པའི་ཀུན་ཏུ་བརྟགས་པའི་བདག་རྟག་པ་**དང་ཆད་པ་ལ་སོགས་པ་**མེད་པར་ལྟ་བ་ཉན་ཐོས་དང་མཐུན་**ཞིང་། **དེ་ལས་ཁྱད་པར་དུ་**ཕུང་པོ་ལྔ་ལས་**གཟུགས་ཀྱི་ཕུང་པོའི་**སྐྱེ་མཆེད་དང་ཁམས་ལས་གཟུགས་ཅན་བཅུ་དང་**ཆོས་ཀྱི་ཁམས་ཀྱི་ཕྱོགས་གཅིག་**རྣམ་པར་རིག་བྱེད་མིན་པའི་གཟུགས་ཏེ་མདོར་ན་གཟུགས་ཀྱི་ཕུང་པོར་གཏོགས་པའི་ཆོས་**ལ་བདག་མེད་པར་རྟོགས་ཤིང་**དེ་གོམས་པས་ནམ་ཞིག་སྲིད་པ་ཐ་མར་**རང་བྱུང་ཆུབ་ཀྱི་འབྲས་བུ་ཐོབ་པའི་དུས་ནའང་ཉན་ཐོས་ལྟར་དགེ་བའི་བཤེས་གཉེན་ལ་མ་ལྟོས་པར།** ཇི་ལྟར་སྒོམ་པའི་ཚུལ། **སྔོན་**དཀར་པོ་རྣམ་པར་མཐོང་བའི་ས་སོགས་སུ་སངས་རྒྱས་ལ་བསྟེན་ཅིང་སྦྱངས་པ་**གོམས་པའི་ཤུགས་ཀྱིས་**བདེན་བཞིའི་རང་བཞིན་ཅན་གྱི་**རྟེན་ཅིང་འབྲེལ་བར་འབྱུང་བ་ཡན་ལག་བཅུ་གཉིས་ཀྱི་**དོན་རྟོགས་ཏེ། དེ་ཡང་སྡུག་བསྔལ་བདུན་སྡུག་བདེན་ཉོན་མོངས་གསུམ་དང་ལས་གཉིས་ཀུན་འབྱུང་། ཀུན་ཉོན་དེ་དག་བྲལ་བ་འགོག་བདེན། དེར་འགྲོ་བའི་ལམ་རྟེན་འབྲེལ་གྱི་དོན་རྟོགས་ནས་གོམས་པ་ལམ་མོ། །རྣམ་པ་གཅིག་ཏུ་ན་ཡན་ལག་བཅུ་གཉིས་རེ་རེ་ལའང་བཞི་བཞི་ལྡན་ཏེ། དེ་དག་རང་གི་བདག་ཉིད་ཐོབ་པ་སྡུག་བདེན། དེ་དག་གཅིག་རྐྱེན་གཅིག་གིས་འགྲུབ་པ་ཀུན་འབྱུང་། གཅིག་འགགས་པས་གཅིག་འགོག་པ་འགོག་བདེན། དེ་དག་འགོག་པའི་ཕྱིར་དེ་ཉིད་ཕྱིན་ཅི་མ་ལོག་པར་སྒོམ་པ་ལམ་སྟེ། དེ་ལྟར་ན་བདེན་བཞི་ལ་དམིགས་པའི་ཡེ་ཤེས་སྐད་ཅིག་མ་བཅུ་དྲུག་ཀྱང་། ཡན་ལག་རེ་རེ་ལ་འབྱུང་བས། །ཡེ་ཤེས་སྐད་ཅིག

མ་བརྒྱ་དགུ་བཅུ་རྩ་གཉིས། སྟོན་གཅིག་གི་སྟེང་དུ་སྐྱེས་ནས་རང་བྱང་ཆུབ་ཀྱི་འབྲས་བུ་ཐོབ་བོ། །དེ་ལྟ་བུའི་**སྒོ་ནས་**སྒྱུ་མ་ལྟ་བུའི་**ཆོས་ཉིད་ཟབ་མོའི་དོན་རྟོགས་**ཏེ། དེ་ཡང་བརྗོད་དུ་མེད་པའི་ངག་ཤིན་ཏུ་འགོག་པའི་ཏིང་ངེ་འཛིན་ལ་གནས་ཀྱང་། བརྗོད་དུ་མེད་དོ་སྙམ་པའི་འདུ་ཤེས་ནི་འཇུག་སྟེ་འཛིན་པའི་རྟོག་པ་མ་སྤྱང་བས་སོ། ། དེ་ཡང་རྟེན་འབྲེལ་ནི་ཀུན་གྱི་ལམ་ཐུན་མོང་སྟེ། ཉན་ཐོས་པས་རྒྱུ་འབྲས་ཀྱི་མཚན་ཉིད་ལ་མངོན་པར་ཞེན་པས་ཕྱི་རོལ་པས་རྒྱུ་འབྲས་ལ་ལོག་པར་རྟོག་པ་སེལ། རང་རྒྱལ་གྱིས་དེ་ལས་ཟབ་ཏུ་རྟོགས་ཏེ། རྒྱུ་འབྲས་ཀྱི་ངོ་བོ་གཟུང་བའི་དོན་དུ་ཡང་མེད་པར་རྟོགས། རྣལ་འབྱོར་སྤྱོད་པས་དེ་བས་ཀྱང་ཟབ་ཏུ་རྟོགས་ཏེ། རྒྱུ་འབྲས་ཀྱི་དངོས་པོ་འཛིན་པའི་བདག་ཏུ་ཡང་མེད་པར་རྟོགས། དབུ་མ་པས་རྒྱུ་དང་འབྲས་བུའི་དངོས་པོ་རང་རིག་པའི་བདག་ཉིད་དུ་ཡང་མེད་པར་རྟོགས་པས་སྤྲོས་པ་ཉེ་བར་ཞི་བའོ། །དེ་ལྟར་ལམ་སྒོམ་ཚུལ་བསྟན་**ནས།** འབྲས་བུ་ནི། ཚོགས་ན་སྤྱོད་པ་དང་བསེ་རུ་ལྟ་བུའི་**རང་བྱང་ཆུབ་ཀྱི་འབྲས་བུ་ཐོབ་པ་ཡིན་ནོ།** **།གསུམ་པ་ནི། བྱང་ཆུབ་སེམས་དཔའི་ཐེག་པ་**ཞེས་རྒྱུའི་སྒོ་ནས་སྨོས་པ་སྟེ། འབྲས་བུ་ནི་གསང་སྔགས་དང་བྱེ་བྲག་མེད་པས་སྔགས་ཕར་ཕྱིན་གཉིས་ཀ་ཐེག་པ་ཆེན་པོར་གཅིག་ཀྱང་། ལམ་གྱིས་བྱེ་བྲག་ཏུ་བྱ་བའི་ཕྱིར་མཚན་ཉིད་ཀྱི་ཐེག་པ་དེ་ལ་**ཞུགས་པ་རྣམས་ཀྱི་ལྟ་བ་ནི། ཀུན་ནས་ཉོན་མོངས་པ་**འཁོར་བ་རྒྱུ་འབྲས་དང་བཅས་པ་**དང་།** **རྣམ་པར་བྱང་བའི་ཆོས་**མྱང་འདས་རྒྱུ་འབྲས་དང་བཅས་པ་དེ་**ཐམས་ཅད་དོན་དམ་པར་ནི་**བདེན་པའི་**རང་བཞིན་**དུ་གྲུབ་པ་གང་ཡང་**མེད་པ་ཡིན་ལ།** དེ་ཡང་དོན་དམ་རང་གི་ངོ་བོ་ནི་སྤྲོས་པ་དང་བྲལ་བ་ལ་བྱ་སྟེ། སྒྲ་དོན་ཡེ་ཤེས་དམ་པའི་ཡུལ་ཡིན་པས་སམ་ཐོབ་བྱ་རྣམས་ཀྱི་ནང་ནས་དམ་པ་ཡིན་པས་དེ་སྐད་ཅེས་བརྗོད་དེ། འདི་ལ་དབྱེ་ན་སྤྲོས་པ་ཕྱོགས་རེ་ཆད་པ་རྣམ་གྲངས་ཀྱི་དོན་དམ་དང་། སྤྲོས་པ་མཐའ་དག་ཡོངས་སུ་ཞི་བ་རྣམ་གྲངས་མ་ཡིན་པའི་དོན་དམ་གཉིས་སུ་ཡོད་དོ། །ཀུན་རྫོབ་ནི་འཁྲུལ་པའི་ཤེས་པ་སྣང་བ་དང་བཅས་པ་སྟེ། ཡང་དག་པའི་དོན་ལ་སྒྲིབ་པས་སམ་བློ་བུར་འཁྲུལ་པའི་བློས་བརྫབས་ཤིང་བརྟགས་ཏེ་རྣམ་པར་བཞག་པས་དེ་སྐད་ཅེས་བརྗོད་དེ། དབྱེ་ན་ཡང་དག་དང་

ལོག་པའི་ཀུན་རྫོབ་གཉིས་ཡོད། **ཀུན་རྫོབ་**དེའི་དབང་**དུ་**བདེན་མེད་ཀྱི་སྣང་བ་**སྒྱུ་མ་ཙམ་དུ་**སྣང་སྟེ། འདིར་ཙམ་སྨོས་ཡང་དག་པར་གྲུབ་པ་གཅོད་དོ། །སྣང་ཙམ་པོ་དེའི་ངོར་རང་རང་གི་བྱ་བ་བྱེད་པ་སོགས་ཀྱི་ནུས་པ་མེད་ཅེས་སྐྱུར་པ་གདབ་ཏུ་མི་རུང་བས་སྤྱོད་ཡུལ་ཡོངས་སུ་དག་མ་དག་སོགས་**སོ་སོའི་མཚན་ཉིད་མ་འདྲེས་པར་ཡོད་དེ་**རང་གཞལ་བྱེད་ཐ་སྙད་ཀྱི་ཚད་མའི་ངོར་གྲུབ་པས་སོ། །དེ་ལྟར་གནས་སྐབས་ཚད་མ་གཉིས་ཀྱི་ངོར་ངེས་པར་བྱ་བ་དང་། མཐར་ཐུག་སྣང་སྟོང་ཟུང་འཇུག་བདེན་གཉིས་དབྱེར་མེད་སྤྲོས་བྲལ་མཉམ་པ་ཆེན་པོའི་ཚུལ་དུ་ལེགས་པར་གཏན་ལ་ཕབ་ནས་སྒོམ་པའི་ལམ་བསྟན་པའི་ཕྱིར་ཤེས་རབ་ཐམས་ཅད་ཀྱི་ནང་ནས་དམ་པར་གྱུར་ཅིང་མཐར་ཕྱིན་པ་ནི་གཉིས་སུ་མེད་པའི་ཡེ་ཤེས་ཡིན་པས། དེས་ཟིན་པའི་སྦྱིན་སོགས་དགེ་བའི་ཆོས་བཅུ་ལ་**ཕ་རོལ་ཏུ་ཕྱིན་པ་བཅུ་**ཞེས་བྱ་སྟེ། འདི་ལ་ཕར་ཕྱིན་གྱི་སྒྲ་ཤེས་རབ་ལས་འདས་ཏེ་ཡུལ་དུ་མ་གྱུར་པ་ནི། ཆོས་ཉིད་སྤྲོས་བྲལ་ལ་བྱ་སྟེ་འདི་ཕ་རོལ་ཏུ་ཕྱིན་པས་དང་། འདིར་འཁོར་བའི་རྒྱ་མཚོའི་ཕ་རོལ་ཏུ་ཕྱིན་པས་དེ་སྐད་ཅེས་བརྗོད་དེ་ལམ་ལ་སྦྱར་བའི་ཚུལ་གཉིས་ཡོད་དོ། །དེ་ལྟར་**སྤྱོད་པའི་**གནས་སྐབས་ཀྱི་**འབྲས་བུ་ས་བཅུ་པོ་རིམ་གྱིས་བགྲོད་པའི་མཐར་**མཐར་ཐུག་གི་འབྲས་བུ་ཉན་རང་སོགས་ལས་ཁྱད་པར་དུ་གྱུར་པའི་སྟོབས་དང་མི་འཇིགས་པ་ལ་སོགས་པའི་ཡོན་ཏན་གྱི་ཚོགས་ཐམས་ཅད་ཡོངས་སུ་རྫོགས་པའི་མཚན་ཉིད་ཅན་གྱི་**བླ་ན་མེད་པའི་བྱང་ཆུབ་ཏུ་འགྲུབ་པར་འདོད་པ་ཡིན་ནོ། །གཉིས་པ་ལ། བསྟན་བཤད་གཉིས་ལས། དང་པོ་ནི། རྡོ་རྗེ་ཐེག་པ་**དེ་**ལའང་**དབྱེ་ན་**རྣམ་པ་གསུམ་སྟེ།** ནང་གི་ཏིང་ངེ་འཛིན་རྒྱུའི་གཙོ་བོ་ཡིན་མོད་ཀྱི་ཕྱིའི་གཙང་སྦྲ་དང་དཀའ་ཐུབ་སོགས་ཀྱི་བྱ་བ་ལ་མ་ལྟོས་པར་དངོས་གྲུབ་མི་ཐོབ་པར་འདོད་པ་**བྱ་བའི་རྒྱུད་ཀྱི་ཐེག་པ་དང་། ཕྱིའི་བྱ་བ་དང་ནང་གི་ཏིང་ངེ་འཛིན་གཉིས་ཀས་གྲུབ་པར་འདོད་པ་གཉིས་ཀའི་རྒྱུད་ཀྱི་ཐེག་པ་དང་། ཕྱིའི་བྱ་བ་ལ་མ་ལྟོས་ཀྱང་ནང་གི་ཏིང་ངེ་འཛིན་འབའ་ཞིག་གིས་གྲུབ་པར་འདོད་པ་རྣལ་འབྱོར་རྒྱུད་ཀྱི་ཐེག་པའོ།** །གཉིས་པ་ལ། བྱ་རྒྱུད། སྤྱོད་རྒྱུད། རྣལ་འབྱོར་རྒྱུད་ཀྱི་རྣམ་པར་གཞག་པ་གསུམ་ལས། དང་པོ་ནི། **དེ་ལ་བྱ་བའི་རྒྱུད་ཀྱི་ཐེག་པ་ལ་**

ཞུགས་པ་རྣམས་ཀྱི་ལྟ་བ་ནི། དོན་དམ་པར་ཆོས་ཐམས་ཅད་རང་གི་ངོ་བོ་**སྐྱེ་འགག་མེད་པ་ལས། ཀུན་རྫོབ་ཏུ་ལྷའི་གཟུགས་ཀྱི་སྐུར་སྒོམ་ཞིང་**ཞེས་བྱང་ཆུབ་ཀྱི་སེམས་དང་དེ་ཉིད་གསུམ་དང་ལྡན་པ་ནི་དངོས་གྲུབ་ཀྱི་སྟོད་དུ་བཤད་དོ། །དེ་ལ་དེ་ཉིད་གསུམ་ནི། བདག་གི་དེ་ཁོ་ན་ཉིད་དང་། ལྷའི་དེ་ཁོ་ན་ཉིད་དང་། བཟླས་བརྗོད་ཀྱི་དེ་ཁོ་ན་ཉིད་དེ། དེ་གསུམ་གྱིས་རིམ་པར་འཁོར་བའི་ཆོས་ཀྱི་རང་བཞིན་དང་། མྱ་ངན་ལས་འདས་པའི་མཚན་ཉིད་དང་། དེ་སྒྲུབ་པའི་ཐབས་ཀྱི་མཚན་ཉིད་རྣམས་བསྡུས་པ་སྟེ། དེ་ལ་བདག་གི་དེ་ཁོ་ན་ཉིད་ཕུང་ལྔའི་དོན་བློས་རྣམ་པར་མ་ཕྱེ་ཙམ་ནི་བདག་ཡིན་ལ། དེའི་དེ་ཉིད་ནི་ཉན་ཐོས་དང་སྒོ་བསྟུན་ན། མུ་སྟེགས་པས་བརྟགས་པའི་བདག་དང་བདག་གི་དང་རྟག་ཆད་སོགས་ཀུན་ཏུ་བརྟགས་པས་སྟོང་པ། ཕུང་སོགས་ཀྱི་ཆོས་ཙམ་མེད་པར་སྐུར་བ་གདབ་ཏུ་མི་རུང་བའོ། །རྣལ་འབྱོར་སྤྱོད་པས་ནི། ཉན་ཐོས་ཀྱིས་བརྟགས་པའི་གཟུང་འཛིན་ཀུན་བརྟགས་ཀྱིས་སྟོང་པ། སེམས་དང་སེམས་བྱུང་རང་རིག་པ་ཙམ་མེད་པར་སྐུར་བ་གདབ་ཏུ་མི་རུང་བ་ཙམ་མོ། །དབུ་མ་པས་ནི། སེམས་ཙམ་པས་རྣམ་པར་མི་རྟོག་པའི་ཡེ་ཤེས་དོན་དམ་པར་ཡོད་པར་བརྟགས་པས་ཀྱང་སྟོང་སྟེ་སྤྲོས་པའི་མཚན་མ་ཐམས་ཅད་ཡོངས་སུ་ཞི་བ་ཉིད་དུ་འདོད་པའོ། །ལྷའི་དེ་ཁོ་ན་ཉིད་ནི་ཆོས་ཉིད་དང་སྒྲ་ལ་སོགས་པ་གསང་སྔགས་ཀྱི་དངོས་པོ་ལྷ་དྲུག་ཏུ་གྲགས་པ་རྣམས་ཏེ། དེ་ཡང་བདག་གི་དེ་ཁོ་ན་ཉིད་གསེར་གྱི་གླེགས་མ་ལྟ་བུ་ལ། ལྷའི་དེ་ཉིད་དངུལ་ཆུ་ཞུན་མ་ལྟ་བུས་བགོས་ཏེ་ལྷར་བསྒོམ་པར་བཞེད་དོ། །བཟླས་བརྗོད་ཀྱི་དེ་ཁོ་ན་དེ་ཉིད་གསུམ། གཟུགས་བརྙན་ཆེན་པོ་གསུམ། དམིགས་པ་གསུམ། ཡན་ལག་བཞི་ལྡན་ཏེ། དེ་ལ་དེ་ཉིད་གསུམ་ནི་ཡེ་ཤེས་མིང་གཟུགས་གསུམ་སྟེ། དེ་ཡང་དོན་དམ་པར་ལྷའི་ཆོས་ཉིད་དག་པ་དང་བདག་གི་ཆོས་ཉིད་མ་དག་པ་གཉིས་རང་བཞིན་དབྱེ་བྲག་མེད་པར་རྟོགས་ནས། དེ་བཞིན་དུ་སྒོམ་པ་སྟེ། ལྷའི་ཡེ་ཤེས་རང་རིག་དག་པ་དང་བདག་གི་ཤེས་པ་རང་རིག་མ་དག་པ་གཉིས་རང་བཞིན་དབྱེར་མེད་པ་དང་། དེ་བཞིན་དུ་ལྷའི་སྐུ་དང་གསུང་ཁྱད་པར་དུ་འཕགས་པར་སྣང་བ་དང་། རང་གི་ལུས་དང་ངག་ཁྱད་པར་ཅན

མིན་པར་སྣང་བའང་བྲེ་བྲག་མེད་པར་ཤེས་ཏེ། དེ་ལ་བརྟེན་ནས་ཀུན་རྫོབ་ཏུའང་ལྷར་བསྒྱུར་ཞིང་བསྐྱེད་དེ་བསྒོམས་པས། འཁྲུལ་པ་དག་པ་ཉིད་འབྲས་བུའི་ངོ་བོར་ལྷར་གྲུབ་པར་ལྟ་བའོ། །གཟུགས་བརྙན་ཆེན་པོ་གསུམ་ནི། ཚུལ་དེ་དང་མཐུན་པར་བསྒོམ་པ་སྟེ་སྐུ་མཚན་དཔེར་གསལ་བ་སྐུའི་གཟུགས་བརྙན། དེའི་ཐུགས་ཀར་བྱང་ཆུབ་སེམས་ཀྱི་རྟགས་ཟླ་དཀྱིལ་བསྒོམ་པ་ཐུགས་ཀྱི་གཟུགས་བརྙན། དེ་ལ་སྙིང་པོ་བཀོད་པ་གསུང་གི་གཟུགས་བརྙན་ནོ། །དམིགས་པ་གསུམ་ནི་བཟླས་བརྗོད་ཀྱི་དུས་སུ་ཡེ་ཤེས་སེམས་དཔའ་མདུན་དུ་དམིགས་པ་ལ། གཟུགས་བརྙན་གསུམ་པོ་དེ་ཀུན་ཀྱང་དམིགས་པར་བྱ་བ་ཡིན་པས་དམིགས་པ་གསུམ་མོ། །ཡན་ལག་བཞི་ནི། དམིགས་པ་གསུམ་བདག་དམ་ཚིག་སེམས་དཔའ་ཟླས་པ་པོ་དང་བཞི་ཆར་ཡང་བཟླས་བརྗོད་ཀྱི་ཡན་ལག་རེ་རེ་ཡིན་པས་བཞིའོ། །དམིགས་པ་གཉིས་དང་ཡན་ལག་གསུམ་སོགས་དེ་ཡིས་བསྡུས་པར་ཟད་དོ། །དེས་ན་རང་ཉིད་ལྷར་མིན་ཀྱང་རྒྱུ་རྐྱེན་གྱིས་ནམ་ཞིག་འགྱུར་སྣང་བས་རྒྱུད་དེ་ལྷར་ལྟ་བའོ། །དེའི་གྲོགས་སུ་རིགས་གསུམ་གང་ལ་མོས་པའི་**སྐུའི་གཟུགས་བརྙན་**བྲིས་སམ་བླུགས་མ་**དང་།** རིགས་གསུམ་**ཐུགས་**ཀྱི་གཟུགས་བརྙན་ནམ་**མཚན་**མ་**དང་**སྟེ། འཆིང་བ་དམ་ཚིག་གི་ཕྱག་རྒྱ། འཛིན་པ་དམ་ཚིག་གི་ཕྱག་རྒྱ། བསམ་པ་དམ་ཚིག་གི་ཕྱག་རྒྱ། བསམ་པ་དམ་ཚིག་གི་ཕྱག་རྒྱ་གསུམ་ལས། དང་པོ་རྣལ་འབྱོར་པས་རྗེར་དྲིལ། གཉིས་པ་ཡེ་ཤེས་སེམས་དཔའི་ཐུགས་མཚན་པདྨ་རྡོ་རྗེ་རལ་གྲི་སོགས། གསུམ་པ་དམ་ཡེའི་ཐུགས་མཚན་བསྒོམ་པ་ལ་བྱའོ། །གསུང་གི་གཟུགས་བརྙན་**བཟླས་བརྗོད་དང་**སྟེ། འདི་ལ་ངེས་པ། བར་མ་ཆད་པ། ཚང་བ་གསུམ། དང་པོ་ཇི་ལྟར་དམ་བཅས་པ་ལྟར། གཉིས་པ་བཟླ་ཚེ་གཡལ་ལུ་མི་ཚིག་སོགས་ཀྱི་སྐྱོན་མེད་པ། གསུམ་པ་གྲངས་མཐར་ཕྱིན་པའོ། །ཕྱིའི་སྤྱོད་ལམ་ཕྱི་ནང་གི་ཁྲུས་སོགས་སྤྱོད་ཡུལ་དག་པའི་**གཙང་སྦྲ་དང་།** བྱ་བ་དང་འཇུག་པའི་**དུས་ཚིག་དང་།** **གཟའ་**ཕུར་བུ་སོགས་**དང་** **རྒྱུ་སྐར་**རྒྱལ་**ལ་སོགས་**རྩིས་ཀྱི་ལ་ཉེ་ཐམས་ཅད་པ་**གཙོ་བོར་**ཕྱིའི་**ཡོ་བྱད་**དང་། **རྒྱུ་**ལྟ་བ་དང་**རྐྱེན་**ཕྱི་ནང་གི་ཡོ་བྱད་སོགས་**ཚོགས་པའི་མཐུ་ལས་**དངོས་གྲུབ་**འགྲུབ་**པར་

འདོད་པའོ། །འདིར་དོན་དམ་སྐྱེ་འགག་མེད་པ་དང་། ཀུན་རྫོབ་ཏུ་ལྷར་བསྒོམ་པའི་ཚུལ་སོ་སོ་ཙམ་བསྟན་གྱིས། ཀུན་རྫོབ་ཀྱི་སྤྱོད་ཡུལ་ལ་དག་མ་དག་ཇི་ལྟར་བལྟ་བའི་ཚུལ་དང་། འབྲས་བུའི་ཁྱད་པར་དག་ནི་མ་གསུངས་ཏེ། འདིའི་དགོངས་པ་ནི། ཀུན་རྫོབ་ཏུ་ལྷར་བསྒོམ་མོ་ཞེས་གསུངས་པ་ཉིད་ཀྱིས། ཀུན་རྫོབ་ཏུ་ལྷར་བལྟའོ་ཞེས་སྨོས་མི་དགོས་ཏེ། ལྟ་བས་ཇི་ལྟར་བཅད་པ་བཞིན་དུ་ཏིང་ངེ་འཛིན་གྱིས་གོམས་པར་བྱེད་པ་ཡིན་ཏེ། གང་གི་ཕྱིར་ལྟ་བ་དང་སྒོམ་པ་ནི་འགལ་དུ་མི་རུང་སྟེ། རིག་པ་དང་ཆང་པར་ལྡན་དགོས་པའི་ཕྱིར་དང་། གསང་སྔགས་ཀྱི་གཞུང་དམིགས་པ་རྣམ་པར་དག་པའི་སྤྱོད་ཡུལ་ཅན་ཡིན་པའི་ཕྱིར་རོ། །གྲུབ་པའི་འབྲས་བུ་ནི། ཐུན་མོང་གི་ལས་དང་དངོས་གྲུབ་དག་མི་མཐུན་ཡང་། མཆོག་གི་དངོས་གྲུབ་བླ་ན་མེད་པའི་བྱང་ཆུབ་མཚུངས་པས་གུད་དུ་མ་སྨོས་སོ། །གཉིས་པ་ནི། གཉིས་ཀའི་རྒྱུད་ཀྱི་ཐེག་པ་ཞུགས་པ་རྣམས་ཀྱི་ལྟ་བ་ནི་དོན་དམ་པར་སྐྱེ་འགག་མེད་པ་ལས་ཀུན་རྫོབ་ཏུ་ལྷའི་གཟུགས་ཀྱི་སྐུར་བསྒོམ་ཞིང་དེ་ཉིད་རྣམ་པ་བཞི་དང་ལྡན་པར་བསྒོམ་པའི་ཏིང་ངེ་འཛིན་ཞེས་བདག་གི་དེ་ཁོ་ན་ཉིད་དང་། ལྷའི་དེ་ཁོ་ན་ཉིད་དང་། ཏིང་ངེ་འཛིན་གྱི་དེ་ཁོ་ན་ཉིད། བཟླས་པའི་དེ་ཁོ་ན་ཉིད་བཞི། དང་པོ་ནི་བདག་དམ་ཚིག་པར་བསྐྱེད་པའོ། །གཉིས་པ་ཡེ་ཤེས་པ་སྤྱན་དྲངས་ནས་སྣ་ཐད་བཞུགས་པའོ། །གསུམ་པ་ནི། བདག་མདུན་གྱི་ཐུགས་ཀ་ན་ཟླ་བ་དང་ཡིག་འབྲུ་བཀླག་སྔགས་བཀོད་པའོ། །བཞི་པ་ནི་དབུགས་དང་སྦྲད་དེ་ཕར་འཕྲོས་ཐུགས་དམ་བསྐུལ། ཚུར་བྱུང་དངོས་གྲུབ་སྟོལ་བའི་དམིགས་པ་དང་བཅས་སྐྲོན་བཙུ་སྦྲང་ལ་བཟླས་པའོ། །ནང་གི་ཏིང་འཛིན་དེ་**དང་།** ཕྱིའི་**ཡོ་བྱད་དང་རྒྱུ་རྐྱེན་**ཚོགས་པ་དང་དམ་ཚིག་མ་ཉམས་པ་**ལ་ལྟོས་པ་གཉིས་ཀ་བསྟེན་པ་ལས་**ཐུན་མོང་གི་གྲུབ་པ་དང་མཆོག་གི་རིགས་བཞི་རྡོ་རྗེ་འཆང་གི་ས་**འགྲུབ་**པར་འདོད་**པའོ། །གསུམ་པ་ལ་བསྟན་བཤད་གཉིས་ཀྱི། དང་པོ་ནི། ཆོས་ཉིད་ཀྱི་དོན་ལ་རིག་པ་རྣལ་འབྱོར་རྒྱུད་ཀྱི་ཐེག་པ་ལ་ཞུགས་པ་རྣམས་ཀྱི་ལྟ་བ་ནི་རྣམ་པ་གཉིས་ཏེ།** ཀུན་རྫོབ་ཏུ་བདག་དང་སངས་རྒྱས་མཉམ་པར་མི་ལྟ་བ་དང་། སྤྱོད་པ་མཉམ་པའི་བརྟུལ་ཞུགས་དང་དུ་མི་

ལེན་པ་ནི་**རྣལ་འབྱོར་ཕྱི་པ་**སྟེ་བསྲུང་མེད་ཀྱི་དམ་ཚིག་ཉམས་སུ་ལེན་མི་ནུས་པར་ཐུན་མོང་གི་སྡོམ་པ་རྣམས་དང་མ་བྲལ་བས་སམ་སྒོ་གསུམ་གསང་གསུམ་དུ་སྒོམ་ནས་མི་མཐུན་པའི་ཕྱོགས་ཀྱི་དབང་དུ་མི་འགྱུར་བས་ན་**ཐུབ་པ་རྒྱུད་ཀྱི་ཐེག་པ་དང་། གོང་ལས་བཟློག་སྟེ་རྣལ་འབྱོར་ནང་པ་**ཅིར་སྣང་བདེ་བ་ཆེན་པོར་དབང་སྒྱུར་བའི་**ཐབས**་མཁས་**ཀྱི་རྒྱུད་ཀྱི་ཐེག་པའོ། །གཉིས་པ་ལ་རྣལ་འབྱོར་ཕྱི་རྒྱུད་དང་། བླ་མེད་རྒྱུད་ཀྱི་རྣམ་བཞག་གཉིས། དང་པོ་ནི། དེ་ལ་རྣལ་འབྱོར་ཕྱི་པ་ཐུབ་པའི་རྒྱུད་ཀྱི་ཐེག་པ་ལ་ཞུགས་པ་རྣམས་ཀྱི་ལྟ་བ་ནི།** ཀྲི་ཡ་ལྟར་**ཕྱིའི་ཡོ་བྱད་ལ་གཙོ་བོར་མི་འཛིན་པར་དོན་དམ་པར་སྐྱེ་འགག་མེད་པའི་**རང་བཞིན་སྣང་ཆར་ཤར་བ་**ལྷ་དང་ལྷ་མོ་དང་། སྒོམ་པ་ལྟ་བ་དེ་དང་**རྣམ་པ་**འདྲ་བའི་རྒྱུད་ཡོངས་སུ་དག་པའི་ཏིང་ངེ་འཛིན་གྱིས་འཕགས་པའི་གཟུགས་ཀྱི་སྐུ་**ཞེས། དོན་དམ་པའི་ལྷ་དང་། སེམས་པའི་བྱེ་བྲག་གི་ལྷ་གཉིས་ནི། དོན་དམ་པ་དང་། ཀུན་རྫོབ་ཀྱི་སྣང་ཆའི་ལྷ་གཉིས་ཡིན་ལ། དེའི་ཆར་གཏོགས་པའི་རྒྱུ་མཐུན་པའི་ལྟར་བསྒོམ་པ་དམ་ཚིག་ཅན་གྱི་སྐྱེ་བོས་བརྟགས་པའི་ལྷ་སྟེ། དེ་ལྟར་གོམས་ན་བདེན་གཉིས་ལྷའི་རང་བཞིན་ཡིན་ཚུལ་མངོན་དུ་གྱུར་པར་བྱེད་པའི་ཏིང་ངེ་འཛིན་ལ་ཡང་མངོན་བྱང་ལྔ་དང་ཆོ་འཕྲུལ་ཆེན་པོ་བཞིའི་སྒོ་ནས་བསྐྱེད་ཅིང་**ཕྱག་རྒྱ་བཞི་དང་ལྡན་པར་**བྱ་སྟེ། སྐུ་ཕྱག་རྒྱ་ཆེན་པོ་སྐུ་དངོས་དང་། དེའི་རྒྱ་ཡིག་འབྲུ་དང་ཕྱག་མཚན་སོགས་སོ། །གསུང་ཆོས་ཀྱི་ཕྱག་རྒྱ་ལྷུགས་སྙིང་རྡོ་རྗེ་རྩེ་ལྔ་སོགས་བསྒོམ་པ། ཐུགས་དམ་རྒྱ་ལ་འཛིན་འཆང་གཉིས་ལས། འཛིན་པ་ཡེ་ཤེས་ལྔ་ཐུགས་སུ་ཆུད་པའི་རྟགས་རྡོ་རྗེ་རྩེ་ལྔ་སོགས་རྣམ་པ་དང་། འཆང་བ་རྡོར་དྲིལ། ཕྲིན་ལས་ལས་རྒྱ་ཐུགས་ཀར་ཧཱུྃ་སྙིང་རྡོ་རྗེ་རྒྱ་གྲམ་ལས་འོད་ཟེར་འཕྲོ་འདུས་འཕགས་པ་སྤྱན་དྲངས་པ་འགྲོ་བའི་དོན་བྱེད་པ་སོགས་ཏེ་དེ་དག་གིས་བདག་ཉིད་ཆེན་པོ་རྣམས་ཀྱི་སྐུ་གསུང་ཐུགས་ཕྲིན་ལས་དང་བཅས་པའི་ངང་ཚུལ་ལས་མི་འདའ་ཞིང་བརྩོན་པར་བྱེད་པའམ། དེ་དང་ངོ་བོ་གཅིག་པར་རྒྱས་འདེབས་པའི་ཚུལ་གྱིས་**བསྒོམས་པའི་**ནང་གི་**རྣལ་འབྱོར་གཙོ་བོར་བྱས་པ་ལས་**ཐུན་མོང་དང་མཆོག་གི་དངོས་གྲུབ་**འགྲུབ་**བར་འདོད་**པའོ།** །གཉིས་པ་ལ། བསྟན་བཤད་གཉིས་ལས།

དང་པོ་ནི། **རྣལ་འབྱོར་ནང་པ་ཐབས་ཀྱི་རྒྱུད་ཀྱི་ཐེག་པ་ལ་ཞུགས་པ་རྣམས་ཀྱི་ལྟ་བ**
ནི་རྣམ་པ་གསུམ་སྟེ། ཐབས་བསྐྱེད་པ་གཙོ་བོར་སྟོན་པ་**བསྐྱེད་པའི་ཚུལ་**མ་ཧཱ་ཡོ་ག་
དང་། ཤེས་རབ་རྫོགས་རིམ་ཤས་ཆེར་སྟོན་པ་**རྫོགས་པའི་ཚུལ་**ཨ་ནུ་ཡོ་ག་དང་།
གཉིས་མེད་ཟུང་འཇུག་གཙོ་བོར་སྟོན་པ་ཨ་ཏི་**རྫོགས་པ་ཆེན་པོའི་ཚུལ་ལོ།** །གཉིས་
པ་ལ། ཚུལ་གསུམ་སྤྱིར་བཤད་པ་དང་། དེ་ལ་འཇུག་པའི་སྒོ་བྱེ་བྲག་ཏུ་བཤད་པ
གཉིས་ལས། དང་པོ་ལ། བསྐྱེད་པ་དང་། རྫོགས་པ་དང་། རྫོགས་པ་ཆེན་
པོའི་ཚུལ་གསུམ་ལས། དང་པོ་ནི། **དེ་ལ་བསྐྱེད་པའི་ཚུལ་ནི།** ནང་རྒྱུད་
གསུམ་པོ་འདི་དག་གིས་བསྐྱེད་ན་ནི་ལྷ་ཡིན་ལ། མ་བསྐྱེད་ན་ལྷར་མི་ལྟ་བ་མ་ཡིན་
ཏེ། རྒྱུ་འབྲས་དབྱེར་མེད་པར་ལྷུན་གྱིས་གྲུབ་པའི་དཀྱིལ་འཁོར་དུ་ལྟ་བར་མཐུན་
པས་སོ། །འོན་ཀྱང་ཏིང་ངེ་འཛིན་གྱིས་རྩལ་སྦྱོང་བ་ལ་རིམ་གྱིས་སྦྱོང་བར་བྱ་བ་ཙམ་
དུ་ཟད་དོ། །དེ་ལ་ཆོས་ཐམས་ཅད་གཟུགས་བརྙན་གྱི་དཀྱིལ་འཁོར་དུ་སངས་རྒྱས་
པར་ལྟ་བ་ལ། རང་བཞིན་གྱི་སངས་རྒྱས་དང་། རྟོགས་པའི་སངས་རྒྱས་དང་།
གྲུབ་པའི་སངས་རྒྱས་གསུམ། དང་པོ་སེམས་ཅན་རྣམས་ཏེ། དེ་ལའང་། སྐྱེ་
བ་རྒྱུའི་སངས་རྒྱས། སྐྱེ་བ་རྟེན་པའི་སངས་རྒྱས། སྐྱེ་བ་མངོན་པར་གྲུབ་པའི་
སངས་རྒྱས་སོ། །དེའི་དང་པོ་ལུས་འགྲུབ་པའི་རྒྱུ་ཁུ་རྡུལ་སེམས་གསུམ།
གཉིས་པ་ཕ་མ་གཉིས་ཀྱི་ལུས་སེམས་ཀྱི་ཁམས་ཐམས་ཅད། གསུམ་པ་རང་གི་
ལུས་མངོན་པར་གྲུབ་པའི་སྐབས་ཏེ། དེ་གསུམ་པོ་ཀུན་ཏུ་རང་བཞིན་གྱིས་སངས་
རྒྱས་པའོ། །གཉིས་པ་རྟོགས་པའི་སངས་རྒྱས་ནི་རིག་འཛིན་གྱི་ས་ལ་གནས་པ་
རྣམས་སོ། །གསུམ་པ་གྲུབ་པའི་སངས་རྒྱས་ནི་དེ་ཉིད་མངོན་དུ་གཟིགས་པའོ། །
འདི་རྣམས་ཀྱང་རང་བཞིན་དང་གནས་སྐབས་ཀྱི་བྱེ་བྲག་ཏུ་འདོད་དོ། །དེས་ན་
སངས་མ་རྒྱས་པའི་ཆོས་མ་དམིགས་ཀྱང་། མ་རྟོགས་པ་རྟོགས་པར་བྱ་བ་དང་།
མ་གོམས་པ་གོམས་པར་བྱ་བའི་ཕྱིར། སངས་རྒྱས་ཀྱི་ས་གསུམ་ལ་བློ་སྦྱོང་བར་
འདོད་དེ། དེ་ཡང་ཀུན་ཏུ་འོད་ཀྱི་ས་ལ་བློ་སྦྱོང་བའི་ཕྱིར་དེ་བཞིན་ཉིད་ཀྱི་ཏིང་ངེ་
འཛིན་རྣམ་པར་མི་རྟོག་པ་སྒོམ་པ་དང་། པདྨ་ཅན་གྱི་ས་ལ་གོམས་པར་བྱ་བའི་ཕྱིར་

ཀུན་ཏུ་སྣང་བའི་ཏིང་ངེ་འཛིན་ཤེས་རབ་དང་སྙིང་རྗེ་འབྲེལ་བ་དང་། ཡི་གེ་འཁོར་ལོ་
ཚོགས་ཆེན་གྱི་ས་ལ་གོམས་པར་བྱ་བའི་ཕྱིར་རྒྱུའི་ཏིང་ངེ་འཛིན་ཡིག་འབྲུ་བསྒོམ་པ་སྟེ་
ཏིང་ངེ་འཛིན་རྣམ་པ་གསུམ་རིམ་གྱིས་བསྐྱེད་དེ། དེ་གོམས་པ་ན་རྟེན་དང་བརྟེན་པའི་
དཀྱིལ་འཁོར་རིམ་གྱིས་བཀོད་ཅིང་བསྒོམས་པས་འགྲུབ་པར་འདོད་**པའོ། །གཉིས་**
པ་ནི། རྫོགས་པའི་ཚུལ་ཨ་ནུ་ཡོ་ག་**ནི།** རྣལ་འབྱོར་རྒྱུད་ཀྱི་གཞུང་ལས་གྲགས་
པའི་སྒོམ་ཞིང་ཉམས་སུ་བླང་བར་བྱ་བའི་དོན་ཐམས་ཅད། བྱང་ཆུབ་སེམས་ཀྱི་རང་
བཞིན་རིག་པ་སྐད་ཅིག་མ་གཅིག་ལ་རྫོགས་པར་གསལ་བར་སྒོམ་ནུས་པའི་དབང་དུ་
གསུངས་པ་སྟེ། དེ་ཡང་གཉིས་ལས་མ་གཡོས་བཞིན་དུ་གཅིག་ཏུ་གསལ།
གཅིག་ཏུ་དབྱེར་མེད་བཞིན་དུ་གསུམ་དུ་མ་འདྲེས་པ་སྟེ། རྒྱ་མཚོ་ལ་གཟའ་སྐར་ཤར་
བའམ། རྫུ་འཕྲུལ་ཅན་གྱི་སྤྱོད་ལམ་བཞི་དུས་གཅིག་ཏུ་སྟོན་པ་བཞིན་ནོ། །དེ་ལ་
དོན་དམ་པར་སྐྱེ་འགག་མེད་པའི་རང་བཞིན་དུ་ལྷུན་གྱིས་གྲུབ་པའི་གཟུགས་བརྙན་གྱི་
དཀྱིལ་འཁོར་**ལྷ་དང་ལྷ་མོ**་ཡི་རང་བཞིན་སྣང་སྲིད་ཐམས་ཅད་སངས་རྒྱས་པའི་
དགོངས་དོན་ལས་མ་གཡོས་པ་**དང**་གཅིག །མཐའ་གང་དུ་ཡང་**རྣམ་པར་མི་རྟོག**
པའི་དོན་དབུ་མ་ཆོས་ཀྱི་དབྱིངས་ལས་ཀྱང་མ་གཡོས་པ་གཉིས་ནི་མ་གཡོས་པ་གཉིས་
ཞེས་བྱ་**ལ།** དེ་ལས་མ་གཡོས་བཞིན་དུ་**ཀུན་རྫོབ་ཏུ**་ཕུང་ཁམས་སྐྱེ་མཆེད་ཐམས་
ཅད་ལྷག་པའི་ཏིང་ངེ་འཛིན་གྱིས་དཀྱིལ་འཁོར་**འཕགས་པའི་གཟུགས་ཀྱི་སྐུའང་གསལ**
བར་བསྒོམས་པ་ནི། གསལ་བ་གཅིག་ཞེས་བྱ་**ཞིང་།** ཅིར་སྣང་ཅི་སྒོམ་ཐམས་
ཅད་ཆོས་ཉིད་བྱང་ཆུབ་སེམས་སྐྱེ་འགག་མེད་པའི་དབྱིངས་སུ་**མཉམ**་པ་ནི་གཅིག་ཏུ་
དབྱེར་མེད་ཞེས་བྱ་**ལ།** **མ་འདྲེས་པ**་གསུམ་ནི། ཐམས་ཅད་ལྷུན་གྱིས་གྲུབ་པའི་
དཀྱིལ་འཁོར་དུ་བསྒོམ་པའང་ཏིང་ངེ་འཛིན་གཞན་དང་མ་འདྲེས། ལྷག་ཏིང་གི་
དཀྱིལ་འཁོར་དུ་སྐུ་མདོག་ཕྱག་མཚན་སོགས་གསལ་བ་ཡང་གཞན་དང་མ་འདྲེས།
གཙོ་གཟུངས་འཁོར་གྱི་དཀྱིལ་འཁོར་དང་བཅས་པ་སོ་སོར་མ་འདྲེས་པར་བྱང་ཆུབ་
སེམས་ཀྱི་རང་བཞིན་རིག་པ་སྐད་ཅིག་མ་གཅིག་ལ་གསལ་བ་སྟེ། དེ་ལྟར་**སྒོམ་པས**
འགྲུབ་བོ། །དེ་ཡང་བརྩལ་མེད་ལྷུན་གྱིས་གྲུབ་པར་སྟོན་ནུས་ཤིང་། ཕྱོགས་

དུས་མཉམ་པ་ཉིད་དུ་སྦྱོར་ནུས་ན་ནི་རྫོགས་ཆེན་དང་ཁྱད་མེད་ཀྱང་། འདིར་སྦྱོར་བ་རྩོལ་བ་དང་བཅས་པ་དང་། རིག་པ་ཕྱོགས་སུ་སྦྱོར། སྐད་ཅིག་མ་དུས་སུ་སྦྱོར་ཏེ་སྐད་ཅིག་ལ་དོན་ཐམས་ཅད་རྫོགས་པར་སྨྲ་རོ། །བསྐྱེད་རྫོགས་འདི་གཉིས་ཀྱི་སྐབས་སུ་ལམ་སྒོམ་ཚུལ་ཙམ་ལས། སྤྱིའི་ལྟ་བ་དང་འབྲས་བུའི་ཁྱད་པར་མ་གསུངས་པ་ནི། དགོངས་པ་གོང་དུ་བསྟན་པ་ལྟར། དོན་དམ་པར་སྐྱེ་འགག་མེད་པ་དང་། ཀུན་རྫོབ་སྒྱུ་མ་ཡོངས་སུ་དག་པའི་ལྷའི་དཀྱིལ་འཁོར་དུ་ལྟ་བ་དང་། བདེན་གཉིས་དབྱེར་མེད་པར་ལྟ་བ་དང་། འབྲས་བུ་བླ་མེད་ཀྱི་བྱང་ཆུབ་ལ་ཐེག་ཆེན་ཐམས་ཅད་ཁྱད་མེད་པས་དབྱེ་མི་དགོས་སོ་ཞེས་དགོངས་པའོ། །གསུམ་པ་རྫོགས་པ་ཆེན་པོའི་ཚུལ་ནི། དེ་ལ་རྫོགས་པ་ཆེན་པོ་ནི་དོན་དང་ཚུལ་གཉིས་ལས། དོན་ནི་ཆོས་ཐམས་ཅད་རང་བྱུང་གི་ཡེ་ཤེས་བྱང་ཆུབ་ཀྱི་རང་བཞིན་དུ་བསྟན་པ་ཡིན་ལ། ཚུལ་ནི་དེ་ལ་འཇུག་པའི་ཐབས་དང་སྒོ་སྟེ། དེ་གཉིས་མདོར་བསྟན་པར་དགོངས་ནས། **འཇིག་རྟེན་དང་འཇིག་རྟེན་ལས་འདས་པའི་ཆོས་**ཀུན་རྫོབ་དང་དོན་དམ་རང་མཚན་དང་སྤྱི་མཚན། དཀར་པོ་དང་ནག་པོ་སོགས་འདི་དང་འདིའོ་ཞེས་དབྱེ་བ་ཇི་སྙེད་པ་**ཐམས་ཅད་**རྣམ་**དབྱེར་མེད་པར་**ཏེ་གང་དུ་དབྱེར་མེད་ན་**སྐུ་གསུང་ཐུགས་ཀྱི་དཀྱིལ་འཁོར་གྱི་རང་བཞིན་**དུ་དབྱེར་མེད་དེ་དཔེར་ན་འཇིག་རྟེན་ཕལ་པ་དང་། ཕྱི་རོལ་མུ་སྟེགས་ཅན་གྱིས་རྣམ་པར་བཞག་པའི་ཐ་སྙད་ཀྱི་མཚན་ཉིད་ཐམས་ཅད་དང་། གང་ཟག་གི་མཚན་ཉིད་ཐམས་ཅད་ཀྱང་། སངས་རྒྱས་པའི་ཆོས་སུ་བསྡུས་ཏེ་བསྟན་པ་བཞིན་ནོ། །ཇི་ལྟར་དབྱེར་མེད་ན་དེའི་རང་བཞིན་**ཡེ་ནས་ཡིན་པར་རྟོགས་ནས་བསྒོམ་པ་**ཡིན་པའི་ཕྱིར་ཏེ་ཞེས་ཚུལ་མདོར་བསྟན་ནས། **དེ་ཡང་རྒྱུད་**གསང་བ་སྙིང་པོ་**ལས།** སྐུ་གསུང་ཐུགས་རྡོ་རྗེའི་རང་བཞིན་ཡིན་པས་རྡོ་རྗེའི་སྒྲས་བསྟན་ཏེ། **རྡོ་རྗེ་ཕུང་པོའི་ཡན་ལག་ནི། །རྫོགས་པའི་སངས་རྒྱས་ལྔ་རུ་གྲགས། །སྐྱེ་མཆེད་ཁམས་རྣམས་མང་པོ་ཀུན། །བྱང་ཆུབ་སེམས་དཔའི་དཀྱིལ་འཁོར་ཉིད། །ས་ཆུ་སྤྱན་དང་མ་མ་ཀཱི། །མེ་རླུང་གོས་དཀར་སྒྲོལ་མ་སྟེ། །ནམ་མཁའ་དབྱིངས་ཀྱི་དབང་ཕྱུག་མ། །སྲིད་གསུམ་ཡེ་ནས་རྣམ་པར་དག** །ཞེས་འབྱུང་སྟེ། དེའི་

དོན་སློབ་དཔོན་གྱིས་རྣམ་པར་སྤྲུར་བར་མཛད་པ། **འཁོར་བ་དང་མྱ་ངན་ལས་འདས་པའི་ཆོས་ཐམས་ཅད་**རིག་པ་བྱང་ཆུབ་སེམས་ཀྱི་རང་བཞིན་ཡིན་པས་**ཡེ་ནས་མ་སྐྱེས་ལ་**སྐྱེ་མེད་སྟོང་པ་ཆེན་པོར་གནས་བཞིན་སྣང་ཆ་རྣམས་འགགས་མེད་དུ་ཤར་བའི་ས་སོགས་རང་རང་གི་**བྱ་བ་བྱེད་ནུས་པའི་སྒྱུ་མ་**རྣམས་**བདེ་བར་གཤེགས་པ་ཡབ་ཡུམ་བཅུ་**དང་སེམས་དཔའ་སེམས་དཔའ་སེམས་མ་**ལ་སྩོགས་པའི་རང་བཞིན་**ལམ་གྱིས་བཅོས་ཤིང་བསྒྱུར་བ་ལྟ་བུ་མ་ཡིན་པར་**ཡེ་ནས་ཡིན་པའི་ཕྱིར།** **ཆོས་ཐམས་ཅད་རང་བཞིན་གྱིས་མྱ་ངན་ལས་འདས་པ་སྟེ།** ས་སོགས་འབྱུང་བ་**ཆེན་པོ་ལྔ་ནི་ཡུམ་ལྔའི་རང་བཞིན་**ཏེ་ས་སངས་རྒྱས་སྤྱན་མ། ཆུ་མཱ་མ་ཀཱི། མེ་གོས་དཀར་མོ། རླུང་དམ་ཚིག་སྒྲོལ་མ། ནམ་མཁའ་དབྱིངས་ཕྱུག་མའོ། །དེ་བཞིན་དུ་**ཕུང་པོ་ལྔ་ནི་རིགས་ལྔའི་སངས་རྒྱས་**ཏེ། རྣམ་ཤེས་མི་བསྐྱོད་པ། ཚོར་བ་རིན་འབྱུང་། འདུ་ཤེས་སྣང་མཐའ། འདུ་བྱེད་དོན་གྲུབ། གཟུགས་རྣམ་སྣང་ངོ་། །**རྣམ་པར་ཤེས་པ་བཞི་ནི་བྱང་ཆུབ་སེམས་དཔའ་བཞིའི་རང་བཞིན་**ཏེ། མིག་ཤེས་ས་སྙིང་། རྣ་ཤེས་ཕྱག་རྡོར། སྣ་ཤེས་ནམ་སྙིང་། ལྕེ་ཤེས་སྤྱན་རས་གཟིགས་སོ། །**ཡུལ་བཞི་ནི་**ཤེས་བཞིར་དགྲེས་བསྐྱེད་**མཛེས་པའི་ལྷ་མོ་བཞིའི་རང་བཞིན་**ཏེ། གཟུགས་སྒེག་མོ། སྒྲ་གླུ་མ། དྲི་ཕྲེང་བ་མ། རོ་གར་མའོ། **དབང་པོ་བཞི་ནི་བྱང་ཆུབ་སེམས་དཔའ་བཞིའི་རང་བཞིན་**ཏེ། མིག་དབང་བྱམས་པ། རྣ་དབང་སྒྲིབ་སེལ། སྣ་དབང་ཀུན་བཟང་། ལྕེ་དབང་འཇམ་དཔལ་ལོ། **།དུས་བཞི་ནི་མཆོད་པའི་ལྷ་མོ་བཞིའི་རང་བཞིན་**ཏེ། དུས་འདས་པ་ནི་བདུག་སྤོས་མ། ད་ལྟར་ནི་པུཥྤེ་མ། མ་འོངས་པ་ནི་སྣང་གསལ་མ། འབྱུང་བར་མ་ངེས་པ་ནི་དྲི་ཆབ་མའོ། **།ལུས་ཀྱི་དབང་པོ་དང་རྣམ་པར་ཤེས་པ་དང་།** **ཡུལ་**རེག་བྱ་དང་**དེ་ལས་བྱུང་བའི་**རེག་པ་སྟེ། བདེ་ཆེན་**བྱང་ཆུབ་ཀྱི་སེམས་ནི་ཁྲོ་བོ་བཞིའི་རང་བཞིན་**ཏེ། དེ་ཡང་ལུས་དབང་གི་གསང་བའི་རྡོ་རྗེ་ཡུལ་དང་ཕྲད་པས་དབང་ཤེས་གཞན་བཅོམ་ཤིང་མི་གནས་པར་བྱེད་པའི་ཕྱིར་སྟོབས་ཆེན་ཁྲོ་བོ་བཞིར་བཞག་སྟེ། རེག་པ་བདུད་རྩི་འཁྱིལ། རེག་བྱེད་ཀྱི་ལུས་དབང་རྟ་མགྲིན། རེག་ཡུལ་སྟོབས་ཆེན། རེག་

ཞེས་གཤིན་རྗེ་གཤེད་དོ། **།རྟག་ཆད་མུ་བཞི་ནི་ཁྲོ་མོ་བཞིའི་རང་བཞིན་ཏེ།** རྟག་པར་ལྟ་བ་གནས་སུ་དག་པ་ལྕགས་ཀྱུ་མ། དེ་བཞིན་དུ་ཆད་པར་ལྟ་བ་ཞགས་པ་མ། བདག་ཏུ་ལྟ་བ་ལྕགས་སྒྲོགས་མ། མཚན་མར་ལྟ་བ་དྲིལ་བུ་མའོ། **།ཡིད་ཀྱི་རྣམ་པར་ཤེས་པ་ནི་བྱང་ཆུབ**་ཀྱི་རང་བཞིན་ཅན་གྱི་**སེམས**་མི་ཕྱེད་པ་**རྡོ་རྗེ**་ལྟ་བུ་ཐམས་ཅད་དུ་དོར་བྱའི་ཆོས་མེད་པའི་**ཀུན་ཏུ་བཟང་པོའི་རང་བཞིན།** ཡིད་དེའི་**ཡུལ་ཆོས་འདུས་བྱས་དང་འདུས་མ་བྱས་ནི་ཆོས་བྱ་བ་མོ་ཀུན་ཏུ་བཟང་མོའི་རང་བཞིན་ཏེ།** **དེ་དག་ཀྱང་ཡེ་ནས་མངོན་པར་རྫོགས་པར་སངས་རྒྱས་པའི་རང་བཞིན་ཡིན་གྱི།** **དེ་ལམ་གྱིས**་གསར་དུ་**བསྒྲུབ་པ་ནི་མ་ཡིན་ནོ།** །དེ་ལྟར་རང་གི་རྒྱུད་ཀྱི་གཞུང་དྲངས་ནས། དེ་དང་མཐུན་པའི་ལུང་གཞན་དག་དྲངས་པའི་ཕྱིར། དཀྱིལ་འཁོར་གསུམ་དུ་སྣང་བའང་རྩ་བ་བྱང་ཆུབ་ཀྱི་སེམས་རང་བྱུང་གི་ཡེ་ཤེས་ཐིག་ལེ་ཉག་གཅིག་ཏུ་བསྟན་པ་**དེ་ལྟར་ཕྱོགས་བཅུ་དུས་གསུམ་དང་ཁམས་གསུམ་ལ་སོགས་པ་འདུས་བྱས་དང་འདུས་མ་བྱས་པའི་ཆོས་ཐམས་ཅད་རང་གི་སེམས་ལས་གུད་ན་མེད་དེ་ཇི་སྐད་དུ།** ཁམས་གསུམ་རྣམ་རྒྱལ་གྱི་རྟོགས་པ་ལས། **རང་སེམས**་ཕྱིན་ཅི་མ་ལོག་པའམ། བློའི་རྩལ་བཞིན་དུ་**སོ་སོར་རྟོགས་པ་ནི།** **སངས་རྒྱས**་དང་**བྱང་ཆུབ**་སེམས་དཔའ་སོགས་**དེ་ཉིད་དོ**་ཞེས་རྟོགས་ན་སངས་རྒྱས། མ་རྟོགས་ན་འཁོར་བའི་སྣོད་བཅུད་དུ་སྣང་སྟེ་**འཇིག་རྟེན་གསུམ་པོ་དེ་ཉིད་དོ།** **།འབྱུང་བ་ཆེ་རྣམས་དེ་ཉིད་དོ།** **།ཞེས་འབྱུང་ངོ་།** **།ཇི་སྐད་དུ**་གསང་བ་འདུས་པ་ལས། **ཆོས་ཐམས་ཅད་ནི་སེམས་ལ་གནས་སོ།** **།ཞེས་ཅིར་སྣང་རང་སེམས་ཀྱི་སྣང་བ་ཙམ་དུ་ཟད་ལ།** **སེམས་ནི་ནམ་མཁའ་ལ་གནས་སོ།** ཞེས་སེམས་ཀྱི་རང་བཞིན་སྐྱེ་མེད་ནམ་མཁའ་དང་འདྲའོ་ཞེས་སོ། **།ནམ་མཁའ་ནི**་མཚན་ཉིད་ཐམས་ཅད་དང་བྲལ་བས་**ཅི་ལའང་མི་གནས་སོ།** **།ཞེས་འབྱུང་བ་དང་།** ལུང་གཞན་ལས་ཀྱང་། **ཆོས་ཐམས་ཅད་ནི**་ཆོས་ཅན་དང་ཆོས་ཉིད་རྣམ་པར་སྒྲུབ་པ་དང་བྲལ་བས་འདི་ལ་འདིས་སྟོང་ཞེས་རྣམ་བཞག་བྲལ་བས་**ངོ་བོ་ཉིད་ཀྱིས་སྟོང་པའོ།** **།ཆོས་ཐམས་ཅད་ནི**་ཉོན་མོངས་པའི་དྲི་མ་ཉིད་ཡེ་ནས་གྲུབ་མ་མྱོང་བས་**གདོད་མ་ནས་རྣམ་པར་དག་པའོ།** **།ཆོས་ཐམས་ཅད་ནི**

སྒྲིབ་པའི་མུན་པ་ཉིད་ཡེ་ནས་མ་གྲུབ་པས་**ཡོངས་ཀྱིས་འོད་གསལ་བའོ།** །**ཆོས་ཐམས་ཅད་ནི་**མི་མཐུན་པ་དང་གཉེན་པོ་གཉིས་སུ་མེད་པས་**རང་བཞིན་གྱིས་མྱ་ངན་ལས་འདས་པའོ།** །**ཆོས་ཐམས་ཅད་ནི་**སྒྲིབ་གཉིས་བྲི་བ་དང་ཚོགས་གཉིས་བསགས་པ་བྲལ་བས་**མངོན་པར་རྫོགས་པར་སངས་རྒྱས་པའོ།** །**ཞེས་གསུངས་སོ།** །**འདི་ནི་རྫོགས་པ་ཆེན་པོའོ། །སྐབས་འདིར་རྩ་བའི་མཆན་སྙིང་གྲུབ། རྫོགས་པ་ཆེན་པོའི་ཚུལ་ནི། བསོད་ནམས་དང་ཡེ་ཤེས་ཀྱི་ཚོགས་རྫོགས་པ། འབྲས་བུའི་ཆོས་ལྷུན་གྱིས་གྲུབ་པའི་ཚུལ་འདི་ནི་དོན་ལ་འཇུག་པའོ། །ཞེས་ཀྱང་འབྱུང་ངོ་། །གཉིས་པ་ལ་འང་། རྟོགས་པ་བཞི་དང་། མཚན་ཉིད་གསུམ་དང་། ཡན་ལག་བཞི་དང་། དཀྱིལ་འཁོར་དུ་འཇུག་པའི་རིམ་པ་སྐྱེ་ཚུལ་བཞིས་བཤད་དེ། དེ་ཡང་རྟོགས་པ་བཞི་ཡུལ་གྱི་ཚུལ་ཏེ་མཚན་གཞིར་བཞག མཚན་ཉིད་གསུམ་ཐབས་ཀྱི་ཚུལ་ཏེ་དེའི་མཚན་ཉིད་དུ་བཞག །བསྙེན་སྒྲུབ་བཞི་ནི་འབྲས་བུའི་ཚུལ་ཏེ་ལ་བརྟན་པའི་མན་ངག་ཏུ་བཞག །ལྷུན་གྱིས་གྲུབ་པའི་དཀྱིལ་འཁོར་དུ་འཇུག་པའི་ཚུལ་ནི་འཇུག་རིམ་དུ་བཞག་གོ །དེ་ལའང་རྒྱུ་གཅིག་པ་དང་ཡིག་འབྲུའི་ཚུལ་གཉིས་ནི་ཡུལ་གྱི་ཚུལ། བྱིན་གྱིས་བརླབས་པར་རྟོགས་པ་ནི་ཐབས་ཀྱི་ཚུལ། མངོན་སུམ་པར་རྟོགས་པ་ནི་འབྲས་བུའི་ཚུལ་ལོ། །དེ་བཞིན་དུ་མཚན་ཉིད་གསུམ་ལ་ཡང་། ཤེས་པའི་མཚན་ཉིད་ནི་ཡུལ་གྱི་ཚུལ། འཇུག་པའི་མཚན་ཉིད་ནི་ཐབས་ཀྱི་ཚུལ། འབྲས་བུའི་མཚན་ཉིད་ནི་འབྲས་བུའི་ཚུལ་ལོ། །བསྙེན་སྒྲུབ་བཞི་ལ་ཡང་། བསྙེན་པ་ནི་ཡུལ་གྱི་ཚུལ། ཉེ་བར་བསྙེན་པ་དང་སྒྲུབ་པ་ནི་ཐབས་ཀྱི་ཚུལ། སྒྲུབ་པ་ཆེན་པོ་ནི་འབྲས་བུའི་ཚུལ་ལོ། །དེ་བཞིན་དུ་འཇུག་རིམ་གསུམ་ལ་ཡང་། ཐོས་པས་མིག་ཕྱེ་བ་ནི་ཡུལ་གྱི་ཚུལ། གོམས་པར་བྱེད་པས་དཀྱིལ་འཁོར་དུ་ཞུགས་པ་ནི་ཐབས་ཀྱི་ཚུལ། གོམས་པའི་མཐུས་མངོན་དུ་གྱུར་པས་དངོས་གྲུབ་ཆེན་པོ་ཐོབ་པ་ནི་འབྲས་བུའི་ཚུལ་ལོ། །དེ་ལྟར་ངེས་པར་བྱས་ནས། དང་པོ་ནི། ཚོགས་གཉིས་རྫོགས་པས་རྫོགས་པ་**ཞེས་བྱ་ལ། དེ་ཡང་ཐེག་པ་འོག་མ་ལྟར་བགྲོད་ཅིང་སྤྱོང་བ་ལ་ལྟོས་པ་མ་ཡིན་གྱི། སྐུ་གསུང་ཐུགས་འབྲས་བུའི་ཆོས་

སུ་གདོད་ནས་ལྷུན་གྱིས་གྲུབ་པས་ཆེན་པོའི་སྡེ་དེའི་དོན་ལ་འཇུག་པའི་ཐབས་དང་སྒོ་ནི་ཚུལ་ཏེ། དེ་ནི་རྟོགས་པ་རྣམ་པ་བཞིའི་ལམ་གྱིས་ཡིད་ཆེས་པར་བྱ་དགོས་ཏེ། རྟོགས་པ་བཞི་ནི། ཐུ་རྒྱུད་ལེའུ་བཅུ་གཅིག་པ་ལས། རྒྱུ་གཅིག་པ་དང་ཡིག་འབྲུའི་ཚུལ། བྱིན་གྱིས་རླབས་དང་མངོན་སུམ་པ། །རབ་ཏུ་རྟོགས་པ་རྣམ་བཞི་ཡིས། །ཐམས་ཅད་མངོན་རྫོགས་རྒྱལ་པོ་ཆེ། །ཞེས་གསུངས་པ་ལྟར། རྒྱུ་གཅིག་པར་རྟོགས་པ་དང་། ཡིག་འབྲུའི་ཚུལ་གྱིས་རྟོགས་པ་དང་། བྱིན་གྱིས་རླབས་ཀྱིས་རྟོགས་པ་དང་། མངོན་སུམ་པར་རྟོགས་པའོ། །དེ་ཡང་རྟོགས་པ་བཞི་འདི་ལ་རིམ་ཅིག་ཅར་གཉིས་ཀྱི་བཤད་པ་འབྱུང་ཡང་འདིར་རྫོགས་པ་ཆེན་པོ་རང་བྱུང་གི་ཡེ་ཤེས་ཐིག་ལེ་ཉག་གཅིག་ཏུ་གཏན་ལ་ཕེབས་པས་ཅིག་ཆར་བ་ལྟར་དུ་བཤད་དོ། དེ་ལ་རྒྱུ་སྟེ་རང་བཞིན་ནམ་གཞི་གཅིག་པར་རྟོགས་པ་ནི་ཆོས་ཐམས་ཅད་དོན་དམ་པར་མ་སྐྱེས་པས་ཞེས་མ་སྐྱེས་པའི་རང་བཞིན་དུ་སོ་སོ་མ་ཡིན་པ་དང་། ཀུན་རྫོབ་ཏུ་སྣང་བ་བདེན་སྟོང་སྒྱུ་མའི་མཚན་ཉིད་དུ་སོ་སོ་མ་ཡིན་པ་ནི་ཐེག་པ་ཆེན་པོ་ཐུན་མོང་དུ་གྲགས་པ་དང་། མ་སྐྱེས་པ་ཉིད་མ་སྐྱེས་བཞིན་དུ་ཆུ་ཟླ་ལྟར་རྒྱུ་དག་མ་དག་སྣ་ཚོགས་སུ་སྣང་ཞིང་རང་རང་གི་བྱ་བ་བྱེད་ནུས་པ་དང་། སྒྱུ་མ་ལྟར་སྣང་བ་ཉིད་སྣང་བཞིན་དུའང་ངོ་བོ་མེད་དེ་མ་སྐྱེས་པས་ན་ཀུན་རྫོབ་དང་དོན་དམ་པར་དབྱེར་མེད་པས་ཟུང་འཇུག་རང་བྱུང་གི་ཡེ་ཤེས་རྒྱུ་གཅིག་པར་རྟོགས་པ་ནི་ལུང་ཟབ་མོ་ལས་གྲགས་པའི་ཐུན་མོང་མ་ཡིན་པའོ། །མདོར་ན་རང་བྱུང་ཡེ་ཤེས་བྱང་ཆུབ་སེམས་ཀྱི་ངོ་བོ་སྣང་སྟོང་དབྱེར་མི་ཕྱེད་པའི་རང་བཞིན་ཡིན་ལ། འཁོར་འདས་ཐམས་ཅད་དེའི་ཚུལ་གཅིག་ལས་མི་འདའ་བ་ནི་རྒྱུ་གཅིག་པའོ། །ཡིག་འབྲུའི་ཚུལ་གྱིས་རྟོགས་པ་ནི། དེ་ལྟ་བུའི་སྣང་སྟོང་དབྱེར་མེད་ཀྱི་རང་བཞིན་དེ་ཉིད་ཀྱང་གདོད་མ་ནས་སྐུ་གསུང་ཐུགས་འབྲས་བུའི་ཆོས་སུ་སངས་རྒྱས་པར་བསྟན་པ་སྟེ། དེ་ལ་ཆོས་ཐམས་ཅད་མ་སྐྱེས་པ་ནི་ཨ་ཡིས་མཚོན་ཏེ་གསུང་གི་རང་བཞིན། མ་སྐྱེས་པ་ཉིད་སྒྱུ་མར་སྣང་ཞིང་བྱ་བ་བྱེད་ནུས་པ་ནི་ཨོཾ་ཡིས་མཚོན་ཏེ་སྐུའི་རང་བཞིན། དེ་ལྟར་རྟོགས་པའི་རིག་པ་སྒྱུ་མའི་ཡེ་ཤེས་མཐའ་དབུས་མེད་པ་ནི་ཧཱུཾ་གྱིས་མཚོན་ཏེ་ཐུགས་ཀྱི་རང་

བཞིན་དུ་རྟོགས་པའོ། །དེ་ཡང་གདོད་ནས་སྣང་སྟོང་ཟུང་འཇུག་གི་ཡེ་ཤེས་དེ་ལ་བསལ་བཞག་གི་བྲི་གང་ནམ་ཡང་མེད་ཅིང་། དེ་ཉིད་རང་བཞིན་རྣམ་པར་དག་པས་འཁོར་བ་ཡེ་སངས་ཆེན་པོ་ཡིན་ལ། དེ་ཉིད་ཀྱི་རོལ་པ་ནི་གདོད་ནས་དཀྱིལ་འཁོར་གསུམ་དུ་གནས་པ་ཡིན་པར་ནི་ཡིག་འབྲུའི་ཚུལ་གྱིས་རྟོགས་པའོ། །བྱིན་གྱིས་རླབས་ཀྱིས་རྟོགས་པ་ནི། རྟོགས་པ་རྣམ་པ་གཉིས་པོ་དེའི་མཐུ་དང་བྱིན་རླབས་ཞེས་པ་སྟེ། དཔེར་ན་རས་དཀར་པོ་ལ་དམར་པོར་བྱིན་གྱིས་རློབ་པའི་མཐུ་བཙོད་ལ་ཡོད་པ་བཞིན་དུ། ཆོས་ཐམས་ཅད་གདོད་ནས་སངས་རྒྱས་པར་བྱིན་གྱིས་རློབ་པའི་མཐུ་ཡང་རྒྱུ་གཅིག་པ་དང་ཡིག་འབྲུའི་ཚུལ་གྱི་མཐུས་བྱིན་གྱིས་བརླབས་པར་ཞེས་ཤིང་རྟོགས་པའོ། །དེ་ལ་ཆོས་ཐམས་ཅད་ཡེ་ནས་སངས་རྒྱས་པ་ཡིན་མོད་ཀྱི་རྟོགས་པ་གཉིས་དང་མི་ལྡན་པ་རྣམས་ལ། དེས་ཕན་འདོགས་པར་མི་འགྱུར་ལ། དེ་གཉིས་དང་ལྡན་ན་ནི་ཕན་ཐོགས་པར་སྣང་བར་འགྱུར་བས། རྟོགས་པ་གཉིས་ཀྱི་མཐུས་ཆོས་ཐམས་ཅད་ཡེ་ནས་སངས་རྒྱས་པར་བྱིན་གྱིས་རློབས་པ་ལྟར་སྣང་བར་འགྱུར་པས་བྱིན་གྱིས་རློབས་པར་རྟོགས་པ་ཞེས་བྱའོ། །མངོན་སུམ་པར་རྟོགས་པ་ནི། སྤྱིར་དབང་པོའི་མངོན་སུམ་སོགས་ཡོད་ཀྱང་འདིར་ཤེས་རབ་ཀྱི་དབང་པོའི་མངོན་སུམ་སྟེ། དེ་ཡང་སོ་སོར་རྟོགས་པའི་ཤེས་རབ་ཉིད་ལ་གོ་བར་བྱ་སྟེ། ཆོས་ཐམས་ཅད་ཡེ་ནས་སངས་རྒྱས་པར་གནས་པ་དེ་ཡང་ཡིད་ཆེས་པའི་ལུང་དང་བླ་མ་བརྒྱུད་པའི་མན་ངག་དང་འགལ་བ་ཡང་མ་ཡིན་ལ་སྟེ། དཔེར་ན་བསྲེག་བཅད་བརྡར་བས་གསེར་ཡིན་མིན། སྐྱོན་ཡོད་མེད་གསེར་བཟང་ངན་ཞེས་པ་བཞིན་དུ། ལུང་གིས་སྒྲོ་ལ་མི་འཁྲུལ། ལུང་ལ་དྲང་ངེས་ལྡེམ་དགོངས་སྣ་ཚོགས་པ་ལ་མན་ངག་གིས་དེའི་སྐྱོན་བསལ་བས་ཡིད་ཆེས། ལུང་དང་མན་ངག་ཡོད་ཀྱང་ཚིག་ཙམ་གྱི་སྒྲ་ཕྱིར་འབྲང་བས་བློའི་གཏིང་དུ་ཉམས་སུ་མ་ལོན་པ་ཡང་ཡོད་པས། ལུང་དང་མན་ངག་གི་ཚིག་ཙམ་ལ་བརྟེན་པ་ཡང་མ་ཡིན་པར་སོ་སོར་རྟོག་པའི་ཤེས་རབ་བམ་རང་གི་རིག་པས་བློའི་གཏིང་དུ་ཡིད་ཆེས་པས་མངོན་སུམ་དུ་རྟོགས་པའོ། །ཞེས་འདིས་ནི་ལུང་གིས་དོན་སྤྱི་ཕྱིན་ཅི་མ་ལོག་པ་ཤེས་པར་འགྱུར་ལ། མན་ངག་གིས་

ལུང་གི་དགོངས་པ་གཞན་དུ་འདྲེན་པ་གཅོད་ཅིང་། ཤེས་རབ་ཀྱིས་མངོན་སུམ་དུ་རྟོགས་པས་ཐོས་པ་ཙམ་ལ་སོགས་པ་ཉིད་དུ་ཞེན་པ་སེལ་ཞིང་གཅོད་པར་བྱེད་པ་ཡིན་ནོ། །དེ་ལྟར་ལམ་གྱིས་ཡིད་ཆེས་པ་ནི། རྟོགས་པ་རྣམ་བཞིའི་དོན་དེ་ཉིད་ཤེས་ཤིང་རིག་པ་ཉིད་རྣལ་འབྱོར་པའི་ལམ་སྟེ། དེའང་མཚན་ཉིད་ཐེག་པར་རྒྱུ་སྦྱོང་དུ་བསྒྲུབས་པའི་འབྲས་བུ་སངས་རྒྱས་ཉིད་ཕྱིས་ནམ་ཞིག་ན་འབྱུང་བའི་དུས་ལ་ལྟོས་པ་ལྟ་བུ་མ་ཡིན་གྱི། ད་ལྟ་ཉིད་དུ་ཤེས་རབ་ཀྱི་དབང་པོས་རང་གིས་མངོན་སུམ་དུ་རྟོགས་ཤིང་ཡིད་ཆེས་པའོ། །གཉིས་པ་ནི། དེ་ལ་ཤེས་པ་དང་འཇུག་པ་དང་མངོན་དུ་གྱུར་པ་སྟེ་མཚན་ཉིད་གསུམ་གྱིས་ཇི་ལྟར་རྟོགས་པའི་རྫོགས་པ་ཆེན་པོའི་དོན་མཐར་ཕྱིན་པར་འགྱུར་ཏེ། དེ་ཡང་། རྟོགས་པ་བཞིའི་ཚུལ་རིག་པ་ནི་གཏན་ལ་དབབ་བྱ་རྒྱུ་ཤེས་པའི་མཚན་ཉིད་དོ། །ཡང་ནས་ཡང་དུ་དེ་ལ་གོམས་པར་བྱེད་པ་ནི་རྐྱེན་འཇུག་པའི་མཚན་ཉིད་དོ། །དེ་ལྟར་གོམས་པའི་མཐུས་དོན་ཇི་ལྟར་བཞིན་མངོན་དུ་གྱུར་པ་ནི་མཐར་ཕྱིན་འབྲས་བུའི་མཚན་ཉིད་དོ། །དེ་ལ་རྒྱུ་ཤེས་པའི་མཚན་ཉིད་ལྟ་བ་དང་། རྐྱེན་འཇུག་པའི་མཚན་ཉིད་སྒོམ་པ་དང་མངོན་དུ་གྱུར་པ་འབྲས་བུའི་ཚུལ་གསུམ་པོ་འདིས་དོན་མཐར་ཕྱིན་པར་བྱེད་པས་ན་འདི་དང་མི་ལྡན་དུ་མི་རུང་བས་ན། མཚན་ཉིད་གསུམ་གྱིས་འབྲེལ་བ་དང་། དགོས་པ་དང་། དགོས་པའི་ཡང་དགོས་པ་སྟོན་ཏེ། དེ་ལ་འབྲེལ་པ་ནི། ཀུན་ནས་ཉོན་མོངས་པ་དང་རྣམ་པར་བྱང་བའི་ཆོས་སུ་བཏགས་པ་ཐམས་ཅད་ཡིག་འབྲུའི་ཚུལ་གྱིས་ཡེ་ནས་སྐུ་གསུང་ཐུགས་ཀྱི་བདག་ཉིད་དང་། རྒྱུ་གཅིག་པར་རྟོགས་པས་རང་བཞིན་གྱིས་སངས་རྒྱས་པའི་དབྱིངས་དང་བྱིན་གྱིས་བརླབས་པར་རྟོགས་པ་དང་མངོན་སུམ་པར་རྟོགས་པའི་དོན་གྱིས་བྱིན་གྱིས་རློབས་པའི་དོན་མངོན་སུམ་དུ་རྟོགས་པ་ནི་རྒྱུ་ཤེས་པའི་མཚན་ཉིད་དེ། དེ་ནི་གང་དང་འབྲེལ་ན་བླ་ན་མེད་པའི་སངས་རྒྱས་སུ་འགྲུབ་པའི་རྒྱུ་ཡིན་པའི་ཕྱིར་དོན་དུ་འབྲེལ་བའོ། །དགོས་པ་ནི་འཇུག་པའི་མཚན་ཉིད་དེ། ཀུན་ནས་ཉོན་མོངས་པ་དང་རྣམ་པར་བྱང་བའི་ཆོས་དང་། སྨན་ལྔ་དང་། བདུད་རྩི་ལྔ་དང་གཉེན་པོ་ལྔ་དང་དུག་ལྔ་ལ་སོགས་པར་བཏགས་པ་གཙང་མི་གཙང་དང་དག་མ་དག་ཐམས་ཅད་ཡེ་

ནས་སངས་རྒྱས་པའི་རང་བཞིན་ཡིན་པས་མཉམ་པ་ཆེན་པོ་ལ་བླང་དོར་མེད་པར་སྤྱོད་པ་ནི་འཇུག་པའི་མཚན་ཉིད་དོ། །དེ་ལྟར་ཞུགས་པ་དེ་ནི་གང་གི་ཕྱིར་དགོས་ཞེ་ན་བླ་ན་མེད་པའི་སངས་རྒྱས་སུ་འགྲུབ་པའི་རྒྱུ་ཐུན་མིན་ཏེ་བླང་དོར་མཉམ་ཉིད་དུ་མ་རྟོགས་པར་སངས་རྒྱས་པའི་ཐབས་ཡོད་པ་མ་ཡིན་པའི་ཕྱིར་དགོས་པའོ། །དགོས་པའི་ཡང་དགོས་པ་ནི་འབྲས་བུའི་མཚན་ཉིད་དེ། ཀུན་ནས་ཉོན་མོངས་པ་དང་། རྣམ་པར་བྱང་བའི་ཆོས་སྤྱི་དང་། སྨན་ལྔ་དང་བདུད་རྩི་ལྔ་སོགས་སྤྱོད་བྱེར་ཁྱད་པར་དུ་བཏགས་པ་ཐམས་ཅད་ཡེ་ནས་སངས་རྒྱས་པའི་མཉམ་པ་ཆེན་པོའི་ངང་དུ་བླང་དོར་མེད་པར་ལྷུན་གྱིས་གྲུབ་པའི་ཕྱིར། སྲིད་པའི་འཁོར་བ་ཉིད་ཡེ་ནས་བླ་ན་མེད་པར་སངས་རྒྱས་པའི་རང་བཞིན་མྱ་ངན་ལ་འདས་པའི་མཚན་ཉིད་དུ་ལྷུན་གྱིས་གྲུབ་པ་མངོན་དུ་གྱུར་པ་ཡིན་པའི་ཕྱིར་འབྲས་བུའི་མཚན་ཉིད་དེ། སྐུ་གསུང་ཐུགས་དུས་རྟག་ཁྱབ་ཏུ་མི་ཟད་པ་རྒྱན་གྱི་ཞེས་ཆོས་ཀྱི་དབྱིངས་གང་བར་ཡེ་ཤེས་ཀྱི་རོལ་པ་ཚད་མེད་པ་སྟེ། དཔེ་གསེར་མིག་གཡུས་སྦྲུས་པ་ལྟར་དང་། འཁོར་ལོ་ཞེས་གདུལ་བྱའི་རྒྱུད་ལ་འཇུག་ཅིང་སྒྲིབ་པ་རྣམས་གཅོད་པར་བྱེད་པ་སྟེ། དེ་ལྟ་བུ་མངོན་སུམ་དུ་གྱུར་པ་ནི་དགོས་པའི་ཡང་དགོས་པའོ། །དེ་ལ་རྫོགས་པ་ཆེན་པོ་ཡེ་ནས་སངས་རྒྱས་པ་ལ་རྒྱུ་རྐྱེན་འབྲས་བུར་བཞག་པ་མི་འགལ་ལམ་ཞེ་ན། དེ་ལྟར་མ་ཧཱ་སོགས་ཐེག་པ་འོག་མའི་གཞུང་གིས་ལམ་བསྙེན་སྒྲུབ་ཡན་ལག་བཞིའི་སྒོ་ནས་འབྲས་བུ་འགྲུབ་པར་འདོད་ལ། སྐབས་འདིར་ནི་དེ་ལྟར་བྱ་མི་དགོས་ཏེ། བསྙེན་སྒྲུབ་རྣམ་པ་བཞི་ཡང་བརྩལ་མེད་ལྷུན་གྱིས་གྲུབ་པའི་རྣལ་འབྱོར་ལ་རྫོགས་པས། རྒྱུ་རྐྱེན་འབྲས་བུར་གྱུར་པའི་དངོས་པོར་དངོས་སུ་ན་མེད་དོ་ཞེས་ལ་བརྡ་བའི་མན་ངག་ཏུ་སྦྱར་རོ། །དེས་ན་ཤེས་པའི་ཡུལ་དང་། དེ་ལ་འཇུག་པ་དང་། དེ་མངོན་དུ་གྱུར་པ་གསུམ་ནི་ཆོས་ཉིད་བྱང་ཆུབ་སེམས་ཀྱི་རང་བཞིན་ལ་ཁྱད་པར་མེད་པས་གཞི་འབྲས་དབྱེར་མེད་རང་བཞིན་ལྷུན་གྲུབ་ཆེན་པོའོ། །གསུམ་པ་ནི། དེ་ལ་བསྙེན་པ་དང་། ཉེ་བའི་བསྙེན་པ་དང་། སྒྲུབ་པ་དང་། སྒྲུབ་པ་ཆེན་པོའི་དོན་ཏེ་བསྙེན་སྒྲུབ་ཡན་ལག་བཞི་པོ་ཡང་རྩོལ་བ་མེད་པར་ལྷུན་གྱིས་གྲུབ་པར་གྱུར་པའི་རྣལ་འབྱོར་ལ་བརྟེན་

པར་བྱའོ། །ཞེས་སྦྱོར་བསྟན་ཏོ། དེ་ལ་མ་ཧཱ་ཡོ་གའི་བསྙེན་སྒྲུབ་བཞི་ལས་
རྫོགས་པ་ཆེན་པོར་ལ་བཟླ་བའི་ཚུལ་རྒྱུ་འབྲས་སུ་སྦྱུར་པའི་འབྱུང་བ་དང་ཁྱུང་པོའམ།
རྣམ་ཐར་གསུམ་མམ། ཐབས་ཤེས་ཟུང་འཇུག་གམ། སྣང་སྟོང་དབྱེར་མེད་
སོགས་ཡབ་ཡུམ་གྱི་ཆར་སྣང་བ་ཐམས་ཅད་ལ་རང་བཞིན་རྩོལ་མེད་ལྷུན་གྲུབ་ཀྱི་ཚུལ་
དུ་སྦྱོར་དགོས་ཏེ། །དེ་ལ་བསྙེན་པ་ནི། གཞི་ཀ་དག་དང་ལྷུན་གྲུབ་ཟུང་དུ་འཇུག་
པའི་བྱང་ཆུབ་ཀྱི་སེམས་ཤེས་པ་སྟེ། དེ་ཡང་ཀུན་བྱུང་གི་ཆོས་ཐམས་ཅད་ཡེ་ནས་
སངས་རྒྱས་པའི་རང་བཞིན་དུ་ལམ་གྱིས་གསར་དུ་བསྒྲུབ་ཅིང་གཉེན་པོས་བཅོས་སུ་
མེད་པར་རྟོགས་པའོ། །ཉེ་བའི་བསྙེན་པ་ནི། ལྟ་བ་དེའི་ངང་ནས་ཕུང་པོ་ལྔའི་
རང་བཞིན་ཅན་བདག་ཉིད་ལྷར་ཤེས་པ་སྟེ། དེའང་ཆོས་ཐམས་ཅད་ཡེ་ནས་སངས་
རྒྱས་པའི་རང་བཞིན་ཡིན་པས། བདག་ཉིད་ཀྱང་ཡེ་ནས་ལྷའི་རང་བཞིན་ཡིན་གྱི།
མ་ཧཱ་སོགས་ཀྱི་ལྟ་བའི་ངང་ནས་བདག་ལྷར་བསྐྱེད་པ་ལྟར་ད་ལྟ་བསྒྲུབ་པ་ནི་མ་ཡིན་
པར་རྟོགས་པའོ། །སྒྲུབ་པ་ནི་ཡུམ་བསྐྱེད་པ་སྟེ། དེའང་མ་ཧཱ་སོགས་ཀྱི་ཡུམ་
བསྐྱེད་པ་ལྟ་བུ་མིན་གྱི་ཡུམ་ཆེན་མོ་ནམ་མཁའི་དབྱིངས་ལས། ནམ་མཁའ་ཉིད་
ཡུམ་ཆེན་མོ་ས་ཆུ་མེ་རླུང་བཞིར་སྣང་ཞིང་། དེ་ཡང་གོ་འབྱེད་པ་དང་།
རྟེན་བྱེད་པ་དང་། སྡུད་པ་དང་། སྨིན་པ་དང་། གཡོ་བའི་བྱ་བ་བྱེད་པའི་ཡུམ་
ཡེ་ནས་ཡིན་པར་རྟོགས་པའོ། །སྒྲུབ་པ་ཆེན་པོ་ནི། ཐབས་དང་ཤེས་རབ་འབྲེལ་
བ་སྟེ། དེའང་ཅི་ལྟར་འབྲེལ་ན། ཡུམ་འབྱུང་བ་ཆེན་པོ་ལྔའི་རང་བཞིན་མེད་པའི་
ཤེས་རབ་དང་ཡུམ་གྱི་མཁའ་སྟོང་པ་ཉིད་ཀྱི་རྣམ་པར་ཐར་པ་ལས། མ་འགགས་
པར་སྣང་བའི་ཕུང་པོ་ལྔའི་སངས་རྒྱས་ཐབས་ཀྱི་ཡབ་སྨོན་པ་མེད་པའི་རྣམ་པར་ད་ལྟ་
ལམ་གྱིས་ཟུང་དུ་སྦྲེལ་བ་ལྟ་བུ་མིན་པར་ཡེ་ནས་ཟུང་དུ་སྦྱུར་པའི་འབྲེལ་པ་ལས།
བྱང་ཆུབ་སེམས་སུ་དབྱེར་མེད་པའི་རང་བཞིན་ལས་སྐྱེ་མཆེད་ཐམས་ཅད་སྲས་སྤྲུལ་པ་
ལྷུམ་དྲལ་དུ་སྦྱུར་པའི་རང་བཞིན་ནི། མ་ཧཱ་སོགས་ཀྱི་ཡབ་ཡུམ་འབྲེལ་བའི་བྱང་
ཆུབ་སེམས་ལས་སྲས་ལྷུམ་དྲལ་འཕྲོ་བ་ལྟ་བུ་མ་ཡིན་ཏེ་ཡེ་ནས་སངས་རྒྱས་པའི་དོན་
ལ། ཡུལ་ཆོས་ཀྱི་དབྱིངས་ཡུམ་སྦྲུམ་ལྟ་བུ་ལ་རིག་པའི་ཡེ་ཤེས་ཡབ་སྦྲུམ་ལྟ་བུར་

རོལ་ཅིང་དེ་ལ་མ་འགགས་མི་དམིགས་དབྱེར་མེད་ཕྱོགས་ཞེན་ཐམས་ཅད་དང་བྲལ་བའི་བདེ་བའི་ཡེ་ཤེས་ཅིར་ཡང་འཆར་བ་རོལ་མོ་ལྷ་བུའི་དགོངས་པ་ཉམས་སུ་མྱོང་བ་ནི། གཉིས་འཛིན་གྱི་ཞེན་པ་རྡུལ་ཕྲན་ཙམ་ཡང་མེད་པས་ཡེ་ཤེས་དགྱེས་པ་དེ་ནི་**བདེ་བའི་མཆོག་**ཡིན་པ་དེ་འདྲ་བའི་**སྒྱུ་མའི་རྒྱུན་ལ་**རོལ་ཞིང་ཉམས་སུ་མྱོང་བའི་ཚུལ་གྱིས་ཏེ། དེ་ཡང་སྐད་ཅིག་མ་འབྲལ་བའི་ངོ་བོ་ཉིད་ཀྱི་རྒྱུན་ནམ་མཁའ་ལྟ་བུའོ། །**བདེ་བའི་དུས་ཉིད་ན་**སྤྲོས་པ་ཀུན་བྲལ་**མཚན་མ་མེད་པའི་**རྣམ་ཐར་གྱི་**དོན་**མཐའ་གང་དུའང་**མི་དམིགས་**ཤིང་**མཁའ་དང་སྙོམས་པ།** བཏང་སྙོམས་ཆེན་པོའི་ར་བ་ལས་མི་འདའ་བ་ནི་ཆོས་ཉིད་རང་བྱུང་གི་ཡེ་ཤེས་ཉག་གཅིག་གི་**ཀློང་དུ་གྱུར་ནས་**བྱེད་རྩོལ་མེད་པར་**ལྷུན་གྱིས་གྲུབ་པ་སྟེ།** དེ་ལ་ཟབ་པའི་རྒྱུ་གཞུང་འཛིན་རང་བྱུང་གི་ཡེ་ཤེས་སུ་དག་ཅིང་མི་འགག་པར་ངོ་བོ་ཉིད་ཀྱི་རྒྱུན་སྣང་བསོད་ནམས་ཀྱི་ཚོགས་དང་། དེ་ཡང་སྤྲོས་མཚན་འཛིན་ཞེན་ཙུང་ཟད་ཀྱང་མེད་པ་ཡེ་ཤེས་ཀྱི་ཚོགས་སོ། །དེ་ལྟ་བུའི་ཚོགས་གཉིས་ལྷུན་གྱིས་གྲུབ་པ་རང་བྱུང་གི་ཡེ་ཤེས་ཆེན་པོ་དེས་**བདུད་རྣམ་པ་བཞིའང་བཏུལ་ནས་མཐར་ཕྱིན་པའི་དོན་འགྲུབ་པའོ།** །དེ་ལ་བདུད་བཞི་བཏུལ་ཚུལ་ནི། བསྙེན་པ་བྱང་ཆུབ་ཀྱི་སེམས་ཞེས་པའི་མཚན་ཉིད་མ་སྐྱེས་པའི་ཏིང་འཛིན་གྱིས་འཆི་བདག་གི་བདུད་བཅོམ། ཉེར་བསྙེན་བདག་ཉིད་ལྟར་ཤེས་པའི་མཚན་ཉིད་སྒྱུ་མ་ལྟ་བུའི་ཏིང་འཛིན་གྱིས་ཕུང་པོའི་བདུད་བཅོམ། སྒྲུབ་པ་ཡུམ་བསྐྱེད་པའི་མཚན་ཉིད་རྡུལ་དང་བྲལ་བའི་ཏིང་ངེ་འཛིན་གྱིས་ཉོན་མོངས་པའི་བདུད་བཅོམ། སྒྲུབ་པ་ཆེན་པོ་ཐབས་ཤེས་ཟུང་དུ་འབྲེལ་བའི་མཚན་ཉིད་མི་དམིགས་མཁའ་དང་སྙོམས་པའི་ཏིང་ངེ་འཛིན་གྱིས་ལྷ་བུའི་བདུད་བར་ཆད་གཡེངས་བའི་བདུད་བཅོམ། དེ་ལྟར་ན་གང་ལ་བདུད་རྣམ་པ་བཞི་འདུལ་བར་བྱེད་པའི་མཐུ་ཡོད་པའི་ལམ་དེ་ནི་རྣམ་པར་དག་པའི་ལམ་ཡིན་ལ། དེ་ཡང་བཙལ་བ་མེད་པར་ལྷུན་གྱིས་གྲུབ་པའི་ལམ་ཆེན་པོའོ། །བཞི་པ་ནི། རྫོགས་པ་ཆེན་པོའི་དཀྱིལ་འཁོར་དུ་འཇུག་པའི་རིམ་པ་སྟེ། དེ་ཡང་ཐེག་པ་འོག་མ་ལྟར་དཀྱིལ་འཁོར་བཞེངས་བཀོད་སོགས་ཀྱི་རྩོལ་བ་ལ་ལྟོས་པ་མ་ཡིན་ཏེ། **ཆོས་ཐམས་ཅད་གདོད་མ་ནས་རྣམ་པར་དག་པའི་**སྒྲ་འཕྲུལ་འདོད་དགུར་འཛེ་བ་**ཡིད་བཞིན་**

གྱི་གཞལ་ཡས་ཁང་ཕྱོགས་དུས་ཀྱི་རྣམ་པས་**རྒྱ་ཡོངས་སུ་མ་ཆད་པའི་འཁོར་ལོ་ཡེ་ནས་བླ་ན་མེད་པའི་**སྟེ་རྟུལ་ཆོན་སོགས་དང་གཟུགས་བརྙན་ཐམས་ཅད་ལས་འདས་པའི་**དཀྱིལ་འཁོར་དུ་འཇུག་པའང་**ཡེ་སངས་རྒྱས་པའི་དོན་རྟོགས་བྱེད་གསང་སྙིང་ལེའུ་བཅུ་གསུམ་པ་མན་ངག་དང་བཅས་པ་རྫོགས་ཆེན་སོགས་**ཐབས་ཀྱི་ཐེག་པའི་གཞུང་**རྣམས་ཐོག་མར་ཉན་པའི་ཤེས་རབ་ཀྱིས་བླ་མ་ལས་**ཐོས་པ་ནི་མིག་ཕྱེ་བའོ།** །བསམ་པའི་ཤེས་རབ་ཀྱིས་དེའི་**དོན་རྟོགས་པ་ནི་དཀྱིལ་འཁོར་མཐོང་བའོ།** །**སྒོམ་པའི་ཤེས་རབ་ཀྱིས་རྟོགས་ནས་གོམས་པར་བྱེད་པ་ནི་དཀྱིལ་འཁོར་དུ་ཞུགས་པ་**སྟེ་དབང་བསྐུར་ཐོབ་པའོ། །དེ་ལྟར་**ཞུགས་ནས་མངོན་དུ་གྱུར་པ་ནི་དངོས་གྲུབ་ཆེན་པོ་ཐོབ་པའོ།** །**དེ་ནི་རྫོགས་པ་ཆེན་པོའི་ཚུལ་འདི་ཀུན་གྱི་ཐུན་མོང་མ་ཡིན་པར་སྟོན་པའི་ཕྱིར་གསུངས་པ། དེ་ལྟར་ཚུལ་འདི་ནི་**མཉམ་ཉིད་**རྫོགས་པ་ཆེན་པོ་**རྒྱུ་འབྲས་ཀྱི་ཐེག་པ་ཐམས་ཅད་**མཐར་ཕྱིན་**པ་སྟེ་དེ་ལས་གོང་དུ་བགྲོད་དུ་མེད་**པའི་དོན་ནོ།** །ལམ་འདིའི་འབྲས་བུ་ནི་**ཡི་གེ་འཁོར་ལོ་ཚོགས་ཆེན་གྱི་ས་ལ་**བཅུལ་མེད་**ལྷུན་གྱིས་འཇུག་པ་སྟེ།** དེ་ཡང་སྤྱིར་མཚན་ཉིད་ཀྱི་ཐེག་པ་སྤྱི་ལས་སངས་རྒྱས་ཀྱི་ས་ཀུན་ཏུ་འོད་ཅེས་བྱ་སྟེ། འདི་ལྟར་འོད་ཟེར་མང་པོ་བཀྱེ་བས་འདུལ་བའི་འགྲོ་བ་སྨིན་དུ་རུང་བར་མཛད་པའི་ཕྱིར་དེ་སྐད་ཅེས་གྲགས་སོ། །རྡོ་རྗེ་ཐེག་པ་སྤྱི་ལས་ནི་སངས་རྒྱས་ཀྱི་ས་གསུམ་དུ་གྲགས་ཏེ། །དེ་ལ་ཀུན་ཏུ་འོད་ནི་ཆོས་ཀྱི་སྐུ་མཚན་མ་མེད་པ་རང་བཞིན་གྱིས་འོད་གསལ་བས་ཀུན་ལ་ཁྱབ་པའོ། །པདྨ་ཅན་ནི་དམིགས་པ་མེད་པའི་ཤེས་རབ་ཀྱིས་ཆོས་ཀྱི་སྐུའི་དོན་ཧེར་ཡང་མ་གཟིགས་པ་ཉིད་མ་ཆགས་པའི་ཐུགས་རྗེའི་གཞི་ཡིན་པའོ། །ཡི་གེ་འཁོར་ལོ་ཚོགས་ཆེན་ནི། དེ་ཉིད་ཀྱི་དུས་ན་ཡེ་ཤེས་དང་མཚན་མའི་དཀྱིལ་འཁོར་གྱི་བདག་ཉིད་བཅུལ་བ་མེད་པར་ལྷུན་གྱིས་གྲུབ་པ་སྟེ། དེ་ལ་ཡི་གེ་ནི་གཉིས་ཏེ། ཡེ་ཤེས་དང་མཚན་མའོ། །མཚན་མ་ལའང་གཉིས་ཏེ་མིང་དང་གཟུགས་སོ། །གཟུགས་ཀྱང་རྣམ་པ་གཉིས་ཏེ། ཡོངས་སུ་རྫོགས་པ་དང་ཆ་ཤས་སུ་སྣང་བའོ། །འདི་ལྟ་བུའི་འབྲས་བུའི་ཆོས་ཀྱི་དཀྱིལ་འཁོར་གྱི་ཚོགས་ཆེན་པོར་ལྷུན་གྱིས་གྲུབ་པ་ནི་ཡི་གེ་འཁོར་ལོ་ཚོགས་ཆེན་གྱི་ས་ཞེས་ཀྱང་བྱ། སངས་རྒྱས་ཀྱི་ས་བཅུ་གསུམ་པ

ཞེས་ཀྱང་བྱའོ། །དེ་ནི་སྐྱེས་བུ་བློ་རྩལ་རབ་ཀྱིས་ཡེ་ནས་སངས་རྒྱས་པའི་དོན་ལ་ཡེ་ནས་སངས་རྒྱས་པར་རིག་ནས་ལམ་གྱི་བྱ་རྩོལ་ལ་མི་ལྟོས་པར་སྐད་ཅིག་གིས་གོམས་པ་དྲག་བརྟུལ་ཏེ་ཅིག་ཆར་དུ་འགྲོ་བ་ཡིན་གྱི། གང་ཟག་ཞལ་གྱི་བསམ་ཞིང་གོམས་པར་བྱ་བ་ནི་མ་ཡིན་ནོ། །སྐྱེ་བོ་ཞལ་གྱིས་འདི་ལྟ་བུའི་དོན་ཐོས་ཏེ་ནན་ཏན་དུ་ཇི་ལྟར་བསམས་ཀྱང་དོན་འདི་ནི་བདེན་ཞིང་ཆེས་ཟབ་པར་ཡིད་ཆེས་པར་མི་འགྱུར་རོ། །ཡིད་ཆེས་པ་དང་ཞལ་གྱི་བློ་ལ་གོ་དཀའ་ཞིང་བདེན་པ་དང་ཟབ་པར་མ་ཤེས་པའི་དབང་གིས་རང་གི་ཉམས་དང་སྦྱར་ནས་གང་ཟག་གཞན་ཀུན་ཀྱང་དེ་དང་འདྲ་སྙོམས་ནས་ཡོངས་ཏེ་རྫོགས་པ་ཆེན་པོ་རྫོགས་པ་རྣམས་དང་ཆོས་ཐམས་ཅད་ཡེ་ནས་སངས་རྒྱས་པ་ནི་ཇུན་ཞེས་སྐྱེས་བུ་རབ་རྣམས་ལ་སྐུར་བ་འདེབས་ཤིང་ཐེག་པ་ཆེན་པོ་སུན་འབྱིན་པའི་བློ་སྐྱེ་བར་འགྱུར་བས་རབ་ཏུ་གསང་བར་བྱ་བའི་དགོས་པའི་ཕྱིར་ཡང་རང་བཞིན་གསང་བའི་ཐེག་པ་ཞེས་སྟོན་པ་ཉིད་ཀྱིས་བཀའ་སྩལ་ཏོ། །དེ་བས་ན་ཆོས་ཐམས་ཅད་ཡེ་ནས་སངས་རྒྱས་པའི་དོན་ལ་ཇི་བཞིན་པར་རྟོགས་ནུས་པའི་བློ་མ་སྐྱེས་བར་དུ་ཐེག་པ་འོག་མ་བས་ཞེས་ལྷ་མི་ཉན་རང་སོགས་ཀྱི་ལམ་གྱིས་འགྲོ་བའི་དོན་བྱས་ན་གདུལ་བྱ་རྣམས་ཀྱི་རྒྱུད་ཚུད་མི་ཟ་བས་ན། སློབ་དཔོན་གྱིས་བློ་དམན་རྣམས་ལ་འཁོར་བའི་སྐྱོན་དང་། མྱ་ངན་ལས་འདས་པའི་ཡོན་ཏན་ལ་བསྔགས་པ་དང་། ཐེག་པ་ཐམས་ཅད་ཀྱི་རིམ་པ་མཐའ་དག་ལ་མཁས་པར་བྱ་བ་དང་། དེའི་དོན་སློབ་མའི་ཉམས་དང་སྦྱར་ལ་རིམ་པས་དྲང་བར་བྱ་བ་ཡིན་གྱི། ཐེག་པའི་ཕྱོགས་འགའ་མི་ཤེས་པས་སློབ་དཔོན་གྱི་ས་བཟུང་དུ་མི་རུང་བར་མདོ་རྒྱུད་དག་ན་རྒྱ་ཆེར་འབྱུང་ངོ་། །གཉིས་པ་ལ། མདོར་བསྟན་པ་དང་། རྒྱས་པར་བཤད་པ་གཉིས་ལས། དང་པོ་ནི། དེ་ལྟར་ལྟ་བའི་ཁྱད་པར་གྱིས་ཡོན་ཏན་གྱི་འབྲས་བུ་འདོད་པའི་ཕྱིར་ལུས་ཀྱི་དཀའ་ཐུབ་དང་རང་གི་ངང་ཚུལ་སྔ་མའི་གནས་སྐབས་ལས་གཞན་དུ་བསྒྱུར་བའི་སྤྱོད་པ་བརྟུལ་ཞུགས་ཀྱང་མི་འདྲ་བའི་བྱེ་བྲག་ཏུ་འགྱུར་ཏེ་ལྟ་བ་མིག་དང་འདྲ་བས་ཇི་ལྟར་བཅད་པ་བཞིན་དུ། དཀའ་ཐུབ་དང་བརྟུལ་ཞུགས་རྐང་པ་དང་འདྲ་བ་རྗེས་སུ་འགྲོ་བར་འགྱུར་བའི་ཕྱིར་རོ། །དེ་ལ་ལྟ་བའི་བྱེ་བྲག་གིས་དཀའ་ཐུབ་ཡོད་མེད་

གཉིས་སུ་འགྱུར་ཏེ། **དཀའ་ཐུབ་མེད་པ་ནི་**གཉིས་ཏེ། ལྟ་བ་ལ་སྒྲུབ་བྱ་མེད་པའི་
དབང་གིས་འཇིག་རྟེན་**ཕྱལ་བ་དང་**ཕྱི་རོལ་**མུར་ཐུག་གོ** །གང་ལྟ་བ་ལ་སྒྲུབ་པར་བྱ་
བ་ཡོད་པའི་དབང་གིས་**དཀའ་ཐུབ་ཡོད་པ་ནི་རྣམ་པ་བཞི་སྟེ།** འཇིག་རྟེན་**རྒྱང་འཕེན་
པ་དང་**ཕྱི་རོལ་**མུ་སྟེགས་པ་སྟེ་**ཐར་པའི་ལམ་དང་རྗེས་སུ་མ་འབྲེལ་བ་**འཇིག་རྟེན་གྱི་
དཀའ་ཐུབ་དང་།** འཇིག་རྟེན་ལས་འདས་པའི་ལམ་དུ་གྱུར་པ་**ཉན་ཐོས་ཀྱི་དཀའ་ཐུབ་
དང་བྱང་ཆུབ་སེམས་དཔའི་དཀའ་ཐུབ་དང་།** **བླ་ན་མེད་པའི་དཀའ་ཐུབ་བོ།** །
གཉིས་པ་ནི། **དེ་ལ་**གོང་དུ་ལྟ་བའི་སྐབས་སུ་སྨོས་པའི་འཇིག་རྟེན་**ཕྱལ་བ་ནི་རྒྱུ་**དང་
འབྲས་བུ་**ལ་རྨོངས་པའི་ཕྱིར་**བླང་དོར་གྱི་གནས་ཅི་ཡང་མི་ཤེས་པས་**དཀའ་ཐུབ་མེད་
པའོ།** །ཕྱི་རོལ་**མུར་ཐུག་པ་ནི་**རྒྱུ་འབྲས་**ཆད་པར་ལྟ་བའི་ཕྱིར་**ཚེ་ཕྱི་མ་ལ་ཕན་པ་དོན་
དུ་མི་གཉེར་བས་**དཀའ་ཐུབ་མེད་པའོ།** **།དེ་གཉིས་ནི་དཀའ་ཐུབ་མེད་པ་སྟེ།
དཀའ་ཐུབ་ཡོད་པའི་ཕྱོགས་ལ།** **འཇིག་རྟེན་རྒྱང་འཕེན་པ་ནི་ཚེ་འདིའི་**བཙན་ཕྱུག་
སོགས་གཞན་ལས་**ཁྱད་པར་**དུ་འཕགས་པ་བསྒྲུབས་པའི་ཕྱིར་**གཙང་སྦྲ་ལ་སོགས་པའི་
དཀའ་ཐུབ་ཅན་ནོ།** **།ཕྱི་རོལ་མུ་སྟེགས་པ་ནི།** **བདག་རྟག་པ་ཞིག་ཡོད་པ་དེ་དག་
པར་བྱ་བའི་ཕྱིར།** ཚ་གྲང་སོགས་ཀྱིས་**ལུས་སྨུན་འབྱིན་ཅིང་**ཕྱོགས་བཞིར་མེད་དང་
སྟེང་ནས་ཉི་མ་སྟེ་**མེ་ལྔ་བརྟེན་པ་ལ་སོགས་པའི་དཀའ་ཐུབ་དང་།** ཁྲི་ཕག་སོགས་ཀྱི་
བརྟུལ་ཞུགས་དམན་པ་ངལ་བ་དོན་མེད་ཕྱིན་ཅི་**ལོག་པར་སྤྱོད་པའོ།** **།ཉན་ཐོས་ཀྱི་
དཀའ་ཐུབ་ནི་འདུལ་བ་ལས།** བསླབ་པ་གསུམ་མདོར་བསྡུས་ཏེ། **སྡིག་པ་ཅི་
ཡང་མི་བྱ་སྟེ།** ཞེས་ཚུལ་ཁྲིམས་ཀྱི་བསླབ་པའི་དབང་དུ་བྱས་ཏེ། མི་དགེ་བ་
བཅུའི་ལས་ཀྱི་ལམ་ལས་ཀྱང་། ཤིན་ཏུ་ལྕི་བ། སྲོག་གཅོད། མ་བྱིན་ལེན།
མི་ཚངས་སྤྱོད། རྫུན་སྨྲ་ལྟ་བུ་ཕམ་པར་གྱུར་པའི་ཆོས་བཞི་སོགས་བྱ་བ་མ་ཡིན་པ་
ལས་ལྡོག་པའོ། **།དགེ་བ་ཕུན་སུམ་ཚོགས་པར་སྤྱོད།** ཅེས་ཤེས་རབ་ཀྱི་བསླབ་
པའི་དབང་དུ་བྱས་ཏེ་བདེན་པ་བཞིའི་དོན་ཕྱིན་ཅི་མ་ལོག་པར་རྟོགས་པའི་ཤེས་རབ་ཀྱིས་
བསྡུས་པ། འཕགས་པའི་ལམ་དང་འབྲས་བུའི་ཆོས་སྤྱད་ཅིང་ཐོབ་པར་བྱ་བ་རྣམས་
སོ། །རང་གི་སེམས་ནི་ཡོངས་སུ་གདུལ། །ཞེས་སེམས་ཀྱི་བསླབ་པའི་དབང་དུ

བྱས་ཏེ་སེམས་ཕྱི་རོལ་གྱི་གཡེངས་པ་ལས་བཟློག་ཏེ་རྩེ་གཅིག་མཉམ་པར་བཞག་པའི་བསམ་གཏན་ལ་བསླབ་པའོ། །ཚུལ་འདི་ནི་སངས་རྒྱས་བསྟན་པ་ཡིན། །ཞེས་ཚད་མར་བྱེད་པའི་ཚིག་སྟེ། ཕྱི་རོལ་དབང་ཕྱུག་སོགས་ཀྱི་ལུང་དང་མི་འདྲ་སྟེ། ཀུན་གྱིས་ཡིད་བརྟན་དུ་རུང་བའི་ཚད་མ་སངས་རྒྱས་ཀྱིས་བསྟན་པ། དམ་པའི་ཆོས་འདུལ་བ་ལེགས་པར་གསུངས་པ་ཡིན་ནོ། །ཞེས་འབྱུང་སྟེ། དེའི་དབང་གིས་**དགེ་བ་དང་མི་དགེ་བའི་ཆོས་ཐམས་ཅད་ཀུན་རྫོབ་དང་དོན་དམ་པར་གཉིས་ཀ་ཡོད་པར་ལྟ་བ་དང་**ཞེས་འདི་ལྟར་ཀུན་རྫོབ་ཀྱི་ཤེས་པ་ལ་སྣང་བའི་ཆོས་གང་དག །དོན་དམ་པའི་ཤེས་པ་ལ་འཆར་སྣང་སྟེ། དེ་བས་ན་གཉིས་ཀར་ཡོད་པ་ཞེས་བྱའོ། །དེའི་དབང་གིས་ལུས་ངག་གིས་**དགེ་བ་ནི་སྤྱོད། མི་དགེ་བ་ནི་སྤོངས་པའི་དཀའ་ཐུབ་དང་བརྟུལ་ཞུགས་ལ་སྤྱོད་པའོ། །གོང་དུ་རང་སངས་རྒྱས་ལྟ་བའི་སྐབས་སུ་བཤད་དུ་བཞག་ནས། འདིར་དཀའ་ཐུབ་མ་སློས་པ་ནི་ཉན་ཐོས་དང་མཐུན་པའི་ཕྱིར་རོ། །བྱང་ཆུབ་སེམས་དཔའི་དཀའ་ཐུབ་ནི།** སེམས་ཅན་ཐམས་ཅད་འཁོར་མཚོ་ལས་བསྒྲལ་བའི་ཕྱིར། ཐམས་ཅད་མཁྱེན་པའི་ཡེ་ཤེས་ཀྱི་སེམས་བསྐྱེད་པ་ནི་སྡོམ་པའི་དངོས་གཞི་ཡིན་ལ། ཐམས་ཅད་མཁྱེན་པའི་ཡེ་ཤེས་དེ་མ་ཐོབ་པར་སེམས་ཅན་གྱི་དོན་བྱེད་མི་ནུས་པས་དེ་ཐོབ་པར་བྱ་ན་རྒྱུ་ནི་བྱང་ཆུབ་ཀྱི་སེམས། རྩ་བ་སྙིང་རྗེ་ཆེན་པོ། མཐར་ཕྱིན་པ་ཐབས་ལ་མཁས་པ་སྟེ། འདི་གསུམ་ནི་མི་ཚར་མི་རུང་ངོ་། །དེའི་མི་མཐུན་ཕྱོགས་རང་བཞིན་གྱི་ཁ་ན་མ་ཐོ་བ། བྱང་སེམས་ལ་ཕམ་པ་བཞི་སྟེ། བྱང་ཆུབ་ཀྱི་སེམས་གཏོང་བ་ནི་བྱང་སེམས་ཡོངས་གཟུང་གི་མི་མཐུན་ཕྱོགས་དང་། སེར་སྣའི་དབང་གིས་སེམས་ཅན་མི་སྐྱོབ་པ་དང་། གནོད་སེམས་ཀྱིས་སེམས་ཅན་ལ་གནོད་པ་བྱེད་པ་གཉིས་ནི་སྙིང་རྗེའི་མི་མཐུན་ཕྱོགས་དང་། དམ་པའི་ཆོས་སྤོང་བ་ནི་ཐབས་མཁས་ཀྱི་མི་མཐུན་ཕྱོགས་ཏེ། དེ་བཞིས་མ་ཟིན་པར་སྙིང་རྗེས་ཟིན་ན་ལུས་ངག་གིས་ཚར་གཅོད་པ་ཡང་བྱ་དགོས་ཏེ། **བྱང་ཆུབ་སེམས་དཔའི་སྡོམ་པ་**ཉི་ཤུ་པ་**ལས།** བྱང་ཆུབ་སེམས་དཔས་ཚར་བཅད་པའི་ལས་ཀྱིས་འགྲོ་བ་འདུལ་བའི་**རྒྱན་དུ་འཚམས་པར་**འགྱུར་ཡང་། ཚར་གཅོད་པའི་ལས་ཀྱིས་འགྲོ་བའི་

དོན་མི་བྱེད་ན་ཡང་ཉམས་པར་འགྱུར་རོ། །རྫུ་འཕྲུལ་བསྟན་པས་བྲིད་པ་དང་སྦྱོ་བ་དང་**བསྡིགས་**པ་**ལ་སོགས་**པ་སྦྱོར་བ་དམ་པ་མིན་པས་འདུལ་ཀྱང་དེ་ལྟར་**མི་བྱེད་**ན་ཡང་ཉམས་སོ། །དེ་ཅིའི་ཕྱིར་ན། བསམ་པ་**སྙིང་རྗེར་ལྡན་ཞིང་བྱམས་**པའི་**ཕྱིར་དང་། སེམས་དགེ་བ་ལ་**སྦྱོར་བ་རྩུབ་ཀྱང་**ཉེས་པ་མེད། ཅེས་འབྱུང་སྟེ།** ཀུན་སློང་**སྙིང་རྗེ་ཆེན་པོས་ཟིན་ན་ཆོས་ཐམས་ཅད་དགེ་བ་དང་།** ལྟར་སྣང་**མི་དགེ་བ་གང་སྤྱད་ཀྱང་**བྱང་སེམས་ཀྱི་**སྡོམ་པ་ཉམས་པར་མི་འགྱུར་ཏེ། བྱང་ཆུབ་སེམས་དཔའི་སྡོམ་པ་ནི་མདོར་ན་སྙིང་རྗེ་ཆེན་པོས་གཞི་བཟུང་ནས་སྤྱོད་དོ། །གསང་བ་བླ་ན་མེད་པའི་དཀའ་ཐུབ་ནི། དམ་ཚིག་ཆེན་པོའི་མདོ་**ཉིད་**ལས།** ཐབས་ཤེས་མཉམ་པ་ཆེན་པོ་བླ་ན་མེད་པ་**སངས་རྒྱས་**ཀྱི་**ཐེག་པར་**བློ་**རབ་**ཏུ་**ངེས་**པའམ་གདེང་དུ་གྱུར་**ན། ཉོན་མོངས་**པ་ལྔ་དང་། **འདོད་**ཡོན་**ལྔ་**ཀུན་ལ་**སྤྱད་ཀྱང་། པདྨ་ལ་ནི་འདམ་**གྱིས་མི་གོས་པ་**བཞིན་ཏེ།** གང་ཟག་མཆོག་**དེ་ལ་**ཉན་ཐོས་ཀྱི་**ཚུལ་ཁྲིམས་**དང་བྱང་ཆུབ་སེམས་དཔའི་སྡོམ་པ་ཐམས་ཅད་ཀྱང་**ཕུན་སུམ་ཚོགས་**པར་འགྱུར་བའོ། །ཞེས་འབྱུང་སྟེ། **ཆོས་ཐམས་ཅད་ཡེ་ནས་མཉམ་པ་ཉིད་ཀྱི་ཕྱིར།** དེ་ལ་**སྙིང་རྗེ་ནི་**ཡེ་ལྡན་ཡིན་པས་འབྲལ་དུ་མི་རུང་བས་**བསྟེན་དུ་མེད་ལ། ཞེ་སྡང་ནི་**རང་མཚན་པ་མེད་པས་**སྤང་དུ་མེད་དེ་**ཡེ་ནས་མཉམ་ཉིད་ཡིན་པའི་ཕྱིར། དེ་ལྟ་བུའི་མཉམ་ཉིད་ཀྱི་བློས་ཟིན་ན་ཅི་ཡང་མི་འགལ་ལོ་ཞེས་དགོངས་པའོ། །མདོར་ན་ཉན་ཐོས་ཀྱི་སྡོམ་པ་ནི་སེམས་ཅན་ལ་གནོད་སྦྱོར་ལས་ལོག་པའོ། །བྱང་སེམས་ཀྱི་སྡོམ་ལ་ནི། དེའི་སྟེང་དུ་ཕན་འདོགས་ལ་ཞུགས་སོ། །གསང་སྔགས་ཀྱི་སྡོམ་པ་ནི་དེ་གཉིས་ཀྱི་སྟེང་དུ་དེ་བཞིན་གཤེགས་པའི་མཛད་སྤྱོད་ཉམས་སུ་བླངས་སྟེ་སྤྱོད་པའོ། །གཞན་ཡང་། ཉན་ཐོས་ཀྱི་སྡོམ་པ་ནི་འདུ་ཤེས་དང་དངོས་གཞིའི་སྒོ་ནས་ལས་གཙོ་བོ་ཡིན་ལ། བྱང་སེམས་ནི་སྙིང་རྗེ་གཙོ་བོ་ཡིན་ཞིང་། གསང་སྔགས་ནི་ཤེས་རབ་གཙོ་བོ་ཡིན་པར་འདོད་དོ། །ཡང་ཉན་ཐོས་ཀྱིས་ནི། སྟོན་གྱི་འཕགས་པ་དགྲ་བཅོམ་པ་རྣམས་ཀྱི་རྗེས་སུ་སློབ་ཅིང་། བྱང་སེམས་ནི་ས་ཆེན་པོ་ལ་གནས་པའི་བྱང་འཕགས་རྣམས་ཀྱི་རྗེས་སུ་སློབ་ལ། གསང་སྔགས་ཀྱིས་ནི་དེ་བཞིན་གཤེགས་པ་ཉིད་

ཀྱི་རྗེས་སུ་སློབ་པའོ། །དེ་ལྟར་ཆོས་མཉམ་པ་ཉིད་མངོན་དུ་གྱུར་ཀྱང་**དེ་ལྟར་**གཏན་
ནས་**མ་རྟོགས་པ་**དང་ཕྱོགས་རེ་ལས་མ་རྟོགས་པ་ཐེག་བརྒྱད་ལ་གནས་པ་རྣམས་**ལ་**
ཐུགས་རྗེ་མི་འབྱུང་བ་མ་ཡིན་ཏེ་དམིགས་མེད་ཀྱི་ཐུགས་རྗེ་ངོ་བོ་ཉིད་ལྷུན་འགྲུབ་ཏུ་
འབྱུང་ངོ་། །མདོར་ན་གསང་སྔགས་མཉམ་པ་ཆེན་པོའི་དམ་ཚིག་ལ་སྤྱོད་པ་ཐམས་
ཅད་ཀྱི་ཐམས་ཅད་དུ་རྣམ་པར་མ་དག་པ་མེད་དེ། **ཇི་ལྟར་ལྟ་བས་ཡེ་ནས་རྣམ་པར་**
དག་པར་རྟོགས་པ་བཞིན་དུ་དཀའ་ཐུབ་དང་བརྟུལ་ཞུགས་ཀྱང་དེ་ལྟར་རྣམ་པར་དག་
པར་སྤྱོད་དོ་ཞེས་གསང་སྔགས་མཉམ་པ་ཆེན་པོའི་དམ་ཚིག་གི་སླར་སྤྱད་པའི་ཚིག་ཏུ་
སྦྱར་བར་མཛད་དེ་ཐེག་པ་འོག་མའི་དཀའ་ཐུབ་དང་བརྟུལ་ཞུགས་ལས་ཁྱད་པར་དུ་གྱུར་
པར་བསྟན་པའོ། །གསུམ་པ་མཇུག་གི་དོན་ལ། གདམས་ངག་གང་ལ་གཏད་
པའི་སྣོད་དང་། བརྩམས་ཟིན་པའི་མཐའ་བྱུང་གདགས་པ་གཉིས་ལས། དང་པོ་
ནི། ལྟ་བ་མཐོ་དམན་གྱི་བྱེ་བྲག་རྣམས་ཕྲེང་བ་བཞིན་དུ་རྒྱུན་ཆགས་སུ་བཀོད་ཅིང་
དགོས་པ་བསྡུས་པས་ན། **ལྟ་བའི་ཕྲེང་བ་**ཞེས་བྱ་ལ་**གསང་བ་**ནི་ཐེག་པ་མཐའ་དག་
གི་དོན་ཚིག་ཉུང་ངུར་བསྡུས་ནས་བློ་ལ་འཆང་བའི་མན་ངག་བཞག་པ་ཡིན་པ་དང་།
ཚིག་ཉུང་ངུ་འདིས་དོན་མང་པོ་རྟོགས་པར་བྱེད་པའི་སྒོ་ནས་སྒྲོན་མ་ཡིན་པས་ནོར་བུ་རིན་
པོ་ཆེ་བཞིན་དུ་སྦས་ཤིང་བཅད་པར་བྱ་བའམ། རྣམ་པ་གཅིག་ཏུ་ན་རྫོགས་པ་ཆེན་པོའི་
དོན་ནི་ཀུན་གྱི་ཐུན་མོང་མ་ཡིན་པས་ཐུགས་རྗེ་ཆེན་པོའི་ཐབས་ཀྱིས་ཀྱང་གསང་བར་བྱ་
བའི་ཆོས་ཟབ་མོ་**འདི་**ནི། ཇི་ལྟར་**དམུས་ལོང་**གཟུགས་མི་མཐོང་བ་དག་ནམ་ཞིག
རང་གི་བསོད་ནམས་ཀྱིས་ནོར་བུ་རིན་པོ་ཆེ་རྙེད་པའམ་**རང་**བཞིན་གྱིས་**ཕྱེ་ནས་མིག**
རྙེད་པ་ལྟར། །ཐོག་མེད་མ་རིག་གི་མདོངས་པའི་སྐྱེ་བོ་ཡང་དག་པའི་དོན་མཐོང་མ
མྱོང་བ་ལས་ནམ་ཞིག་སྔོན་གྱི་བསོད་ནམས་ཀྱིས་དགེ་བའི་བཤེས་གཉེན་དང་ཕྲད་ནས།
དེའི་དབང་གིས་ཤེས་རབ་གསུམ་གྱི་མིག་རྙེད་དེ། **ཤེས་རབ་**དང་**ཐབས་ཀྱི་རྩལ་**
རྙེད་པའམ་**འཆར་བའི་**རང་བཞིན་རྫོགས་པ་ཆེན་པོའི་སྣོད་དུ་གྱུར་པའི་**སྐྱེས་མཆོག་ཡོད**
ན་དེའི་དོན་དུ་གྱུར་པའི་གདམས་ངག་རིན་པོ་ཆེ་འདི་དེ་དང་**ཕྲད་པར་གྱུར་ཅིག** །ཅེས་
སྨོན་ལམ་དུ་མཛད་པའོ། །གཉིས་པ་ནི། **ལྟ་བའི་ཕྲེང་བ་ཞེས་བྱ་བའི་མན་ངག**

སློབ་དཔོན་ཆེན་པོ་པདྨ་འབྱུང་གནས་བོད་ཡུལ་ནས་སྔར་གཤེགས་ཀར་བྲག་དམར་མཆོ་མོ་འགྱུལ་གྱི་ནེ་ཐང་དུ་དགུང་གསུམ་བཞེས་ནས་ལྷ་སྲས་ཁྲི་སྲོང་ལྡེ་བཙན་དང་རྗེ་འབངས་ལ་འགྲེས་ཞུག་གི་དུས་སུ་མཛད་པ་རྫོགས་སོ། །ཞེས་པའོ། །འདི་བྲིས་དགེ་བས་ཆོ་རབ་ཐམས་ཅད་དུ། །པདྨ་འཇམ་པའི་རྡོ་རྗེ་སྙིང་ལ་ཞུགས། །ཡང་དག་ལྟ་བའི་ཟབ་གནད་ཀུན་རྟོགས་ནས། །འགྲོ་ལ་རྒྱལ་བའི་ལམ་བཟང་སྟོང་གྱུར་ཅིག །མི་ཕམ་པས་ཐུན་པར་གཅིག་ལ་བྲིས་པ་མངྒ་ལཾ།། །།ཞེས་འཇམ་མགོན་སྨྲ་བའི་སེང་གེ་མི་ཕམ་འོད་གསལ་རྡོ་རྗེའི་ཕྱག་མཚན་སོར་བཞག་ལ་གསང་བའི་བདག་པོ་བློ་གྲོས་མཐའ་ཡས་ཀྱིས་མཛད་པའི་འགྲེལ་བའི་ས་བཅད་ཀྱིས་བརྒྱན་ཏེ་རབ་ཆོས་དོན་འགྲུབ་ཞེས་པ་ས་མོ་ལུག་གི་ལོར་ཞེ་ཆེན་རི་ཁྲོད་དུ་ཞལ་བཤུས་ཤིང་སྡེ་སྣོད་འཛིན་པ་ཆེན་པོ་མཁན་ཆེན་བླ་མ་ཀུན་བཟང་དཔལ་ལྡན་ནས་ཞུས་ཆེར་མཛད་དེ་ལེགས་པར་གཏན་ལ་ཕབ་པའོ། །རྒྱལ་བ་རིག་འཛིན་བརྒྱུད་པའི་མན་ངག་བཅུད། རྒྱལ་དབང་པདྨའི་ཐུགས་མཆོར་བསྒྲིལ་བ་ལས། །རྒྱལ་བློན་ལས་ཅན་འཁོར་ལ་གདམས་པའི་ཕུལ། །རྒྱལ་བསྟན་འཛིན་པ་རྣམས་ཀྱི་གཅེས་ནོར་ལགས། །དུས་ཀྱི་མཐར་ཡང་སྐྱོབ་པ་མཆོག་དེ་ཡི། །ཐུགས་བསྐྱེད་སྨོན་པའི་རེ་ཁྲ་མ་རྨུས་པས། །ཉེ་བརྒྱུད་བྱིན་རླབས་དང་ལྡན་བདུད་རྩིའི་ཆབ། །ཡོངས་སུ་སྤྱོད་འདི་སྐལ་བ་ཅིས་མི་བཟང་། །དེ་སྐད་འཇམ་མགོན་བླ་མའི་ཕྱག་མཚན་གཞུང་། །གུས་པས་བཤུས་ལ་རང་བློས་མ་བསླད་སླམ། །འོན་ཀྱང་ནོངས་གྱུར་གང་མཆིས་བདག་བློའི་སྐྱོན། ། ཆོས་སྐྱུན་ལྡན་པ་རྣམས་ཀྱིས་བཟོད་པར་མཛོད། །དེ་ལས་བྱུང་བའི་རབ་དགེ་དྲི་མེད་ཀྱིས། །ཐེག་མཆོག་བསྟན་པའི་པད་ཚལ་རྒྱས་པ་དང་། །བདག་ཀྱང་སྐྱེ་ཀུན་པདྨའི་བྲན་གྱུར་ཏེ། །ཡང་དག་ལྟ་བའི་ལམ་བཟང་སྟོང་གྱུར་ཅིག །ཅེས་པའང་འཇམ་དབྱངས་བློ་གྲོས་རྒྱ་མཚོས་སྨྲས་པ་དགེ། ། །།

INDEX

a barren women's son 45
A Garland of Views . . . . v, xvii
a rope seen as a snake 20, 45
a short explanation of the nine vehicles iii
A Warehouse of Gems v
a yogin's path 25, 72
actuality 35, 39, 89, 96
adventitious . . . . xlv, 49, 89
affliction . . . 10, 21, 25, 26, 43, 44, 73, 75, 89, 96, 108
aggregates, dhātus, and āyatanas 20, 45, 62
Akaniṣhṭha . . . . xv, 14
Akṣhipāda 4, 5
all dharmas are by nature nirvana 23, 24, 65
almighty god 42
alpha-purity 75
animal sacrifices 42
animate and inanimate 90
annotations 87, 88
Anuyogatantra . . . . . xxxiii, xxxiv, xxxviii
appearance and rebirths 90
approach and accomplishment . 75
  accomplishment 75
  close approach 75
  great accomplishment 76
arousing the mind 83, 90
articulated speech xiv
Assurance 84, 91
Atiyoga . . x, xi, xiii, xxix, xxxiii-xxxvi, xxxviii, xl, 59
Atiyoga of Mahāyoga . . . xxxvi, xl
Atiyogatantra . . . . xxxiii-xxxv, xxxviii
attainments . xxxii, xlv, 49, 56, 58, 68
austerities and yogic conducts . . . . xix, 28, 29, 81, 83, 85
authoritative statement 25, 71, 91
authoritative statement and foremost instruction 71
authoritative statements . . . . . xvi, xviii, 33
Autonomy school 9
Avalokiteśhvara's Yogic Disciplines 9
beyond-worldly views . . . . . iii, xi
bodhichitta 11, 52, 91, 95
bodhisatva . xiii, xxx, xxxi, 20, 21, 23, 24, 28, 29, 34, 35, 44, 48, 49, 57, 64-66, 77, 81, 83-85, 91, 95, 96, 105

bodhisatva vehicle . xiii, xxxi, 20, 21, 44, 48, 49, 85
Bṛihaspatika 38
Bṛihaspati's system 38
buddha-nature 39, 89
Buddhist views xxix
causal and fruitional vehicles . . 48
causal samādhi of syllable letters 61
causal vehicle 48
cause and effect . . xxiii-xxv, xxvii, 6, 19, 20, 28, 35, 38, 40, 41, 48, 60, 78, 81, 105, 106, 109
Chārvāka . xiii, xx-xxvi, xxviii, 3-6, 19, 28, 34, 36-40, 81
Charyātantra . . . xxxii, xxxiii, 52
clinging . . xxxvi, 12, 39, 48, 76, 77, 91
compassionate activity . 29, 35, 79, 85, 86, 92
compendium of important Nyingma texts viii
complete liberation 34, 40
complete purification . . 21, 25, 26, 44, 73, 75, 108
complete purity . . . 11, 23, 24, 27, 29, 55, 64, 66, 70, 78, 85, 92, 108
completion stage . . . x, xxxiv, 1, 2, 12, 59
concept label 92
concept labels 40, 65, 78, 92
confusion xxx, xlv, 49, 53, 70, 71, 92, 93, 105
consciousness . . xlv, 9, 20, 23, 45, 49, 50, 53, 60, 65, 74, 90, 93, 94, 97, 107
Consequence school 9
containers and contents . . . 66, 93
contrivance 93
conventional vehicles . . . iv, xxxi, xxxii
conviction . 24, 25, 28, 68, 71, 72, 79
conviction by the path 25, 72
conviction explained 68
countless views of sentient beings 19
creation and completion . . . xxxiv, 12, 34, 59, 63
creation of the female consort 27, 75, 77
creation stage x, xxxiv, 1, 2, 12, 59
cross over 67, 75, 93
cyclic existence . 90, 92, 94, 98, 102
definition of austerities and yogic conduct 80
definition of bhagavat 35
definition of the two stages xxxiv
definition of Ubhaya xxxiii
definition of unsurpassed tantra xxxiv
deity vii, x, xviii, xix, xxix, xxxiv, 11, 12, 14, 26, 35, 52-56, 58-60, 62, 75, 77
detailed explanation of the entrance to great completion 59, 67
dharmadhātu . . 20, 22, 46, 62, 74, 76, 94, 108
dharmakāya 78, 79, 99
dharmatā 8, 10, 12, 21, 35, 43, 47, 51, 53, 57, 62, 66, 74, 77, 94
dharmatā enlightenment mind . 74
dharmatā free of elaboration . . 51
dharmins 42, 69
dhātu . . 20, 22, 46, 62, 74, 76, 90, 94, 108
direct perception . . . xxxv, xxxix, xliii, 24-26, 50, 68, 69, 71, 72, 74, 96, 97
discursive thought 95

Dispelling the Darkness of the Ten Directions . . . . viii, xii, 1
eight levels of accomplishment 47
eighteen sub-schools 7
elaboration 48, 49, 51, 76, 95
electronic editions 113, 114
electronic texts 114
eleventh chapter 68
emptiness . xxii, 10, 27, 35, 50, 64, 69, 70, 75-77, 94, 95, 100
endeavour . . . xxxv, xxxix, 63, 74, 75, 78, 79, 95
endeavour-less, spontaneously-existing mode 75
Endurance World 3
enlightenment . . xxvii-xxxii, xlvi, 4, 8, 11, 20, 21, 23, 26, 27, 43, 44, 47, 48, 51, 52, 54, 56, 61-66, 69, 74-77, 83, 90-92, 95, 96, 98-100, 102, 105, 107, 108
enlightenment mind . . . 11, 23, 26, 27, 52, 54, 64-66, 69, 74-77, 83, 90, 91, 95
entity . . 12, 24, 42, 44, 49, 52, 53, 59, 69, 76, 96, 107
eternal self . . 19, 20, 28, 41, 42, 81
etymology of "great completion" xxxix
evil deed 29, 82, 96
explanation of the Bodhisatva Vehicle 48
explanation of the secrecy of great completion 79
explanation of the views of outsiders 36
expression of worship 33
extremely secret level . . . . . x, xiii
Extremely Vast Word of the Nyingma viii
fictional . . xliii, xliv, 9, 21, 22, 24, 49, 50, 52, 53, 55-58, 62, 69, 83, 90, 97, 108
five aggregates . 23, 36, 40, 52, 65, 75, 76
Followers of Sutra 45
foremost instruction iii, iv, vii, x, xvi-xviii, xl, 13, 19, 25, 30, 33, 67, 71, 74, 85, 86
Foremost Instruction section . . xl
Foremost Instruction, "A Garland of Views" 19
four castes of Hindu culture . . . 8
four great miracles 58
four limbs of approach and accomplishment 75
four modes 67, 68
four realizations . xlii, xliii, 25, 67-69, 72
realization in direct perception 69
realization through the mode of syllables 69
realization of single cause . . 69
realization through blessing 69
four seals 22, 58
four suchnesses 22, 56
four truths of the noble ones 20, 47
four types of austerities 81
the bodhisatva austerities . . 83
the śhrāvaka austerities 81
four types of māra 27, 77, 78
four types of view 38
fruition dharmas existing spontaneously 24, 67
fruition mode 67, 68
fruitional vehicle 48
fruitions . . . . xxix, 34, 43, 51
Garland of Views . . . . v, viii, xvii, xxxv, 30, 86
Gelug xxx

general explanation of the three modes 59, 60
Good Aeon 3
grammar texts 112
grammatical names . xi, xiv, 13, 34
grasped-grasping . 9, 48, 53, 77, 97
great accomplishment . 26, 27, 76, 77
great bliss 27, 57, 65, 76, 98
great bliss illusion 27, 76
great completion . . . iv, vii, x-xiii, xvii-xix, xxix, xxxiii, xxxv-xl, xlii, xlvi, 1, 2, 12, 14, 15, 22-24, 33, 34, 59, 60, 63, 67-69, 72, 74, 75, 78-80, 86, 90, 92-95, 100, 102, 104, 105, 112, 113
  etymology of "great completion" xxxix
  levels of the Great Completion teaching xl
  mistranslations promoting misunderstanding . xxxviii
  origin and meaning of the term great completion . . . xxxvii
great equality of primordial buddhahood 26, 74
great female consort . . . 27, 75, 76
great gadgetry of illusion 12
Great Vehicle . . 11, 49, 69, 79, 95, 96, 98-100
Guhyagarbha . . . iii, viii-x, xii, xiv-xvi, xl, 1, 13, 14, 33, 64, 68, 78, 80
Guhyagarbha Tantra . . . iii, viii, ix, xii, xiv-xvi, xl, 1, 13, 14, 64, 68, 80
Guhyasamāja 66
habituation . 21, 25, 27, 47, 55, 58, 61, 68, 72, 78, 79, 97
having four limbs . . 53, 54, 67, 75
having the four seals 22, 58
higher samādhi 62
highest spiritual teaching available xxxv
illusions 21, 23-25, 50, 63, 64, 69, 70
illusions like moons in water 24, 69
immeasurable palace 27, 78
in superfact . . 9, 21, 22, 53, 55, 58, 62, 63, 67
in the fictional . . 9, 21, 22, 24, 49, 52, 53, 55-57, 62, 69
indivisible in one 61
inner tantras . . . . . ix, xi, xiii, xiv, xxxiv, xxxvi, xxxvii, 60, 61
inner yoga vehicle 22, 57
innermost level of the great completion teaching . . . xxxvi
inseparable appearance-emptiness 69, 70
inspace 12, 13, 27, 77
intent xi, xiii, xxxi, 33, 38, 39, 71, 83, 99
interdependent origination . . xliv, 21, 47, 48
interior space 12
Iśhvara 4, 6, 41, 42
Jamgon Kongtrul viii
Jamyang Lodro Gyatso . . . v, viii, 33, 88
jñānasattva 54, 56, 105
Ju Mipham Namgyal . . . . viii, 32
Kagyu . . . . xxx, 111, 112
Kanāda 4, 5
Kāśhyapa 7, 39
kāya 78, 79, 99, 100
kayas and wisdoms 100
Khenpo Padma Tsering ix
Krīyatantra . xiii, xxxii, xxxiii, 11, 21, 34, 52, 54, 58
Lama Kunzang Palden 87

latency 100
Lesser Vehicle 47, 90, 98, 100
letters .. xi, xiv, xlvi, 13, 14, 34, 61
levels of seeing the wholesome . 47
levels of the Great Completion
teaching iv
locale owners 41
Lodro Gyatso ...... v, viii, 33, 88
Lodro Thayay 87
Longchen Rabjam .. i, iii, iv, viii, ix, xlix, 113
Longchenpa .... xv, xvii, xix, xx, xxii, xxvii, xxxv, xxxvii, xxxix, 4, 6
luminosity 12, 24, 67, 94, 100
Madhyamikas 48, 53
Mahāparinirvāna Sutra 37
Mahāsaṃghika 7
Mahāsaṃghika school 7
Mahāyogatantra . xxxiii, xxxiv, 12
Mahā-sammitīya school 8
male and female bodhisatvas .. 64
male and female sugatas ... 23, 64
manifest complete buddhahood
.... 23, 24, 66, 67
mantra recitation 52, 54
Mañjuśhrī 19, 33, 35, 65
māra 27, 77, 78, 101
meaning of all dharmas being
primordial buddhahood 28, 80
meanings and usages of great
completion xxxviii
meanings of the names of the
tantras xxxii
memory aid xvi
mere appearances 50
method and prajñā aspects . xxxiv
method mode 67, 68
migrator 101
mind ... xi, xiii, xv, xvii, xx, xxiii-xxvi, xxx, xxxi, xxxix, xl, xliv, xlv, 1, 2, 8-14, 21, 23-29, 34, 36, 40, 44, 46, 48-50, 52-54, 57-61, 64-71, 73-77, 80, 82-93, 95-109
Mind Only 8, 9, 48, 98, 103
Mind, Space, and Foremost
Instruction sections xl
mind's nature is unborn 66
Mipham .. i, viii, ix, xvi, xviii, xx, xxii, xxiii, xxx, xxxv, xlii, xliv, 4, 32, 34, 35, 87, 124
Mipham's commentary .. viii, ix, xxix, xxxi, xxxiv, 13
Mipham's notes xix
mode of completion . xxxv, 22, 59, 61, 63
mode of creation 22, 59, 60
mode of great completion . 22-24, 34, 59, 63, 67, 68, 78
moments of consciousness 45
more about foremost instruction
.... iii, xvii
Nature Great Completion . xiii, 2, 15, 80, 86, 102
nature of rigpa 64
nihilism xxv, xxvi, 4-6, 23, 28, 38, 39, 43, 65, 81
nine and three vehicle
presentations xxx
nine vehicles .... iii, vii, ix, x, xiii, xix, xxi, xxii, xxix-xxxii, xxxvii, xl, xlvi, 113
nirvana ... 1, xxxviii, 2, 23, 24, 26, 28, 37, 49, 52, 55, 64, 65, 67, 70, 74, 80, 90, 93, 99, 111
noble ones 20, 46, 47, 59, 82
non-dual unification 59
not understanding . xiii, xx, xxiv, xxvi, xliii, xliv, 3, 8, 19, 20, 28, 38-40, 79, 101

Nyāya 4, 5
Nyingma tradition ix
object mode 67, 68
Ṛiṣhi Kapila 4, 5
one all-encompassing space . xxxvii
one great juncture xxxvii
order of entry into the maṇḍala 67
outcastes 8
outer and inner tantras defined xxxiii
outer tantras xxxiii
outer yoga vehicle 22, 57
outflow 102
outflows 43, 77, 102
outsiders 34, 36, 39, 43, 64
pacification of elaboration . 48, 49
Padmasambhava . i, iii-v, vii-ix, xii, xiii, xv, xvi, xviii-xxii, xxiv, xxvi, xxvii, xxix, xxx, xxxiii-xl, xliv, 3, 5, 6, 19, 33, 34, 38, 39, 43, 55, 63, 64, 86, 104, 124
Padmasambhava's teaching ix, xv
  basis for the teaching ix
  content of the teaching . . xviii
  more about foremost instruction xvii
  purpose of the teaching xv
  the title xvi
Padmasambhava's teaching . . . iii, viii, ix, xii, xv, xviii-xx, xxix, xxx, xxxv, xxxvi, xxxviii-xl, 6
pāramitā . . . 10, 11, 21, 34, 35, 49, 51, 76, 77
Particularists 45
Paryanta . . xxvi, 6, 19, 28, 34, 36-39, 41
Paryantika iii, xiii, xx, xxv-xxviii, 5, 6, 28, 38, 39, 41, 81
past and future lives . . . xxiv, xxv, 19, 39, 40
path without outflows 43
paths to enlightenment xxxi
permanence . . 4-6, 20, 23, 39, 40, 43, 45, 65
phrase linkers xiv
Phyal ba . . . . . . iii, xiii, xxii, xxiv, xxviii, 3, 4, 19, 28, 34, 36-40, 81
pinnacle vehicle xxxvi
prajñā . xxxiv, xxxix, 7, 10, 11, 27, 30, 35, 36, 40, 45, 51, 59, 61, 62, 71, 72, 75-79, 82, 84-86, 103
Prajñāpāramitā 10, 11, 76, 77
pratyekabuddha . xxx, xxxi, 7, 20, 34, 44, 46-48, 51, 80, 83
pratyekabuddha vehicle 20, 44, 46
preface 33
presentation of the Unsurpassed or Anuttara Tantras 59
presentation of the Vajra Vehicle 51
presentation of the Vehicle of Characteristics 44
presentation of three vehicles . xxx
presentation of Ubhayatantra . 56
presentation of Yogatantra 57
primally unified appearance-emptiness 70
primordial female consort . 27, 75
primordial space ix
primordially manifest complete buddhahood 23, 66
primordially spontaneously-existing . . . . xi, xii
primordially-liberated mind inspace 12
profound meaning of the dharmatā 21, 47
profound topics of Mahāyoga . . x
qualities needed in a master . . . 80
rational mind . xlv, 25, 36, 50, 61,

71, 93, 103
rdzogs pa chen po 102
realization . . . . iv, xxxiii, xxxviii, xxxix, xlii, xliii, 7, 8, 12, 24-27, 61, 66-72, 75, 76, 86, 91, 103, 104
realization in direct perception 24, 25, 68, 69, 71
realization of single cause . . 24, 69
realization through blessing . . . 24, 25, 69, 70
realization through the mode of syllables 24, 25, 69, 70
Realization Victorious Over the Three Realms 66
rebirth 8, 46, 47, 90, 101
reference-less compassionate activity 85
relationship, need, and core need 25, 72
reminder . . . . xvi, 19, 34
rigpa . xxxv, xliii, 25, 55, 61-64, 70-72, 76, 104
ritual cleanliness . 11, 21, 52, 54, 55
Sāṃkhya 5, 41, 42
Sakya xxx
samādhi of suchness 61
samādhi of total appearance . . . 61
Samantabhadra . . . ix, x, xii, xv, xl, 1, 14, 23, 65, 80
Samantabhadri 23, 66
samayasattva 54, 56, 105
samsara . 1, xxi, xxiii, xxxviii, 2, 4, 6, 7, 23, 26, 28, 46, 49, 51, 55, 64, 66, 70, 74, 80, 83, 90, 92-94, 98, 99, 101, 104, 106, 107
samsara's containers and contents 66
Sanskrit "avagamana" xlii
Sarvāstivāda school 7
Satva and sattva: 104
secret . . . x, xi, xiii, xiv, xvi-xviii, xxxi, xl, 2, 10-13, 28, 30, 33-35, 53, 55, 65, 79, 80, 84-87, 105
secret garland of views 30, 86
Secret Mantra xvi, 10, 11, 35, 55, 85
secrets of enlightened body, speech, and mind 12
seed-syllables 67
self-arising wisdom . xxxix, 63, 66, 69, 77, 105
self-enlightenment 8, 20, 21, 47, 48
short explanation of the nine vehicles . . . . xix, xxix
conventional and unconventional vehicles xxx
signlessness 27, 76, 77
single cause xliii, 24, 25, 67, 69, 70
single unique sphere . . . xxxix, 66, 69, 108
single unique sphere of self-arising wisdom . . . . xxxix, 69
single unique sphere of wisdom 108
six unconventional vehicles . xxxii
something beyond prajñā 51
spiritual friend 20, 47, 86
spontaneous existence . 60, 68, 74, 75, 105, 106
Sthavira school 7
study and translation of Tibetan texts 113
study program 113
subject headings viii
sugata 23, 64, 65, 106
superfactual . . . x, xliii, 24, 45, 58, 69, 83, 90, 106-108
superfice 93, 107
Sutra of the Recollection of Dharma

. . . . 82
Sutra Petitioned by Kāśhyapa . . . 39
tantra means "continuity" . . xxxii
tantra of capability 22, 57, 58
tantra of method 22, 57, 59
tantras . . . . ix, xi, xiii-xv, xxi, xxii, xxx, xxxii-xxxvii, xxxix, xl, 10, 13, 33, 39, 48, 55, 59-61, 69, 80, 89, 93, 95, 96, 113
tantras are texts xxxii
tantric vehicles xxxii
tathāgata . ix, xi, 1, 54, 61, 85, 107, 108
ten levels 21, 51
ten non-virtuous actions 82
ten pāramitās 21, 51
terminology . iv, xxix, xxx, xxxvi, xl-xlii, xliv, xlv, 67, 75, 98, 103
Tīrthika . . . . iii, xiii, xx-xxii, xxv-xxviii, 4, 6, 19, 20, 28, 34, 36, 37, 39, 41, 45, 46, 52, 62, 64, 81, 83, 107
the activities of a tathāgata 85
the authentic . . xi, xiii, xix, xxviii, xxxi, xliii, xlv, 3, 4, 7, 8, 10, 33, 34, 36, 39, 49, 86-88, 107
the bodhisatva vow . . . 29, 84, 85
the colophon 85
The Dharmadhatu Treasury . xxxix
the female consorts 76
the five great female consorts . . 27
the formal title xvii
the four great elements 20, 45
the four realizations . xlii, xliii, 25, 67, 68, 72
the four seals explained 58
the Great Assembly of Letter Wheels 27, 61, 78, 79
The Great Completion Resting Up Trilogy xlvi
the great unification xxxv
the level Having Lotuses 61
the level of The Great Assembly of Letter Wheels 27, 61, 78
the level Total Light 61
the male consorts 27, 76
the meaning of the essence, Completion Stage 1
the mode of completion . . . xxxv, 22, 59, 61, 63
the mode of creation . . 22, 59, 60
the mode of great completion 22-24, 34, 59, 63, 67
the pinnacle teaching of great completion . . . . iv, xxxv
the samaya of the great equality 85
the sudden approach 69
the tantra of capability . 22, 57, 58
the three characteristics . . . 25, 67, 68, 72, 102
the three complete emancipations 75, 76
the three suchnesses 52
the three trainings 81
the śhrāvaka vow 85
The unconventional tantra vehicles
  the pinnacle teaching of great completion xxxv
  the unconventional tantra vehicles xxxi
the unsurpassed ones' austerities 84
the vessel 15, 85
thirteenth chapter . . . iii, vii-x, xii, xv-xix, xl, xliii, 5, 13, 14, 78, 80
three bad migrations 39
three buddha levels explained . . 78
three buddha-levels 61
three characteristics . . . 25, 67, 68, 72, 102
three families 54

three vehicles . . . xxix, xxx, 11, 98
Tibetan grammar 112
Tibetan texts . . v, xxxiii, xxxviii, xli, xlii, 105, 112-115
Tibetan word "rtogs pa" xlii
title . . . iii, vii, viii, xvi-xviii, 33-35
total affliction . 21, 25, 26, 43, 44, 73, 75, 108
total affliction and complete purification . 21, 25, 26, 44, 73, 75, 108
transcendence of the world . . xiii, xviii, xxviii, xxix
transliteration of Sanskrit . . . xlvi
Treasury of Oral Instructions . . viii
truly complete buddhahood xxxviii
twelve links each with four truths 47
Twenty Verses on Bodhisatva Vows 84
two accumulations . . 8, 67, 68, 77
twofold creation and completion 63
Ubhayatantra . . xiii, xxxii, xxxiii, 21, 56
Ubhayatantra means xxxiii
Uḍḍiyāṇa . . . . xxxvii, xxxix
śhrāvaka . xiii, xxx, xxxi, 7, 20, 28, 29, 34, 44, 46-48, 51-53, 57, 80, 81, 83-85
śhrāvaka vehicle 20, 44
śhrāvaka, pratyekabuddha, and bodhisatva vehicles . . . xxx, 44
Śhrī Singha College ix
śhūdra caste 8
Ulūka 5
unconventional vehicles . iv, xxxi, xxxii
unending enlightened body, speech, and mind 26, 108
unification . . xxxiv, xxxv, xxxviii, 12, 59, 64
unsurpassed enlightenment . . . 21, 51, 56, 63
Unsurpassed Tantra . . . . xxxiv, 58
un-compounded phenomena . . 45
un-stopped 102
Vaiśheṣhika 4, 5, 42
vajra master . . . . xv, 14
vajra vehicle . x, 11, 35, 51, 64, 80, 99, 105
Vajradhara 56
vajras of enlightened body, speech, and mind . . . . xi, 1, 12, 64
valid cognizer 50, 108
Vehicle of Characteristics . . 8, 10, 20, 35, 43, 44, 49, 72
vehicle of the vajra . 20, 21, 44, 52
vehicles of characteristics 39, 49, 78
vidyādhara 60, 87, 105
view of the perishing collection 40
view, meditation, and conduct . . . . xxxi, 93
views leading to emancipation . vii
views of ignorance 20
views of outsiders 36
views of the nine vehicles . vii, xiii, xxx
visualizations 53, 54
Viṣhṇu 4-6
wheel of ornamentation . . 26, 108
wisdom . . xxxix, 1, 6, 9, 10, 12, 24, 25, 33, 43, 46, 47, 49, 51, 53, 62, 63, 66, 67, 69, 70, 74, 76, 77, 79, 83, 92-94, 96, 99, 102-109
wishlessness 27, 76, 77
without endeavour . . xxxv, 78, 79
worldly views . . . . iii, xi, xix, xxi, xxii

wrongdoings 83
Yogacharins 48, 53
yogantantras explained xxxiii
Yogatantra . . xiii, xxxii-xxxiv, 11, 12, 21, 22, 34, 52, 57, 58, 61
Yogatantra means xxxiii
yogic conduct . . 28, 29, 36, 81, 85
Zhechen Monastery . . . viii, ix, 87
"completion" tantra xxxiv
"great completion" tantra . . xxxiv
"method" tantra xxxiv